We've Always Had Paris . . .
and Provence

We've Always Had
Paris . . .
and Provence

A SCRAPBOOK OF OUR LIFE IN FRANCE

Patricia and Walter Wells

HARPER

An Imprint of HarperCollins*Publishers*
www.harpercollins.com

HarperCollins books may be purchased for educational, business,
or sales promotional use. For information, please write: Special
Markets Department, HarperCollins Publishers, 10 East 53rd Street,
New York, NY 10022.

FIRST EDITION

Designed by Emily Cavett Taff

Library of Congress Cataloging-in-Publication Data is available
upon request.

ISBN: 978-0-06-089861-8

08 09 10 11 12 QV/RRD 10 9 8 7 6 5 4 3 2 1

For **Rita and Yale Kramer,**
great friends who sent us on our way,
and for
Colette and Jean-Claude Viviani,
who welcomed us into their French family

Acknowledgments

PATRICIA:

Twenty-eight years of Thank You is rather a lot, but I am taking a stab at remembering all the fabulous people who have improved our lives over the years:

First thanks go to my friend, mentor, and journalism professor Wilmott Ragsdale, who was the first to urge me to "be bold!" The first to insist that I "go for it!"

There were so many friends and family who helped us get going on our way in the early years, and special thanks go to Craig Claiborne, Julia Child, Lydie and Wayne Marshall, Maggie and Al Shapiro, Catherine O'Neill and Richard Reeves, Lee and Berna Huebner, Vivien and Roger Cruise, Steven Rothfeld, Julee Rosso, Susy Davidson, Martha Shulman, Wendy Moonan, Jonathan Kandell, Bill McBride, Stewart McBride, Denise Lioté, and Susy Piochelle.

Throughout my career, several agents, editors, publishers, and publicists ushered books through the system to allow a fertile collection of titles today, with special thanks to Susan Lescher, Amanda Urban, Peter Workman, Suzanne Rafer, Carolyn Reidy, Maria Guarnaschelli, Susan Friedland, Harriet Bell, Jonathan Burnham, Gail Winston, Lisa Ekus, and Carrie Bachman. Special thanks to all at HarperCollins who have given attention to this book: to Sarah Whitman-Salkin, who attended to every detail; to Emily Cavett Taff for her lovely design; and to Christine Van Bree for the winning jacket design.

Special thanks to all the friends and assistants who have helped allow these books to see the light of day: Susan Herrmann Loomis, Jane Sigal, Sarah Greenberg, Laura Washburn, Heather Mallory, Alexandra Guarnaschelli, and Elisabeth Hopkins.

Throughout my years of food writing, many editors gave me extra care and attention, and thanks go to Arthur Gelb, Nora Kerr, Mike Leahy, Nancy Newhouse, Pamela Fiori, Malachy Duffy, Linda Wells, Donna Warner, Ila Stangner, and Katherine Knorr.

My love and knowledge of food in Paris would be far less rich without the friendship of Lionel Poilâne, Apollonia Poilâne, Joan Richardson, Philippe Alleosse, Marie Quatrehomme, and Joël Thiebaut.

In the dining room, the kitchen, and the wine cellar, my life has been eternally enhanced by contact with Joël Robuchon, Guy Savoy, Jean-Claude Vrinat, Alain Dumergue, Claude Udron, Philippe Marquet, Frédéric Anton, Benoit Guichard, Philippe Goubert, Philippe Braun, Eric Lecerf, Maguy and Gilbert Le Coze, Antoine Hernandez, Yves Gras, Juan Sanchez, and Fabrice Langlois.

As we grew, so did our circle of close friends, and special thanks go to Eli Zabar and Devon Fredericks, Johanne Killeen and George Germon, Andrew Axilrod and Allyson de Groat, Rolando Beramendi, Ina and Jeffrey Garten, Todd Murray, Dorie and Michael Greenspan, Mike Bee and Julie Selzer, Marcella Butler, Kathy Griest, Marianne Tesler, Lee and Missy Isgur, Pat Thompson and Jim Bittermann, Sheila and Julian More, and Carole Allen. I am forever grateful to my sister, Judith, and brother-in-law, John Jones, for their friendship and support over the years.

In Provence, our days are forever enlivened and enlightened by the fine people who make up the rich texture of our lives there, including, over the years, Josiane and Christian Deal, Josiane and Corrine Meliani, Eliane and Aymar Beranger, Guy and Tina Julien, Raoul and

Flora Reichrath, Jean-Louis Martin, Jean-Benoît and Catherine Hugues, Marlies and Johannes Sailer, Jean-Louis and Mireille Pons, Roland Henny, Frank Peyraud, Gilles and Severine Diglé.

Over the years, students in my classes in both Paris and Provence have been a constant source of inspiration, and though they are too numerous to mention, I thank them all for their insight, wisdom, patience, and most of all, continued support and friendship.

WALTER:

Jim Sterba of the *Wall Street Journal* and once upon a time a buddy at the *New York Times* sent a credit-where-it's-due reminder soon after learning that we were working on our memoirs. Even thirty years after the fact it was good to have the explanation.

"It starts in Sag Harbor," Sterba wrote, "a summer house rental with Judy Klemesrud, and threats to hit your croquet ball all the way to Federico's down the hill.

"Flash forward: I'm in Southeast Asia. I run into Mort Rosenblum of AP and he says the *NYT* and *WP* can't agree on whose turn it is to edit the *IHT*, so they picked him. Mort's editing/supervisory experience is minimal. He asks me if I know anyone who can manage the paper. I say something like, 'Walter Wells, no question.' Who's he? I tell him he's the best editor I know. I say Mort would be lucky to get Walter . . .

"I assume that if the French Legion of Honor comes with remuneration, my finder's fee is in the mail . . ."

And so a long list of people to thank starts with Sterba and moves on to Mort Rosenblum, who took Sterba's advice. Add to that journalistically my staff at the *Trib* and especially Sam Abt, Sarah Alexander, and Elisabeth Hopkins, all of whom were there in very different ways to steady my hand through some unsteady times.

Profound thanks to Mike Getler, John Vinocur, and Dave Jones, bosses, colleagues, and valued friends.

To Arthur Sulzberger and Howell Raines, who brought me back to the *Trib* after I had quit the first time.

To a number of colleagues at the *New York Times* who counseled me almost back into that fold—Allan Siegel, Michael Oreskes, Andy Rosenthal, John Geddes, Jill Abrahamson, Bill Keller, Janet Robinson.

To Alison Smale for her wisdom and even more for the pleasure of working with her for much of my second tour at the *Trib*.

To Nadège de Noailles, always a voice of sanity and good sense.

To a number of professional counselors over the years, but especially John Morris, Richard Eder, Richard McClean, and Michael Golden. And to David Halberstam.

To Jean Love, favorite aunt and source of inspiration since an early age. And to Keith Love, oldest and best friend.

To Samuel Okoshken, for many reasons, most recently for vetting much of this manuscript.

A deep nod to Gail Winston, a real pro as an editor if ever there was one. She took two disparate manuscripts and skillfully crafted them into one. And another grateful nod to our agent, Amanda Urban, whose advice was always welcome, if not always followed.

And of course to everyone Patricia has already named.

Contents

PART III

Our Private Universe

PART IV

World Enough

List of Recipes

We've Always Had Paris . . .
and Provence

PREFACE:
Go for It!

*Our "formal" wedding portrait, taken in a photo
booth in Times Square, September 1977.*

WALTER:

We were young—okay, we were youngish, thirty-three and
thirty-six—and, though it seems absurd now, at the time we
thought we had already overachieved our ambitions. Daily journalism
moves you from story to story, from deadline to deadline. You angle for
better assignments, you don't think much about winding up as editor.
If Patricia and I had goals, they involved working at great newspapers
and living in interesting places. In New York, at the *Times*, we were
a lot further along than maybe we had expected to be when we met
our first deadlines in Milwaukee (Patricia) or South Carolina's piney
woods (me).

Patricia had come to the *Times* from the copy desk of the *Wash-*

ington Post Style section. She landed in Washington (with the guy she calls the starter husband) the week of the Watergate break-in, and she moved to New York just about the time that *All the President's Men* was released.

The hiring procedure for copy editors at the *Times* involved a try-out. Upon rare invitation, and after a careful consideration of résumé and application, the candidate spent a week working at the newspaper. Patricia's tryout started on July 4, 1976, the date of the American bicentennial, celebrated in New York with a huge harbor parade of "tall ships," sailing vessels from around the world whose ages were closer to the Republic's than to our own.

As we both like to recall, she walked into the *Times* newsroom on West Forty-third Street that day with my name in her pocket, a note that said "Walter Wells, 3rd floor." I was duty editor on the national desk, and she reported to me, with super-short hair, a tight blue-jean skirt, and open-toed shoes. "Pretty girl," I thought. I also thought she belonged to someone else. Not to a husband—one of the things I knew about her was that her marriage was over. But her sponsor for the tryout, her "rabbi," in *Times*-talk, was my immediate boss on the *Times* national desk. So, making a wrong if predictable assumption, I thought our contacts would be professional at most.

I was also extracting myself from a relationship with a woman I remember now as Adèle H. I was hardly Lieutenant Pinson, but her obsession as she trailed me around the Upper West Side was the kind that makes some men take to the high seas. I hadn't fled bodily, but I was in the mood to cool it, not hot things up with a woman who I thought was there for someone else. And just to wrap up one last detail, I too was divorced. My starter marriage had ended ten years earlier in Virginia. I had come to New York for my own *Times* tryout soon after.

Our first meeting outside the office was professional, a welcome-to-New-York lunch at a French restaurant (what else?) called Du Midi on West Forty-seventh Street. Our second date was a real one, dinner at an Indian restaurant called Nirvana and then the symphony afterward. The Scythian Suite was on the program at Lincoln Center, and Patricia liked Prokofiev. Other dates followed, of course. Patricia accused me of being slow on the uptake, but she moved to New York in August and I had a closet in her apartment by Christmas. The next spring we contracted to buy an apartment together. So maybe I was slow, but my steps were all purposeful, taking us toward our life together.

Walter in the spring of 1977 at Patricia's West End Avenue apartment, with our first coulibiac of salmon, an Easter specialty.

Our courtship revolved around food and kitchens. We first redid my kitchen, then hers, then the one we bought together. We took cooking lessons from Lydie Marshall, John Clancy, and Giuliano Bugialli. Dinners at Le Cygne and Lutèce, two of New York's best tables in the 1970s, bracketed our wedding, which was considerably less formal than the meals. Having both been married before, and living in New York distant from both families, we decided to do the deed at City Hall. With the single required witness—Keith Love, my cousin and best friend—we went to One Centre Street, took a number, and waited our turn. The ceremony concluded with the "thunk" of the time clock that the justice of the peace used to make the time of the marriage precise and official.

"Go for it" was the standard phrase of encouragement and we used it often, whether to egg on a double-dip of Häagen-Dazs or sign up for a group rental in Sag Harbor for the summer. When the *Times* began adding its original Home and Living sections—suddenly bursting from leaden seriousness into three and then four sections with a daily lifestyle section—"go for it!" was the phrase I used first to push Patricia to the editing staff of the dynamic new sections. And then again, when the *Times* needed another food writer to help fill the new space.

We were crossing Forty-fourth Street, returning to the office after lunch, and Patricia was expressing doubts about applying for the opening. The doubts weren't about her competence, but involved whether she wanted to stay at the *Times* or quit to work on a book idea. I couldn't imagine leaving the *Times* for anything, so I said, "Go for it." And she went back to the office and did just that. She got the job and though she didn't love everything about it, the experience and the credential of being a food writer for the *Times* served her well.

Meals as well as mottos led us eventually to France. Because of food we were Francophiles. And because of Paris, too. Both of us had been there before, though not together, and we were besotted with the romance of the city. Throughout our courtship we tested our commitment in a lot of ways, and one of them involved the fantasy of living in France: "If I got a job at the *Herald Tribune*, would you quit at the *Times* and move to Paris with me?" was a question we each asked the other.

Then it turned into more than idle chatter. In 1978 the *Times* was shut down by a strike and we were out of work for two months. A couple of really positive things resulted from not having regular income. The first was that we realized we could be happy outside the intense, all-consuming atmosphere of the *Times* newsroom. The second was that because of being without salary for two months, we got a big tax refund. And so in 1979 we suddenly had enough money for a long trip to France. We put together all our vacation time and holidays and went for a three-week gastronomic tour. We moved from one starred restaurant to the next, mostly in France but in Brussels too, burping along as our bodies tried to adjust to the overload of rich food. It was a challenge I felt I could handle over the long term.

And during that time, I got the *Trib*'s job offer. The call came while we were staying at the Hotel Amigo in Brussels, and our pillow-talk question about a fantasy life was now foreplay of a very different kind.

"Go for it," we said, and we did. We didn't realize we were jumping from the high dive; we didn't know if there was water in the pool. But the consequences of that motto have been a fairly fabulous life, and that life is what these stories are about. Most of them are about things that happened to us. But being journalists, some are about things that we observed, discovering life in France and all the things we say "*vive la différence*" about. Good stories are meant to be told, and we tell ours with considerable amazement at our good fortune. And of course with the hope that you'll enjoy reading them.

PATRICIA:

In 1976 when I was still in DC, trying to decide whether or not to accept the *New York Times* offer, I asked the advice of my colleagues. The chorus was loud, and negative. I remember one friend's response was "Why would you leave the gorgeous town of Washington for that dark hole of New York City! Besides, you'll end up living in a six-hundred-dollar-a-month cell!"

My friend Kathryn was one of the few who gave words of encouragement. "Look," she said, "you can always come back to DC if it doesn't work out. Remember, the only thing in life that is irreversible is having children."

I was beginning to understand the word "reversible." I was separated, and divorce papers were in the works when I took the elevator to the *New York Times* third-floor newsroom and reported for duty to Walter Wells. (I like to say that at that point I was NEVER going to be interested in men again, but being the practical gal that I am, I began a list of potential contenders just in case I ever changed my mind. Walter Wells was soon at the top of that list.)

As Walter notes, we met, courted, and on September 9, 1977, we "eloped." It was the year of Woody Allen's *Annie Hall*, so, fittingly, my costume included a gorgeous green tie from Walter's collection, along with a beige silk blouse, brown corduroy vest, and brown wool skirt.

The very next day I had my first *New York Times* byline as Patricia Wells.

I was a new hire at the *Times*, working first as an editor on the daily culture desk and soon afterward for the new Style sections called Home and Living. The *Times* needed another food writer, I raised my hand, and they gave me a chance.

Food and cooking have been a passion since my childhood days in Wisconsin. I was lucky enough from an early age—third grade, in fact—to know what I wanted to be when I "grew up." I wanted a career in newspaper journalism. But back then, being a food writer was about as sexy and appealing as Betty Crocker. I didn't want to be Betty Crocker, so as I began my career it never occurred to me that I might combine my dual passions. Walter calls me a lapsed Catholic and a reformed vegetarian. I often joke that I am the only person who ever gave up vegetarianism for a career.

I was never militant about my meatless diet, so I willingly renounced vegetarianism to bring a broader palate to my job as a junior food writer. But I'll never forget my shock the day that, as he gave me the new assignment, assistant managing editor James Greenfield whispered, "You don't have to eat meat, just say you do." It wasn't a Jayson Blair moment, but it was not the kind of moral direction I expected.

The *Times* has never had a reputation as an easy place for journalists to work, and my early years there were brutal. Like rookies every-

We elope at Manhattan's City Hall, September 9, 1977:
Patricia in pure Annie Hall with a Karen Carpenter
haircut. What bangs!

where, I was exposed to a natural amount of hazing, but it felt much worse. The restaurant critic, Mimi Sheraton, seemed to make me a special target. I thought she did her best to get most of my assignments killed. I was young, ambitious, energetic, and apparently a problem for her in a way I could not understand.

Greenfield also leaned on me hard, calling me into his office one day to say that my writing was "just not authoritative." Yet there was no guidance on how to be "authoritative." In those days I would run around the Reservoir in Central Park before heading for the office, repeating with every laden step, "It's not always going to be like this, it's not always going to be like this."

Despite all the criticism, or perhaps because of it, I made a vow to "show them," to not let them win the battle. Even though my subject matter was limited to local and regional stories—the then-fledgling New York City farmers' markets, tales of artisanal goat cheese makers, apple growers, maple syrup farmers in upstate New York—I developed a technique of researching each story until every minute question had been answered. I found that if I researched the death out of every subject, the facts and story would fall into place, and voilà! my voice suddenly became more authoritative. (About that time, the British wine author Hugh Johnson told me about how he went about penning the

December 1979. The New York Times *throws a going-away party for us before we move to Paris. Note Patricia's perm and Walter's three-piece suit.*

terse, well-written prose that accompanies his compact *Pocket Guide to Wine.* He wrote the first volume seated in a small room facing a mirror, on which he had written "5 facts per line." His editor came in, scratched out the five, and replaced it with a seven.)

In 1979 when we were faced with the decision of leaving New York City for Paris, I decided not to ask advice from friends my age, but rather Walter and I looked around at people a generation older, people whose lives seemed to have turned out quite well. To a person, they encouraged us to go. But the most potent advice of all came from food editor Craig Claiborne: "If you have to ask the question, you don't deserve to go." And so our decision was made!

Winter 1979, leaving our brand-new dream kitchen on Central Park West:
We still use the same copper and Kitchen Aid!

SEDUCTION DINNER:
POLENTA with CHUNKY FRESH TOMATO SAUCE

In the fall of 1976, when we were courting, Walter prepared an elegant dinner party, the one we soon began to refer to as the "Seduction Dinner." The first course was polenta shaped in a ring mold and topped with tomato sauce. Years after we were married I got up the courage to let him know a detail of that dinner. "Do you remember the polenta from the Seduction Dinner? I hate to tell you, but the polenta was rancid." That would have been the case back then, for what Americans then used as polenta was actually Quaker cornmeal from a cardboard canister. The cornmeal probably sat around on the shelves for ages, and of course became rancid. The original polenta recipe is lost to history. Walter remembers it coming from an obscure Italian cookbook. Here, then, is an updated recipe using real polenta.

EQUIPMENT: A nonstick 1-quart ring mold.

> 1 quart whole milk
> 1 teaspoon fine sea salt
> ½ teaspoon freshly grated nutmeg
> ¾ cup instant polenta
> 1 cup freshly grated Parmigiano-Reggiano cheese
> Chunky Fresh Tomato Sauce (recipe follows)

1. In a large saucepan, bring the milk, salt, and nutmeg to a boil over high heat. (Watch carefully, for milk will boil over quickly.) Add the polenta in a steady stream and, stirring constantly with a wooden spoon, cook until the mixture begins to thicken, about 3 minutes.

2. Remove from the heat. Stir in the cheese, blending thoroughly. The polenta should be very creamy. Pour into the ring mold and let cool. Unmold at serving time and fill with the fresh tomato sauce. Serve in thick slices with ample portions of the sauce.

8 servings

NOTE: The aphrodisiac effects of nonrancid polenta have not been established.

CHUNKY FRESH TOMATO SAUCE

This is a quick rustic tomato sauce that can be put together in a matter of minutes, yet tastes as though you may have labored for hours. Just use the freshest, most flavorful tomatoes you can find.

EQUIPMENT: A large heavy-duty casserole; a food mill fitted with the coarsest screen.

> 1 tablespoon extra-virgin olive oil
> 3 pounds garden-fresh tomatoes, rinsed, cored, and quartered
> 1 tablespoon coarse sea salt
> Several celery leaves
> Several fresh or dried bay leaves
> 1 plump head fresh garlic, cloves separated and peeled
> Hot red pepper flakes to taste (optional)

1. In a large heavy-duty casserole, combine the oil, tomatoes, salt, celery leaves, bay leaves, garlic, and hot pepper flakes, if using. Cook, uncovered, stirring regularly over moderate heat until the tomatoes have collapsed and are cooking in their own juices, about 15 minutes. Taste for seasoning. Remove and discard the celery leaves and bay leaves.
2. Place the food mill over a large bowl. Using a large ladle, transfer the sauce to the food mill and purée into the bowl. (Store, covered, in the refrigerator for 3 days or the freezer for 3 months.)

5 cups sauce

NOTE: What I learned: This makes a rather rustic sauce that will have seeds. If you prefer a more refined sauce, pass through the fine screen of the food mill.

PART I

Setting Out to Live a Fantasy

AH, PARIS!

LEARNING MORE THAN FRENCH
Our Lemon Chicken with Roasted Onions
Chiberta's Nouvelle Cuisine Raw Duck Salad

SEEING THINGS

RULES, RULES, AND MORE RULES
Johannes's Picnic Couscous Salad

REALITY STRIKES
Judy's North Carolina Pork Barbecue

MAKING YOURSELF UP
Celery, Tarragon, Spinach, and Chicken Salad

PUT YOURSELF ON VACATION
Red Sea Squid Pasta

LA VIE EN ROSE
Frédy Girardet's Fresh Foie Gras in Vinaigrette

1

{ Ah, Paris! }

WALTER :

Like any fantasy, it was supposed to be ephemeral. It was also supposed to be transcendent. But here I was, stuck in airport traffic and the only question in my head on that dismal January morning was "What have I gotten Patricia and me into?" The taxi was nudging its way into the bumper-locked queue of cars snaking toward Paris, snuffed or so it seemed by the smoky pea soup that often passes as wintertime air, and my abs and glutes knotted in involuntary acknowledgment that our gamble of moving to Paris could be a really bad bet.

A colleague who had also recently left the *Times* had spent months making his decision, with neat lists of pros and cons and extensive conversations with various newsroom counselors. Far less methodical than he—also younger, with no children and more blitheness of spirit—I had done none of that. My lists were all in my head and consisted mostly of people in New York I would miss and things in Paris I wouldn't have to miss anymore. My colleague was looking for a career opportunity and my interest was mostly in a little adventure—a couple of years at the

International Herald Tribune. My friend ended up staying away from the *Times* for about two years, then he went back. I never did.

Slumped in a battered taxi that was barely moving and blind in the fog, I had just begun learning Paris's best kept secret: its gray, damp weather. January's short, sunless days are especially depressing. All Frenchmen who can afford it (and they save up so they can) seek a sunny antidote to winter's depths either on an Alpine ski slope or on some Club Med beach. Not me. I was headed in the other direction, swept along by what I counted on being adventure and what I now feared might just be naïveté.

Ironically, the fog reinforced one bit of clarity. I knew already that living in Paris would not be like visiting Paris, but I hadn't appreciated what that really meant. My previous trips to France had lasted days or weeks and had been marked by an epiphany at some museum or cathedral and a lot of feel-good time at sidewalk cafés or strolls in the long summer twilight. Vacation syndrome is dangerously seductive. You actually believe that this magical place you have come to allows you to be the contented, stress-free person you really are. There's a lot of vacation syndrome in Paris.

And now fog or not, traffic jam or not, I was about to become a Parisian. And in two weeks, when Patricia had closed up the New York apartment, she would join me. The magic of that idea was powerful. Paris was the ultimate destination in my map of the universe. Even more than New York, Paris offered glamour and excitement as a place to be. And it was exotic. After eight years in New York—and still considering it my true home—I wanted an overseas adventure.

Exoticism aside, the immediate requirement, shelter, had been temporarily solved by Lydie and Wayne Marshall, New York friends who were generously lending us their apartment for several weeks in exchange for fitting some of their furniture into the small shipping container that Patricia had stayed behind to fill with clothes and other basic needs. We left everything else behind to be there when we returned. The Marshalls' little apartment, on the Rue des Entrepreneurs

in the 15th arrondissement, provided a place to sleep plus the experience of a quiet working-class neighborhood. When I had described
the neighborhood to a colleague at the *Times*, I had called it "not very
interesting." "There is no such thing as an uninteresting *quartier* in
Paris," he corrected me. Maybe not, but it did seem remote from Paris's
chic, mythic center.

In our sparsely furnished living room at Rue Daru, with an exhibition
of paintings by our French tutor, the artist Denise Lioté.

And so did my next stop, the *Herald Tribune* offices. After the taxi
finally crawled to the 15th and I dropped off my bags, I got onto the
Métro and headed for Neuilly. The paper had moved several years earlier from Rue de Berry off the Champs-Elysées. Its new offices, in a
plush suburb on the western edge of Paris, are only four Métro stops
beyond the Arc de Triomphe, so it wasn't geography that made it feel
remote.

I had visited the *Trib* for the first time four months earlier and had
left the job interview feeling very dubious about giving up my staff
job at the *New York Times* for this. Patricia and I were also in love with

the idea of being New Yorkers. When I was growing up in the Carolina Piedmont, television had just begun the great cultural leveling that over time washed away a lot of America's regionalism. The excitement and sophistication flowing down the coaxial cable all emanated from New York. I had wanted to be at the wellspring for a long time before I got there.

Another Southerner, Willie Morris, wrote a book in those years called *North Toward Home*, and the title described a path that had beaconed to me since third grade. Miss Frances Love, our teacher at the little school in McConnells, South Carolina, talked to her unwashed, barefoot charges about her trips to Manhattan. One day she got so excited as she talked of that place far, far from our Faulknerian hamlet that she turned to her blackboard and sketched the three most noteworthy skyscrapers of our day. Her chalk drawings did little credit to the Old World angles of the Flatiron Building, or the elegant symmetry of the Empire State Building, or the Chrysler Building's Art Deco frou-frou. But the crude chalkboard images stuck in at least one young mind eager for impressions from the outside, and I recalled my early teacher's drawings when I moved to New York and began directly sharing her enthusiasm for the city.

Yet thoughts of working in Paris had grown, and I persuaded myself that it would be tantamount to a temporary reassignment, since the *Times* was one of the *Trib*'s owners. I also encouraged myself to believe that I would be moving from one legendary news operation to another. But the legends were made of different stuff—it was clear from the first instant that the *Trib*'s mythic reputation was much bigger than the tiny, impecunious reality.

So those were the pulls and the tugs as I had tried to reach my part of the decision about accepting the offer. Meanwhile, my *Times* bosses' principal strategy for trying to keep me was to make dismissive judgments about the *Trib*. You can *visit* Paris, said one, emphasizing the obvious. It's boutique journalism, said another. "Going to Paris is a lifestyle choice, but staying here is a career choice."

"I know," I replied, with far more callow smugness than smarts.

I was hardly on Abe Rosenthal's scope. The crusty executive editor had little time for production editors—he regarded us as necessary technicians, but not of the Brahmin class. But I felt a bizarre pride when he took enough notice to call me "shithead" in front of a large group of my peers. He told me that if I was considering leaving the *Times*, it probably meant that I should.

Meanwhile, from Paris there was little or nothing. The editor, Mort Rosenblum, himself new to the job, called from time to time to confirm the offer. But he could propose no moving expenses, nor money for a hotel or temporary apartment. One future colleague wrote a friend at the *Times*: "Whatever Wells thinks he has been offered, he should get it in writing. Promises don't mean very much around here."

It was in this atmosphere that Patricia and I had gone back and forth on the Paris offer. The gamble seemed greater for her—I would have a job, but she would be giving up a staff job for the uncertainty of freelance writing. Also, I had assurances that I could return to the *Times*, and whatever the shortcomings of the *Trib*, I could certainly take it for two years. And back at the *Times*, I would have "foreign experience" and experience managing a staff, not just deadlines.

But we had made the decision, and there I was settling into the Marshalls' tiny apartment awaiting Patricia's arrival in mid-January.

When she got there and we unpacked, I was surprised to see that one of the items that the Marshalls had put in our Paris-bound container was a new ironing board still bearing its $29.95 price tag. We had left our own behind in the West Side apartment for the renters who were subletting it. After settling in and looking for a Paris ironing board, we were shocked to find that the cheapest model cost 320 francs, or the equivalent then of eighty dollars. It was the kind of sticker shock we never got used to, especially not with the exchange rate of the period, which hovered around four francs to the dollar. We had given up two New York salaries for one in Paris, one that when multiplied by four sounded like a lot. But the dollar's exceptional weakness made the math very misleading. The apartment search drove home the point. Rent would cost us more than twice as much as our two-bedroom apartment in a doorman building on Central Park West.

One of our great Paris friends, Al Shapiro, told us more than once: "If you came to Paris to save money, you bought the wrong ticket." Like a lot of Al's observations, it was as funny as it was right on.

The crispest memories of those early days involve prices. Besides the eighty-dollar ironing board, there was the radio that cost us both a week's walking-around money, one hundred dollars. It allowed us to listen to any of the stations then on the air, about a dozen of them, all blah-blah all the time. And most memorably, there was also the hundred dollars' worth of smoked salmon that I watched friends wolf down at a Sunday brunch.

But the best thing about that brunch was the bagels. Having rejected all that we had found as not up to New York standards, Patricia made a batch from scratch, and they were delicious.

There are also the memories attached to the details of settling in, all of them unfamiliar. We got to know the appliance stores to buy a refrigerator, a clothes washer, a stove powered both by electricity and by gas. Why? Well, the salesman explained, if ever the electricity goes out, or the gas fails. Then he added ominously, "If ever there's a war . . ." revealing a frame of reference that was totally foreign. Subsequently, we became aware of the number of times that French acquaintances would say "*pendant la guerre* . . ."

There were frequent trips to various government offices and long waits once there. *Fiche d'état civil* was a new vocabulary expression, as were *carte de séjour* and *carte de travail*. We had to go for an interview at the neighborhood Commissariat de Police, where the interviewer talked to us about our new president, Ronald Reagan, "*star de série B*," and the old one, Carter, "*un grand naïf.*" His eyes brightened when both of us said we had been divorced. "How many times?" he wanted to know, then seemed disappointed when we said only a humdrum once apiece.

Walter whips up an omelet in the Rue Daru kitchen.

Much of the early immigrant experience was often entertaining, but it was also hard. I could have cried the Friday night I got home—I was at the office until after the paper closed at midnight—and found Patricia on a stepladder painting yet another room. I felt guilty about what I had gotten her into and I was also not happy at seeing how I was going to spend the weekend. And we both did cry the night I came home and found Patricia already in tears. I realized how lonely she was and remember saying to her, "This is the worst mistake I have ever made and it's the worst time of my life."

Whatever I had gotten us into, the fantasy was under way.

Top: *Walter at the Arc de Triomphe during our first Paris snowstorm:*
He has always loved hats!
Bottom: *In our Rue Daru dining room.*

2

{ Learning More Than French }

PATRICIA:

When we landed in Paris, I spoke not a word of French, and since Walter knew at least a hundred words and several conjugations, I considered him totally fluent. That gave me the wifely right to demand, "Call the real estate agent [banker, plumber, . . .]." And he usually did.

It was one of our first days in Paris, and Walter got off the phone after speaking to a real estate agent. With a huge smile of relief he looked up to announce "It sounds like Audrey Hepburn's dream apartment."

I had visions of dancing up those winding, red-carpeted stairs in soft black ballerina shoes. I would be perfectly coiffed and my shiny red nails perfectly manicured. I would be dressed in black and white Chanel, made up to perfection.

We got Audrey's dream and more. Or less. Moving into a rental apartment in Paris in 1980 was a bit like buying a used car without seats, steering wheel, or tires. Rock-bottom bare is what you got: few light fixtures and if there were fixtures, no lightbulbs; no appliances (unless you made a cash deal with the previous tenant); no curtains or draperies; and in our case, a kitchen without a single drawer. Most walls had not been painted since 1905 when the elegant gray stone Haussmannian apartment building was constructed. Much of the old tile floor in the kitchen had given way, and in the center of the high-ceilinged room hung a makeshift clothes drying rack with a pulley, right out of *The Honeymooners*.

But we had class! (The French call it *standing*.) There were marble fireplaces with beveled mirrors above carved mantels in every room. Romantic floor-to-ceiling windows overlooking a well-tended inner courtyard. A bathroom with a white porcelain sink so big you could almost bathe in it. And oak floors that seemed to speak of all those tenants who had come before us. There were funny quirks from another era, like a little buzzer on the floor of the double living room (that rang in the kitchen to call the maid), an ancient toilet with a pull chain for flushing, a sixth-floor walk-up maid's room for the servant we would never have, and a cool, damp *cave* for storing all those precious Bordeaux we were certain to collect on romantic weekend outings.

Clearly, we had a lot of learn about our fantasies. Because we did not intend to stay for long, we moved only a handful of boxes and a few basic pieces of furniture from New York, but the day our goods arrived we found the building's tiny elevator was suddenly out of order. The movers hauled everything up the three flights of winding red-carpeted stone stairs on their backs. Only later did we realize why the elevator was out of service: We had failed to slip the concierge a handful of francs as a "consideration" beforehand.

Even before we installed ourselves on Rue Daru that February, I began exploring the neighborhood, not far from the Arc de Triomphe. One weekday before 5:00 p.m., I happened upon the huge outdoor market on the Rue Poncelet. The day was frightfully damp, it was already pitch dark, with daylight in depressingly short supply, but as I walked in wonderment past stall after stall of brilliantly fresh produce, beautiful poultry and rabbits with their furry feet still attached, sparkling fresh fish and shellfish direct from Brittany and the Mediterranean, I looked up at the red, silver, and gold holiday decorations and I cried. I could not believe my good fortune. (And little did I know what an important role that market would play in my daily life for some twenty years.)

Soon Walter was leaving our new home as early as nine each morning, and sometimes not returning until somewhere around 2:00 a.m., when the *IHT*'s last edition had finally been "put to bed" then argued over. As soon as he left for work I entered the spare bedroom to write on my blue-gray Smith Corona portable electric typewriter. There were days that I felt I had a gun to my head: Write! Make some money!

I had been completely in favor of the move, even though I was giving up my dream job as a reporter for the *New York Times* in exchange for a promise of nothing. (Then I still believed in two years I would be back at my desk at the *Times*. This was just going to be a sabbatical in Paris.)

But reality hit soon: I was lost in the language, I had little promise of freelance work beyond a few connections at such New York magazines as *Food & Wine* and *Travel + Leisure* and some vague promises from my old bosses at the *New York Times*. With a New York City mortgage to pay off and four francs to the dollar, money was scarce.

Walter and I had been married only two years and by most standards we were still newlyweds. We didn't think so then, of course, but our marriage was about to be put to a royal test. He was off struggling with a disorganized newspaper and a habitually disgruntled staff. I felt totally alone.

I remember that I cried a lot in the beginning. My one solace was running, and run I did. Each morning I'd don my running togs and head for Parc Monceau, where a daily hour's run was the routine. Willie Nelson and Anne Murray were my favorite singers then, and I'd stick their tapes into my bulky Walkman and they'd carry me around the 1-kilometer (0.6-mile) route—around and around. I came to love the ultra-romantic marble statue of Chopin playing the piano that stood at one end of the park, as well as the strange fake Greek ruins that flanked the other end. In fact it was in those early days in Paris that I created the credo I stick to even now: "If you run five miles before nine in the morning, nothing bad can happen to you the rest of the day." And it usually didn't. Running was my psychological insurance policy. It also became my religion.

I had been to Paris only once before, in January of 1973, a glorious week filled with exploration, culinary excitement, and elegance. But the thought of ever living there was beyond my wildest dreams.

As I look back on our first months as residents, I realize that I did have one great luxury then: time—practically all the time in the world. That didn't make up for the absence of assignments. I left New York that January of 1980 with a specific idea: to write a book that would be called *The Food Lover's Guide to Paris*. I was convinced that there were enough other visitors and even Parisians themselves who were fascinated not just by the city's restaurants, but also by the bakeries, pastry shops, wine bars, chocolate shops, and markets, all the truly fun things that happened between meals in Paris. The problem was I hadn't found a single New York publisher who agreed with me. Before leaving New York, I spoke with Judith Jones, the illustrious editor at Knopf who carried Julia Child through much of her publishing career. Judith, whose love of Paris is legendary, listened to my passionate proposal and responded, "It's a book I'd love to buy, but I can't publish it. It will never sell."

I know now, but didn't know then, that perseverance, persistence, and an unwillingness to take no for an answer would be much-needed traits throughout my career in France. They would also serve me well in shaping my work. I developed a simple strategy: I'd get the assignments separately and write the book chapter by chapter. I would show a publisher that the idea was a good one!

My first big freelance assignment was an article on the bakers of Paris, for *Travel + Leisure* magazine. It was my first chance to examine every Paris neighborhood as a reporter, and I felt like a giant sponge,

*In front of restaurant L'Ami Louis, foie gras land,
with friends Lydie Marshall and Heidi Trachtenberg.*

absorbing characters and experiences, flavors and aromas, all new and exotic to me. I remember seeing now-defunct wood-burning ovens that baked huge, wholesome loaves and met for the first time the famed Lionel Poilâne and his father, Pierre, who walked Rue du Cherche-Midi in his signature navy beret. Thankfully, I didn't need to know much French for most of the research. I visited maybe twenty bakeries, purchased their specialties, then back at home sampled, noted, and rated. I narrowed it down to the best half dozen or so, and bravely (read stupidly) called one of the *boulangeries* to set up an appointment. At that time I thought that if I mimicked the fast-paced speech of the French, maybe some of my mistakes would be camouflaged. I asked the person on the other end of the phone for an appointment, explaining who I was and what I was doing. But the response came back, "*Madame, je ne comprends pas un mot que vous avez dit.*" (Lady, I don't understand a word you have said!) I embarrassedly hung up the phone, headed for the Métro, and about thirty minutes later appeared at the bakery, explaining it all over again. This time, with a bit of sign language and some false stops and starts, I got through the interview and eventually got the story.

I wasn't quite as lucky with an interview with Frédy Girardet, the Swiss chef who was then considered one of the best in the world. The night before taking the train from Paris to Crissier, near Lausanne, Switzerland, I sat up translating my questions, word for word, from the English-French dictionary. I considered this simply an insurance policy, since I was certain that any chef of his stature would speak English.

Was I in for a surprise! Not only did chef Girardet not speak English, he spoke French with a Swiss accent so thick I could barely understand him. (Only later did I find out that he DID speak English, only not to the much mistrusted band of food journalists.) I thought I had myself well covered: I spent the entire day in the kitchen, taking copious notes, and tape-recorded every word of our halting conversation. The story was written, then accepted, with one little request for additions: "Do you think you could have a few more quotes from the chef?" my editor queried. My tape recorder saved the day, and the editor received a few more samples of chef Girardet's wisdom.

My French is far from perfect, but it's good enough to get me through live French television and radio shows, though I still shy away from those, fearing I won't understand the questions. I once even thought of hiring a specialist to help me lose my distinct American accent but years later when my French editor advised me not to lose my "adorable" accent, I finally felt off the hook.

But my fractured French could not diminish my enthusiasm or excitement of being of a journalist in Paris. I was interviewing bakers and chefs and shopkeepers, not rocket scientists. How badly could I misunderstand?

Our move to France conveniently coincided with the expansion of the *New York Times* Travel section, and the editor, Michael Leahy, liked my ideas and was eager to run regular articles about Paris restaurants and food shops. Though a contract was distant, soon the contents of my future book were rolling out of my typewriter as I raced around town reporting on wine bars, tea salons, and cafés, sampling croissants from some twenty different patisseries, finding the perfect lemon tea cookie or madeleine, and relishing the lavish displays of produce, meats, fish, and poultry from the city's many markets.

By September of that year, there was an opening for the post of restaurant critic at the *IHT* and I jumped in. I was going to prove them all wrong, especially one *New York Times* colleague who had sneered "You will NEVER make a living as a full-time food writer in Paris!"

My first IHT press pass.

~◌◦~

Our Lemon Chicken
with Roasted Onions

People often ask what Walter and I eat at home, when it's just the two of us. More often than not I'll suggest a simple roast chicken, and Walter will second that, and that has been true since our early days in Paris. In this sublime recipe, the chicken is stuffed with lemons, and halved onions are placed cut side down in the roasting pan, so they absorb all the delicious juices. Most often, we will serve this with a simple mushroom salad and steamed green beans. The next day I'll make chicken salad for lunch and a rich chicken stock from the leftover carcass.

EQUIPMENT: An oval roasting pan, just slightly larger than the chicken (about 13 by 9 inches), fitted with a roasting rack.

> 1 fresh farm chicken (3 to 4 pounds), at room temperature, with giblets
> Sea salt
> Freshly ground black pepper
> 2 lemons, preferably organic, scrubbed, dried, and quartered lengthwise
> 1 bunch fresh thyme
> 2 tablespoons unsalted butter, softened
> 6 onions, halved but not peeled

1. Preheat the oven to 425°F.
2. Generously season the cavity of the chicken with salt and pepper. Place the giblets, lemons, and thyme in the cavity. Truss. Rub the skin with the butter. Season all over with salt and pepper.
3. Place the onions cut side down in the roasting pan. Place the roasting rack over the onions.
4. Place the chicken on its side on the roasting rack. Pour about ½ cup water into the bottom of the pan to help create a rich and pleasing sauce later on. Place in the center of the oven and roast, uncovered, for 20 minutes. Turn the chicken to the other side, and roast for 20 minutes more. Turn the chicken breast side up, and

roast for 20 minutes more, for a total of 1 hour's roasting time. By this time, the skin should be a deep golden color. Reduce the heat to 375°F. Turn the chicken breast side down, at an angle if at all possible, with the head end down and the tail in the air. (This heightens the flavor by allowing the juices to flow down through the breast meat.) Roast until the juices run clear when you pierce a thigh with a skewer, about 15 minutes more.

5. Remove from the oven and season generously with salt and pepper. Transfer the chicken to a platter, and place on an angle against the edge of an overturned plate, with head down and tail in the air. Cover loosely with foil. Turn off the oven and place the platter, with the plate underneath at an angle, in the oven with the door open. Let rest a minimum of 10 minutes and up to 30 minutes. The chicken will continue to cook during this resting time.

6. Meanwhile, prepare the sauce: Remove the onions to a platter. Place the roasting pan over moderate heat, scraping up any bits that cling to the bottom. Cook for 2 to 3 minutes, scraping and stirring until the liquid is almost caramelized. Do not let it burn. Spoon off and discard any excess fat. Add several tablespoons cold water to deglaze (hot water will cloud the sauce). Bring to a boil. Reduce the heat to low and simmer until thickened, about 5 minutes.

7. While the sauce is cooking, remove the lemons, giblets, and thyme from the cavity of the chicken. Carve the chicken into serving pieces and transfer to a warmed platter. Chop the giblets and add them to the platter. Squeeze the lemons all over the pieces of poultry, extracting as much juice as possible. Place two onion halves on each plate with the chicken. Strain the sauce through a fine-mesh sieve and pour into a sauce boat. Serve immediately.

4 to 6 servings

WINE SUGGESTION: When I think of roast chicken I often think of a light, young Beaujolais Villages, such as one from the village of Saint Amour.

CHIBERTA'S NOUVELLE CUISINE
RAW DUCK SALAD

In November of 1980 as one of my first pieces for the *International Herald Tribune*, I reviewed Chiberta, then the Paris restaurant of the moment. I wrote, "To be serious about food and miss Jean-Michel Bédier's superb *nouvelle cuisine* is akin to skipping a pilgrimage to Fauchon and Michel Guérard on Place de la Madeleine." I raved about his duck salad: raw paper-thin slices of *magret de canard* draped atop a bed of spinach, showered with shallots, chives, and sherry vinegar. This hardly seems daring today, but back then it was revolutionary. I like to set out the garnishes and allow guests to season their own duck. I also prefer lemon juice over vinegar as a seasoning, so I offer both options.

EQUIPMENT: An electric slicer or very sharp knife; 4 chilled salad plates.

> One 12- to 16-ounce duck breast (*magret de canard*), skin, fat, and silverskin removed
> 4 cups baby spinach leaves, rinsed and dried
> Several tablespoons Classic Vinaigrette (recipe follows)

> GARNISH AND SEASONING:
> 2 whole shallots, peeled, halved, and finely minced
> Finely minced chives
> Extra-virgin olive oil
> Best-quality sherry wine vinegar or quarters of fresh lemon
> Freshly ground black pepper
> Fleur de sel

> Toasted slices of crusty bread for serving

1. Wrap the duck breast in plastic wrap and place in the freezer for 1 hour, to make it easier to slice. With an electric slicer or a very sharp knife, cut the duck breast lengthwise on a slight bias into 16 thin slices. Transfer to a plate, cover with plastic wrap, and let

thaw at least 10 minutes before serving. (The duck slices can be refrigerated for several hours before serving.)

2. Place the spinach leaves in a large bowl and toss thoroughly with just enough vinaigrette to coat them lightly and evenly. Taste for seasoning. Distribute the salad among four chilled salad plates. Drape the slices of duck breast on top of the greens. Allow each guest to select from the number of garnishes, as well as their quantity. Serve with crusty toasted bread.

4 servings

NOTES: Chiberta, on the Rue Arsène Houssaye near the Arc de Triomphe, is still a popular Parisian restaurant, now owned by chef Guy Savoy. The gourmet shop, Fauchon, is still on the Place de la Madeleine, but Michel Guérard's specialty shop is no longer there.

Magret de canard can be found in some specialty markets in the U.S. and can be ordered online in the U.S. from D'Artagnan at www.dartagnan. com. Ask for moulard duck breasts, which weigh an average of 1.6 to 2 pounds.

CLASSIC VINAIGRETTE

EQUIPMENT: A small jar with a lid.

> 2 tablespoons best-quality sherry wine vinegar
> 2 tablespoons best-quality red wine vinegar
> Fine sea salt to taste
> 1 cup extra-virgin olive oil

Place the sherry vinegar, red wine vinegar, and salt in the jar. Cover and shake to dissolve the salt. Add the oil and shake to blend. Taste for seasoning. The vinaigrette can be stored at room temperature or in the refrigerator for several weeks. Shake again at serving time to create a thick emulsion.

About 1¼ cups vinaigrette

3
{ Seeing Things }

WALTER:

Paris has been so much a part of my life with Patricia that it's ironic to remember that it was with another girl that I first saw the city. I hadn't intended to—I set out for London. But after a week the girlfriend persuaded me to come with her to the other side of the Channel.

It was love at first sight. Not with the girl—she's long gone. On our last night together, standing on the Pont du Carrousel, the lights along the Quai du Louvre reflected in the Seine, I wanted to sound meaningful (and avoid any further involvement with my tour guide) so I said, "I'll be back to stay." I'm sure that I sounded only trite. Millions have done the same thing, surely, standing on one bridge or another, because Paris exerts such a powerful romantic pull. Couples come to get engaged, for a honeymoon, to revive a marriage, or just to renew commitment.

When Patricia and I first came to Paris together it was on a lark, one week out of that three-week gastronomic tour of France. When we moved there it was to be an interlude, a couple of years away from our high-pressure New York jobs. It turned out that there was more stress in my Paris job, but outside the newsroom, Paris offered some of the deliverance I had wanted. While living in New York, I remember saying in the course of a long and fitful dialogue with a friend—a therapist, actually—that I would welcome some elegance in my life. "That's asking a lot," she said.

Looking for a bit of elegance…

A lot? How could it be a lot? I wasn't asking for Park Avenue sumptuousness, or for "living large," as an expense-account-envious friend would put it. Just a little class. Sidewalks where no one was spitting, or piling garbage, or commanding "Gimme a quarter, buddy" as New York's panhandlers did in those days. Yet not in some drive-through burg that squatted along the road to somewhere else. I wanted to exercise my pretensions in a world capital, one with excitement and texture.

Paris provided that. It was clear from the outset that my life was better in Paris—at least it was clear through the rose-colored glasses that I dared not take off for the first six months, determined as I was to make things work out after the move. Life was better, I told myself, even though most days it didn't feel better. The glasses helped not just vision but imagination. For instance, watching people at cafés or on the Métro, I could tell that they were happy and content. Looking around the Métro now, I wonder who the hell I might have been looking at back then. But whatever I was seeing, with hindsight it's obvious that the decision was right and the determination was right, too.

Why Paris? What was it about the city that pulled us there and kept us? Well, how high is the sky?

It's not that the answer is elusive, or the answers, because there are millions of them in words and images and none of them are more adequate than grunts and blurs. The ones that are adequate are personal and intense and they have grown and changed over thirty years. I don't remember now how many of my own answers were obvious in 1980. But both as a new arrival and as a longtime resident, a hundred times a day if not a thousand I found something that brought passing delight: a vista along the Seine or clouds roiling in a silvery sky; the Eiffel Tower twinkling over a 7th arrondissement neighborhood; a pedestrian looking warily upward when he realizes that the way in front of him is dappled with pigeon droppings; the roar of the fountain in front of the Hôtel de Ville, louder even than the traffic on the expressway running alongside; the eager looks of the customers waiting in line at Pierre Hermé on a big feast day, eager to get inside and buy their chocolate treats but apprehensive that when they get to the counter there won't be anything left, even at those prices; the breathy alto of the flutes of the (fake?) Peruvian band down in the Châtelet Métro station; the cars driven onto the sidewalks and abandoned there for the duration of a movie or dinner; the way women look you in the eye when they catch you noticing them; the way older men still wear suits and ties on weekdays when they go to read their papers in the cafés, and ascots on weekends when they walk with their wives or lovers.

These pictures and sounds hang there in my mind's eyes and ears, to be called up and relished. There are other things that center me—

literally, like *Point Zéro* in front of Notre Dame, from which all distances are measured in France; or in a more symbolic way, the Statue of Liberty in the Luxembourg Gardens. That calls me to reflect on America, which as an idea is endlessly gleaming and bright and which as a place is always home.

Those are small, quiet pleasures, not grand ones like the emotional wash that comes when you turn a corner inside Notre Dame and see the big rose window with the sun bright behind it, or glimpse Sacre Coeur in the distance, tall skinny beehives up there on the Butte Montmartre, or the Eiffel Tower's hourly glitz disappearing into a misty evening sky.

Beauty abounds in Paris, and it's mostly self-conscious. Even the scrims put up to hide restoration at the national monuments are decorated with big pen-and-ink sketches of the buildings they're covering. Several years ago when the old flower stalls at the Madeleine were replaced with snappy new ones, a friend bemoaned such tarting up as evidence of a house-proud city administration. But having missed the decrepit charm that Eugène Atget's photographs made so romantic, I take what I can get, including all the tarting up. The primping is simply French, like the orderly public plantings and the greenswards that are to be looked at and not lain on. PELOUSE EN REPOS say the cute signs now (lawn resting). We were late for Atget's Paris, but we have seen a kinder, gentler approach evolve. In the 1980s, the signs weren't cute but authoritarian, as were the whistle-empowered park policemen who ordered you off the grass if you dared to sit down on it.

Those park police were reality. In time they helped smudge my rose-colored glasses and dim my vision. Our fantasy life began looking like plain old life. But even in focus, with its warts exposed and worries uncalmed, Paris has always remained more than just scenery. It's not that we never looked back at our life in America and never thought of returning. But when we did, the tug of Paris and the life we have there overwhelmed those thoughts. We made the original decision because of that tug, and it remains a powerful magnetic field.

4

{ Rules, Rules, and More Rules }

"Je Vous Donne la Règle"

PATRICIA:

After settling in, one of the first things we had to deal with was learning the language. So beginning on a morning in late January 1980, and for the next two years, Walter and I took the Métro from our neighborhood Courcelles station on the Right Bank to Montparnasse on the Left Bank for our daily French lesson. Most mornings after it was over we stopped for a cup of espresso at the Dôme café and fantasized as to what the place was like when Hemingway sat there near a coal heater, writing. It was one of many Parisian fantasies.

Our French tutor, Denise Lioté, is a fine contemporary artist who still lives in a true artist's loft in Montparnasse. Each morning we would climb the six floors to her sky-lit studio and begin our French adventure surrounded by a series of oil paintings in progress, most of them calming, ethereal pastels—lots of blue grays and orangey pinks reminiscent of tender clouds or sunsets in the making.

It was there that we began to learn the biggest rule of all: France is full of rules. We quickly learned that living in France can in fact be quite easy, for there is a rule for each and every moment of the day, each and every situation, each and every word, gesture, movement. So it seems that if you followed all the rules, life would be a breeze. But learning the rules is not always *évident*, as the French say.

I don't take readily to foreign languages nor do I cave in easily to stiff rules. So in speaking French, I would learn to get my message across by weaving in and out of sentences, re-forming them so that I did not have to use a form or a tense I did not know. Probably because I was a beginner, Denise let me get by with that, but our next tutor, the fashionable Susy Piochelle, cut me no slack. She would often have me in tears as she scolded me after one of my dodgy, roundabout phrases. "*Je vous donne la règle!*" (I will give you the rule) she would announce.

There were rules, rules, and more rules. One of the earliest rules we deciphered was what we came to call the Orange Juice Trick. We went to many formal dinner parties in those days, terrifying events where I feared I would not understand a word that was said and would make an embarrassed fool of myself. Always, following dessert, we would retire to the living room. Men would gather at one end, women at another, Cognac would be offered, cigarettes and cigars would be lit, there would be coffee. Then a short time later, like clockwork, a large crystal and silver pitcher—usually Christofle—filled with chilled orange juice would appear. We would sip the orange juice and everyone would go home. It took us a while to understand the rule: Orange juice was the signal that it was time to leave. How clever! No embarrassingly long evenings, no one lingering on past their welcome. The host and hostess did not have to say a word. Everyone knew the Orange Juice Trick and everyone obeyed it. Life in France was beginning to seem simpler. Only later did we learn what an intelligent signal the orange juice was: The vitamin C helps counteract the alcohol and may even prevent hangovers, for it speeds up the metabolism of alcohol by the liver.

Another Parisian goodbye trick is to ask, "Who needs a taxi?" That's slightly more subtle than our American host who went around turning out the lights.

I am also not very good at French history or the succession of kings and emperors, so when we went to the elegant silver shop, Puiforcat, to buy monogrammed silver cups as baby presents, we learned another rule. I had chosen a rather decorative cup and wanted to have it engraved with a modern block Art Deco script. The saleswoman gasped at my unforgivable lapse of taste: "You cannot mix Louis XV with Charles X. It is just not done." I begged and cajoled, requested again and again, insisted. She would not budge. She would rather lose a sale then permit such an obvious faux pas!

Not far from the Puiforcat shop, on Boulevard Haussmann in those days, sat the elegant stationery store Vendel Shakespeare. Of course we needed engraved cards with our new Paris address but, again, had to learn some new rules. PATRICIA AND WALTER WELLS is the way we wanted the card to read. Again, lose a sale if you must, but the saleslady put her foot down on that. It had to be MONSIEUR ET MADAME WALTER WELLS. Then she whispered in a low voice, fearing that someone might overhear, "You know, some young people do it these days, but they soon regret it."

We were hindered in furnishing our new apartment by two main issues: lack of money and lack of vocabulary to purchase what we needed. At that time, the once-elegant, then-dowdy department store Magasins Réunis was just a few blocks away, and their basement was a handyman's dream, full of every kind of screw, nut, bolt, tool a handyman or *bricoleur* could want. Our apartment had a very handy *garde-manger*, a sheltered, screened pantry about a foot deep, two feet wide, and two feet high, beneath the window in the kitchen. In the cooler winter months, the pantry served us well, and one could store fruits and vegetables there, a sort of ecologically correct refrigerator substitute. But ours had not been used or refurbished in decades and the wire mesh screen—there to protect the pantry's contents from the insects and the elements—needed replacing. We hunted down just what we needed in the basement of Magasins Réunis and brought the roll of screening to the salesclerk. He asked if the screen was to be used for a garde-manger. We said yes. His response was a direct, "*Pas pour garde-manger!*" with a stern wagging of the finger. Dumbfounded, once again, we saw that the man would rather lose a sale than sell us screening that he deemed incorrect. We waited around until he went on a break, found another salesperson, and insisted the screening would, of course, never see the light of day in a garde-manger! We installed the screening that day in 1980, and to this day, I am sure it still lines the pantry in that Rue Daru apartment.

The 1980s was an era of lots of fancy, stylish pantyhose with stripes, polka dots, and floral patterns. I guess I wore a lot of navy blue then, for I remember searching from one department store to another for striped navy blue pantyhose. I could not figure out why I found not a single pair, anywhere. I finally gathered the courage to ask a saleswoman, who quickly gave me La Règle, speaking as though any fool would know: "*Mais Madame, la fantaisie n'existe pas en bleu marine!*" *Fantaisie* was the word for any kind of patterned pantyhose and the Rule was that there would be no patterned stockings in navy blue, only black. Who makes those rules?

Years later, after having lost quite a bit of weight, I took piles of designer clothes to a luxury resale shop. I had several lovely Armani suits I had purchased in New York City. One was navy blue. I was again informed that not only did Parisian women not wear *bleu marine* but they did not wear Armani!

Few people—save for savvy professional photographers—realize that it is illegal to be photographed professionally at certain Paris monuments or parks without advanced written approval from the city as well as a permit for a single shot. The Eiffel Tower, the Place de la Concorde, and Parc Monceau are at least three that I know of. One day, years later, I was being photographed for a profile of me in *Figaro Magazine*. The photographer knew of the rule, informed me, and we decided to take a chance, seating me on a park bench in Parc Monceau. Sure enough, a few shutter clicks into the session, a policeman came by, asking for the famed *permis*. From all the photographer's gear, it was clear that he was a professional. But the photographer announced that he was a friend just taking a friendly portrait. The policeman knew better, but didn't press the point. So, as always, we waited until he went away, and then we went on about our business. The picture ran full-page the next week in the weekly Sunday magazine.

One day while researching a story in Brittany, my friend the photographer Steven Rothfeld and I—both avid oyster fans—visited a produce market with an oyster stand. The morning menu included six oysters and a glass of white Muscadet wine enjoyed at a little bar. We both agreed that it was too early in the day for wine, but not for oysters. So we asked if we could have six oysters and a Perrier instead. The waitress was flummoxed and had to ask her boss. She returned, clearly frustrated, and totally unable to understand how anyone would want to change the rules. "*Mais vous n'êtes plus dans la formule!*" she announced, looking at us total morons who did not understand La Règle. We finally got our oysters and our Perrier, with a lot of chuckling and head-shaking along with it. I think we paid the price of oysters and wine, but the laughter was worth the price of admission.

One summer in late August we had planned a catered picnic at a clearing at the top of one of our favorite hiking spots in Provence, just above the village of Gigondas. It was an extremely hot and dry summer, and many parks were closed to all traffic, including hikers, for fear of forest fires. The park above Gigondas was officially closed, but both the chef catering the picnic and the winemaker in attendance assured us that we were well within La Règle. But sure enough, just as we were finishing our elegant feast on the wooden picnic tables beneath the pines, the local forest rangers spotted us and stopped to scold. The winemaker, Yves Gras, jumped in and told them that we were important clients who had reserved the meal months in advance and he couldn't say no to us. The rangers were calmed, and left.

About thirty minutes later, my friend Julie and I were hiking back down to the village and crossed the rangers once more. The Catholic girl in me began solemn apologies, but they stopped us short. "*Madame*," they assured me, "*c'est interdit! Mais toléré.*" Okay, that was a totally new rule to me: Forbidden. But tolerated. What did I say about it being easy if you just follow the rules?

I have already made it clear that I don't write in French. But that doesn't keep me from sending off formal and flowery letters from time to time, cribbed from one of the most useful books in French, called *500 Lettres Pour Tous Les Jours: Savoir Écrire en Toutes Circonstances*, or *500 Letters for Everyday Life* (Larousse, 2004). The Larousse tome allows even an idiot to create perfectly penned notes that will fit into any situation.

My favorite is a thank-you note to send to your hostess following a weekend at her family château. The first line reads "*Quelle douce merveille . . .* " (What a gentle and marvelous visit) which we transformed into *quelle douche merveille* (what a marvelous shower!) thanking our plumber for our lovely new bathroom! I'm not sure it was a joke or that he got it, but we still quote the line and laugh.

French rules of the table can be so complex and *catégorique* that they would send even the most well-mannered to dine alone, in peace. One of my favorite rules concerns cheese: Diners must never take seconds of cheese, for that would send two insulting signals to the hostess: First, you didn't get enough to eat during the earlier part of the meal, a true affront. Second, that the food prepared by the hostess was not good enough, so you need to make it up with food that she clearly did not make!

Other rules I love:

> If you entertain on Friday, you must serve fish,
> no matter what your religion.

> If you don't know your guests well, do not serve organ
> meats, rabbit, pork, shellfish, or rare meat.

> You may serve seconds of the first course and main
> course, but never soup, salad, cheese, or fruit.

If any guest at the table takes seconds of the first and second course, the host and hostess are obliged, by etiquette, also to take seconds.

Women never pour their own wine. But men at the table are told to be vigilant, for it is bad manners for anyone ever to be left with an empty glass!

And who gets served first? In this order: the women, then the guests of honor, the hostess, the men in order of descending age, the host, and finally, the children.

Seating arrangements can be the most complicated of all, enough, again, to dine alone without any rules. My favorite detail is the order in which women have rank at the table: widows first, followed by a married woman, a divorced woman, a single woman. And what if you are a single host or hostess? Single hostesses must never seat a man, either married or single, directly across from her. Single hosts must never sit across from a married woman if her husband is absent.

Breaking all the rules: We sat chef Joël Robuchon to my right at a special dinner. Only decades later did we learn that the local mayor had seniority in seating!

"Do you know what a foul is in basketball?" my friend asked, clearly anticipating a dorky technical response. So with a tiny, almost Gallic shrug, I let him give his own answer: "It's when the referee blows the whistle."

Ah, now that's a rule to live by.

There are rules aplenty in France, and being a foreigner has sometimes meant keeping an ear out for a whistle—in other words, getting by with an approximate relationship to the rules. And that says something about the basic tolerant nature of the culture. For despite all the rules—*règles, avis, préceptes, ordres, consignes,* and even *arrêtes,* as laws are known—differences are tolerated. To a certain extent. The nail that sticks up gets pounded down, say the Japanese. In French the expression is more poetic: The nail that stands out summons the hammer.

Yet the idea of rules—*les règles*—is basic to life. (Very basic, in fact, because a woman's period is her *règles.*) The importance of rules is evident in how many expressions are built around the word. When accounts are settled or a dispute, they are *réglé.* When everything is normal, it is of course *normale,* but it's also *en règle.* A piece of equipment that meets the norms is *réglementaire.* Something *pas régulière* is quantitatively worse than something that is *pas logique.* And a *situation irrégulière* is one that you want to avoid because—if anyone is there to blow the whistle—it can lead to a fine, like being caught on the Métro without a ticket. In the language of the young, who often shorten words down to an essential syllable or two, something out of whack is "*pas réglo.*"

The rules of grammar are more daunting than an array of forks on the table because you confront the rules every time you open your mouth, let alone put pen to paper. Just look at how the accent waggles metronome-like from grave to acute and back again over variations of *règle.*

When our French tutor would say, "*Je vous donne la règle,*" it often followed a tolerant smile at some barbarism. "Anyone would understand what you mean," she would say, "but it's not French."

Madame Piochelle was not a member of *L'Académie Française*, but her instinct to police the use of the language was strong enough to earn its gratitude. If she didn't make us remember all the rules of grammar, she certainly made us understand that they were better enforced than no-parking signs.

To the unruly American grammatical mind, perhaps no French effort at being French is more puzzling than the studied defense of the language. Paul-Marie Coûteaux, in *Être et Parler Français* (Perrin, 2006), provides a wonderfully recondite definition of the language: "Language is so much more than a means of communicating," he writes (my translation). "It is a way of conceiving the world, of life, of one's place in the world, and perhaps even of one's sense of life itself."

Needless to say, none of the several versions of *Webster's* on my shelf supports that theory, nor does my four-volume *Harrap's French-English Dictionary*.

But Mr. Coûteaux's argument does bring this rush of clarity. The French language is to words as the American flag is to cloth: sacred and a blazon. It is an intimate bond between the Frenchman and his nation, and it is a symbol to be fought for and over, not just spoken.

೫೦

JOHANNES'S PICNIC COUSCOUS SALAD

The day that I learned the remarkable French expression—forbidden but tolerated—we sampled this delicious couscous salad as part of a splendid picnic prepared by chef Johannes Sailer of restaurant Les Abeilles in the Provençal village of Sablet.

EQUIPMENT: A fine-mesh sieve; a food processor or a blender.

1½ cups medium-grain instant couscous
3 tablespoons freshly squeezed lemon juice
1 tablespoon extra-virgin olive oil
1½ teaspoons fine sea salt
1 pound red-ripe tomatoes, cored and quartered
⅛ teaspoon ground Espelette pepper (or dried Anaheim chile or ground mild chile)
⅛ teaspoon ground cayenne pepper
1 green bell pepper, cut into very fine dice
2 tablespoons chiffonade of fresh mint leaves

1. Place the couscous in a very fine sieve and rinse thoroughly under cold running water. Place in a large bowl. Toss with a fork to fluff. Set aside.
2. In a food processor or a blender combine the lemon juice, oil, salt, tomatoes, Espelette pepper, and cayenne. Process to blend. Pour the mixture into the couscous and toss with a fork to blend. Fluff until the grains are evenly separated. Cover and set aside, occasionally fluffing and tossing the grains, until all the liquid has been absorbed, about 3 minutes.
3. Add the diced pepper and mint. Toss to blend. Taste for seasoning. (The couscous can be prepared up to 8 hours in advance, covered, and refrigerated.)

8 servings

WINE SUGGESTION: That day our current winemaker and friend Yves Gras brought several bottles of his white Sablet wine, a blend of Viognier, Grenache Blanc, and Bourboulenc grapes, offering a great balance of fruit and acidity.

5

{ Reality Strikes }

WALTER:

It was a joke, one that we repeated often because often it seemed true: We came to Paris for my job and we stayed for Patricia's. But even as her career blossomed, the *Trib* was always the financial glue that held us there. Over time my job evolved into a great career. But in the beginning it almost ended our marriage.

I arrived with solid experience as an editor. I could conceive stories and manage assignments. I could work copy into publishable shape, design handsome pages, and write good headlines. But I was the kind of newsroom manager who thinks that competence is skill enough. It took a while to learn that it takes more, but a boss helped me. A boss who—we said, those of us on his bad side—had learned his own management skills while questioning Japanese POWs. He followed me to the paper by a year. Our relationship started out well, but that didn't last and the conflict with him completely destabilized me. It took me a stupidly long time to learn that home is where you go for love, not to relive job anxieties.

Patricia's generosity of spirit is nearly boundless, but her patience knows tight limits. She accepted my late hours and frequent weekend work, but not the negative anger that my boss had set to smolder. Sometimes a whine is the fastest way to get the whack you deserve, and Patricia's threat to move out was an effective whack. So we made another deal: I worked on anger management, and she stayed. No boss lasts forever, not in journalism. The one who hired me had already been fired and number two was not serving a lifetime appointment. Soon enough there would be a third and a set of other things to learn to manage.

Journalism has ended a lot of marriages, but the *International Herald Tribune* was unlikely grounds for divorce. The paper started as the *Paris Herald* when it was founded in 1887 by James Gordon Bennett Jr., son of the owner of the *New York Herald*. A social exile from New York, he was inspired to start the Paris edition, according to the legend, because he heard an owl hoot in the middle of the night. If that suggests the founder was quirky, that would be right. There had been a succession of owners when I was recruited in 1980, but the *Trib* was still quirky. It was also fragile and underresourced.

For example, there was in 1980 a single photocopier, secure in the advertising department and available to the news department only until 7:00 p.m. The editing terminals, installed just two years before, thunked and rattled as they sent stories and headlines into the ether as often as to a typesetter. The newsroom was strictly an "I'm all right, Jack" kind of shop.

Although there were new computers it was not all that different in spirit from the Rue de Berri newsroom that produced the paper Jean Seberg hawked on the Champs-Elysées in *Breathless*. The 1960 film classic offered a link to glamour for the paper's ink-stained staff, some of them committed and talented and some marginal hangers-on. By the time I got there, the paper had moved to other offices, but the claims on Parisian glamour were still insistent. There was the glamour of our hometown, of course, but also because of our A-list readership. Indira Gandhi, Leonard Bernstein, Anne Bancroft, Helmut Schmidt,

George Kennan, Valéry Giscard d'Estaing, and Queen Sofia of Spain were among the scores of people who told me at one time or another how much they loved the paper. Walter Cronkite said that mine was the only other title in journalism he had ever wanted.

But the most glamour derived from the ownership, an improbable linking of the *New York Times*, the *Washington Post*, and Whitney Communications, the remnants of the *New York Herald Tribune*.

For a brief period, William S. Paley, who founded CBS, was one of three co-chairmen, along with Katharine Graham and Arthur Ochs Sulzberger. (And yes, Mrs. Graham wanted to be called co-chairman.) For both Sulzberger and Graham, the *Trib* was more noblesse oblige than bottom line. The *Trib*'s meager earnings paled against the international prestige of presiding over the chief independent source of news from America. Because the *Trib*'s coverage reflected the dominant postwar American internationalist worldview, it was highly valued in foreign ministries and chanceries. It was also beloved by Americans traveling or living abroad, and it was admired by journalists in other countries as a gold standard.

Viewed from outside, it was a world-class institution, one of the first bridgeheads in globalization. When I got inside, what marked it was major upheaval. Between 1977 and 1981, a beloved editor had been fired; the paper had been relocated to the Paris suburbs and converted to computerized editing and typesetting; the change had derailed relations with the craft unions; more than half the editing staff had left and been replaced; there was a new publisher; and the editor in chief who had hired me had been fired.

I think now that under the circumstances, naïveté served me better than any management skills I might have had. But thanks to a lot of help from several staff members, I began seeing progress. We rationalized staffing and procedures and focused on hiring that would build newsroom strengths and not just fill the daily roster.

And with encouragement from Patricia it was occurring to me that I could take a night off now and then. And on March 30, 1981, I

*Walter did not work ALL the time: He also made marvelous
and elegant French-style strawberry shortcake.*

did. I left the office about eight and joined her for dinner in a bistro
near our apartment. After a relaxed dinner we went for a long walk,
from the Place des Ternes near where we lived, around the Arc de
Triomphe and over to the Trocadéro to look out at the Eiffel Tower.
On our stroll back we stopped to have a glass of wine on the terrace
of the Brasserie Lorraine. Still not understanding very much French,
I noticed how often people at other tables were saying "Reagan" or
"*l'Amérique.*"

"Something has happened," I said to Patricia. "Let's go home." It was
before the days of cell phones and beepers, and I had left no number
because I didn't know where I would be. It was the last time I did that.

At midnight when we walked through our front door the phone
was ringing. "Reagan has been shot," Richard Berry, the duty editor
told me. "He's alive. We missed some circulation but we got the story
into all the editions that went out and we'll soon be locking up the

last one." After a few questions on content and display, I congratulated him on the job he had overseen. But I was crestfallen not to have been there making the decisions.

The next morning I was at the door when the concierge delivered the mail and the paper with it to see how the staff had handled the story. Quite well, frankly, given the small amount of time they had to deal with it. Having coffee with Patricia I said, "I bet they had fun." And then, after a pause I added, "I should have been there."

"Look," she said with a note of comfort in her voice. "You can't always be there. And you already know that you won't always have fun working there, and probably not anywhere else. So let's have fun living here."

She had a point.

Judy's North Carolina Pork Barbecue

Nothing satisfies like comfort food! Every now and then—especially during some of the tougher times—Walter and I would think back to what we missed from "back home." My sister, Judy Jones, stepped in to save us with this Southern barbecue recipe. When we returned home on visits to Walter's family in South Carolina or to my sister, her family, and my mother in North Carolina, pork barbecue often played a role. We even brought back a slow cooker from Target on one of our many trips home. The first time I purchased the pork to make this in our Paris kitchen, the butcher asked me what I was going to do with it. I wanted to respond in a deep Southern accent, "Pork barbecue, honey."

EQUIPMENT: A slow cooker.

Pork
A lean Boston pork butt, about 4 pounds
1 cup cider vinegar
2 tablespoons light brown sugar
1 tablespoon fine sea salt
½ teaspoon hot red pepper flakes

Barbecue Sauce
3 cups cider vinegar
⅔ cup light brown sugar
½ cup ketchup
2 tablespoons hot sauce (Texas Pete brand is recommended, though we can't get this in France!)
1 teaspoon fine sea salt
1 teaspoon freshly ground black pepper
1 teaspoon Worcestershire sauce

1. Combine the pork, vinegar, brown sugar, salt, and hot pepper flakes in the slow cooker. Cover and cook at a low setting for 10 hours. Remove the meat and chop, carefully removing and discarding any fat. Return the meat and juices to the cooker.

2. While the meat is cooking, prepare the barbecue sauce: In a large saucepan, combine the cider vinegar, brown sugar, ketchup, hot sauce, salt, pepper, and Worcestershire sauce. Bring to a simmer over medium heat and stir until the sugar melts. Let marinate for several hours, refrigerated.
3. Before serving, add the barbecue sauce to the cooked, shredded pork in the slow cooker. Cook on low for 30 minutes to 1 hour before serving. This dish freezes very well.

16 servings

BEVERAGE SUGGESTION: We enjoy this with a good, cold beer.

6

{ Making Yourself Up }

PATRICIA:

Something about the word "expatriate" really rankles. My online dictionary defines it inoffensively just as someone who has moved abroad. But there's the implication of banishment or rejection, and that's not what happened. Like most of our friends who live abroad, Walter and I have never rejected anything of our native culture. When we left the United States to settle in Paris, it was to gain some journalistic experience and understand another culture before returning to New York. As we have stayed, we have continued to grow with new experiences, taking the best of each culture and applying it to ourselves and our daily lives.

For me, being a journalist in a foreign country is the best job of all. For journalists must remain impartial observers. It's best not to be an insider. As a foreigner and a journalist, I get to observe French culture without having to apologize for it, even to myself.

But I discovered another advantage to being a foreigner: I got to make myself up. One day I looked around at all of our Anglophone friends and realized that most of them—journalists, lawyers, authors—

were self-employed and had made a decision that living abroad was life enhancing. They were in Paris because they made a specific choice—even if the choice was simply to stay. I realized that I liked being surrounded by self-made friends, people who were not there because it was the only place they could make a living.

With that realization came another, that I had handed myself the opportunity for my own self-invention. Back in New York, I had been hazed as that "country" girl from the Midwest (many New Yorkers still think that Milwaukee—or Columbus or Raleigh—is a hick town with no redeeming qualities).

But after arriving in Paris, I sat down and realized that the French had no idea who Patricia Wells was, at least who she was back in America. I could have had a Ph.D. from Harvard or wealthy parents or some other pedigree. But, no, I was born in Wisconsin to a department store buyer and a stay-at-home mom. My ancestors were German and Italian immigrant farmers and I went to the state university.

But since none of those facts mattered to the French, I could be whoever I wanted to be. I could be simple or outrageous, I could play by the rules or not. To the French, I was just another American. There was no other pedigree.

I could not imagine a more refreshing situation. What freedom! But also what a challenge, what a responsibility. There were no guidelines, no plans—I had to write them. There were no set goals. That was for me to create. It was exhilarating and frightening at the same time.

One of my goals came to fruition in the fall of 1982. My agent Susan Lescher set up a meeting with Peter Workman, one of New York City's most original publishers and a man of unusual vision. I came with a grab bag of book ideas, but we quickly agreed that my guide to Paris food was the best of the pack. I was elated.

By that time I had become a freelance machine, saying yes to every two-bit writing job that came my way. (I was always afraid that if I said no, it would be a curse, and the well would dry up.) In fact, there were many days when, upon awakening, even before getting out of bed, I would count the number of assignments that were overdue. My recurring dream was that I had a review due the next day and the night before wandered from restaurant to restaurant, finding sign after sign that read *Fermé*.

As I set out to work methodically on *The Food Lover's Guide to Paris*, I realized that I couldn't do it by myself. At that time, the Left Bank cooking school La Varenne—established by British-born food writer Anne Willan—was in its heyday. Students who attended the English-language school provided me with a wide assortment of willing food lovers: young, energetic, and hungry young Americans.

I don't know whether I found Susan Herrmann or she found me, but by the spring of 1983 I had made my first hire. Susan had graduated from La Varenne and like many Americans in love with Paris, was willing to do almost anything to stay there.

The Food Lover's Headquarters on Rue Daru.

With our Rue Daru "spare bedroom" office as our headquarters, we would spend Mondays mapping out our research routine. We were very systematic. I had created files for every chapter I thought would

An early Métro pass identity card.

be important, from tea salons to pastry shops, markets to wine bars, kitchen shops, and chocolate makers. Working on my portable type-writer, we created lists by arrondissements, noting every shop that might be worth a visit.

Tuesday through Friday, we took to the streets for field research. I would be out the door by 7 a.m.—my favorite time in Paris, when the streets are almost empty save for a lone concierge scrubbing a sidewalk or waiters setting out café tables—and Sue and I would meet at an appointed outdoor food market. We were strict, and didn't allow ourselves to wander or leave the day's arrondissement. By noon, we would have visited a market or two, several cafés, a handful of *boulangeries* and pastry shops, and maybe a few kitchen shops. Our purses bulged with goodies. Each day brought a new restaurant for lunch. It's hard to imagine, but in 1983, women—especially women unaccompanied by men—simply did not dine out at lunchtime.

We all still laugh about our first visit to Pile ou Face (Heads or Tails), then an elegant little restaurant near the Bourse, or stock exchange. We were the only women there, we fell instantly in love with the place, and obviously asked more questions than the normal businessman diner. When we left, the owners—a trio who in time became good friends—said to one another, "Who were those babes?"

We walked and we walked. I was young enough then not to need to be too concerned about the caloric intake of the day, and Sue is a naturally lean gal. But we still had rules about our daily consumption. As we canvassed the city on foot, sampling flaky croissants, buttery almond-flavored financiers, fragrant quiche warm from the oven, we followed the Food Lover's Law: We could only take one bite. No matter how good. One bite and then put it into our trusty sacks. Actually, an awful lot of our treasures ended up in the hands of the many homeless who lived on the streets back then, and more often than once they made it clear that a drink or a Métro ticket would have been more welcome. And when we dined out at lunch if the bread was not up to our standards, we simply reached into our sacks and pulled out a treasure.

I look upon those days with envy today. Everything was new, bright, exciting. There were so many first-time experiences, so many thrilling new tastes. People were real, dedicated, eager to share their stories. Many a night, as Walter walked in the door from work I would shout with joy, "I just had one of the best days of my life!" Walter would respond, "You say that three times a week."

After lunch and more shops, Sue and I would return to Daru to type up our notes on carbon paper, so that we each had a copy of the day's events and reactions. Yes, these were the days before home photo-copiers. But also the days before faxes, FedEx, even Post-it's! I did get my first home computer just as we finished work on *The Food Lover's Guide to Paris*. But no matter, we still had to send our copy to New York via standard mail.

As I look back, I never made it easy on myself and asked a lot of myself. I could have settled for just a guidebook with names and addresses but wanted more. Recipes. A complete glossary of French and English food terms. Photographs had to be included, as well as little quotes and boxes filled with history, lore, and humor. When the book came out in the spring of 1984, it was a fine hit. The nicest comment ever came from an American Airlines flight attendant who saw the book but didn't recognize me and commented, "Oh yes, the book that cracks the code."

We had cracked the code to Paris. We made it possible for every American who came to the city to feel comfortable, knowledgeable in ordering that steak rare, daring to sample that warm foie gras, willing

In my black-and-white polka-dot Yves Saint Laurent dress during the early 1980s: Girl reporter at work!

to take the Métro out to the 20th arrondissement to sample Bernard Ganachaud's crusty sourdough bread, or confident that they knew what to swoon over when they could get a table at Jamin, the new hit restaurant.

Likewise, restaurateurs, chefs, bakers, and chocolate makers returned the compliment: "You have the nicest readers," they would say over and over again. Who wouldn't want enthusiastic, well-informed clients walking into their establishments?

I was touching fame, but far from reaching for fortune. The advance for the first book was $17,500 and I spent much more than that on research. And even though times were lean, Walter never suggested that I should go out and "get a real job." For that I will be eternally grateful because it has made all the difference.

CELERY, TARRAGON, SPINACH, AND CHICKEN SALAD

I've already gone on record saying that I could eat chicken every day. The Paris markets are full of great poultry vendors. In fact, when we moved to Paris, the Rue Poncelet market had two meat butchers and three poultry vendors. We still get super-fresh chicken, with feet and head still attached to attest to their freshness. And since chicken stock is one of the most valuable ingredients in my everyday larder, I naturally have plenty of delicious, moist poached chicken on hand. This is one of my favorite ways to use that lean protein, with plenty of celery for crunch, tarragon for its fiery tang, and capers and cornichons for a finishing touch of acidity. The spinach adds great color, as well as flavor.

1½ cups diced celery
¼ cup finely minced fresh tarragon leaves
3½ cups cubed cooked chicken (about 1 pound)
2 tablespoons capers in vinegar, drained
12 cornichons, cut at a diagonal into thin slices
2 cups baby spinach leaves, washed and dried
¼ cup light cream
2 teaspoons French mustard
½ teaspoon fine sea salt
Freshly ground black pepper

1. In a large bowl, combine the celery, tarragon, chicken, capers, cornichons, and spinach. Set aside.
2. In a small bowl, combine the cream, mustard, and salt, and whisk to blend.
3. Pour the dressing over the ingredients in the bowl and toss to evenly coat. Season generously with pepper. Serve.

4 servings

WINE SUGGESTION: A fresh-tasting Sauvignon Blanc is a great match for tarragon's bright, herbaceous flavors. A house favorite is the Quincy from Domaine Mardon.

7

{ Put Yourself on Vacation }

"Mettez-Vous en Vacances!"

PATRICIA:

It was a dry, hot July afternoon in a small local supermarket in Provence. I stopped dead in my tracks and almost laughed out loud as I confronted the display of espadrilles, the playful rope-soled cloth shoes made in the Basque region in southwestern France.

There they were, a sure sign of summer, in every color of the rainbow, some solid, some brilliant stripes. The sign above the display shouted in big, bold red letters: METTEZ-VOUS EN VACANCES! (PUT YOURSELF ON VACATION!)

The French seem to believe that they invented vacation. They sure have enough of it, and make the very best of every millisecond of their beloved *vacances*. (I love the fact that the noun is feminine, and plural. What good would it be if there was only ONE singular day's vacation!)

Truth be told, for a largely Catholic nation, the French never seem to appear guilty about anything, especially their God-given right to forty-four days off each year. But who's counting? In fact, my good friend Fabrice Langlois, sommelier at the renowned Châteauneuf-du-Pape estate Château de Beaucastel, says it best: The way the French are different from everyone else in the world is that they feel absolutely no guilt about pleasure. Especially when it comes to the pleasure of food, wine, and vacation!

As one who grew up—yes, Catholic—in America's Midwest, vacation was simply not a very big part of my life. My father, a linens buyer for the now-defunct Gimbels department store, had two measly weeks of vacation each year. One week was taken in the winter, ostensibly to do handyman projects around the house. Inevitably, dad would throw his back out on the first day of vacation, instantly putting an end to any household repairs.

Without exception, the second week was taken during the last week of June, perhaps because there were no special department store sales that week. We always drove the 300 or so miles north to my mother's family's dairy farm in Comstock, Wisconsin, staying in a lake cottage hidden in the pines, swimming, fishing, and visiting family. This was the 1950s, and the thought of leaving the state for vacation was unheard of. (We did sometimes drive south of the border, to Illinois, to purchase—of all things—margarine by the case. The wicked nonbutter was then outlawed in America's dairyland!)

My first realization of the dead-serious nature of the French vacation came early in 1980, our first year in France. Even though we had no children, we could not help but be aware of—as well as affected by—the fifteen-day February *vacances scolaires* or school vacation. (How could it come so soon after the Christmas shutdown? And why do the French never say two weeks, it is always *quinze jours*, or fifteen days. They are always stretching it!)

Suddenly I found the stores closed, markets all but bare, hours reduced, streets empty. But weeks later, when life returned to normal, the capital was filled with a miraculously lean, super-tanned populace. They were back from ski vacations, of course! Parisians looked like cartoon characters, parading about in their smooth, bronzed bodies as badges of honor, walking advertisements for their winter ritual, as if to say: "I took my vacation, and I found sunshine!"

But it didn't take us long to realize WHY the Parisians flock to the sun as often as possible. (An American friend who lives in France once said, "Whatever the French do, they all do together.") You too would seek out the sun if you lived some six months of the year under a depressing monolithic blanket of gray.

I remember one particularly grim, typically rainy Paris day in winter. It seemed as though daylight slinked in somewhere around nine-thirty in the morning and raced out around four in the afternoon. At two-thirty in the afternoon it was so dark on the somber bus I was riding that the driver had to the turn on the lights. As he did passengers let out a long, collective sigh of angst. (To give you some idea of how bad it is, the city of Nice in the south of France revels in an average of 2,779 hours of sunshine each year. Paris manages less than 1,814, and most of those are gleaned in the summer months. The capital sees a mere 539 hours of sunshine each winter.)

These were the days before people talked about SAD disease, winter depression and malaise brought on by a simple lack of light. It was also before the ultra-tan was simply considered very bad judgment.

As one who is self-employed, I work—in some manner or another—seven days a week. And Walter and I remain American to the core when it comes to taking vacations. We get away, but there's always work. For at least twenty years, we spent every month of August in Paris. Usually, the only other resident in the entire apartment building was the concierge, who had wisely taken her vacation in July and returned to an empty, low-maintenance building in August.

As if to lord it over us nonvacationers, many Parisian boutiques, often shuttered for parts of both July and August, sport huge signs blaring *BONNES VACANCES!* or HAVE A GOOD VACATION! Sometimes shopkeepers will even leave a chatty little message about where they're going and why. Our local oyster supplier in the 6th arrondissement once left a detailed note taped to the door of his shop, describing how long he would be gone and how he would be tending the oyster beds so that we could profit from them come *la rentrée*, the celebratory moment in September when all the *aoûtiens*—as people who go on vacation in August are known—flood back from *les vacances*.

On assignment for European Travel & Life: *The story was on romantic inns of Tuscany. We didn't have to work too hard at that!*

A second realization of how sacred vacation is to the French came just a few weeks after that February school vacation. I don't remember the assignment now, but it required lining up a series of interviews. I'd managed all the courage I could and picked up the telephone. (I am still unashamedly phonaphobic when it comes to speaking French on the telephone.) After I stammered through my attempts to set up an interview in the next week or so, person after person would reply, matter-of-factly, "*après Pâques*" (after Easter). I was dumbfounded. It seemed incredible to me that life in all of Paris had to stop until after Easter some weeks later. I could not believe that Parisians—whose tans had not even yet begun to fade—were already starting the countdown to the next, big *vacances*!

On a working vacation as "non-rev celebs"
on the Sea Goddess *in the Mediterranean.*

Actually, one of my favorite pastimes is to observe the French on vacation. They get into it completely with a proper costume for each region, each season, each sport. It seems that people who may be sour and serious the rest of the year turn into, well, children during those long and lazy days of vacation. It is also quite endearing to witness families (father, mother, three children, each a well-calendared two years apart) at their best, everyone relaxed, doing what they love together, whether it's running from the waves along the Atlantic coast, sharing a hair-raising midnight hike to the top of Mont Ventoux in Provence, or getting off the high-speed train *ensemble*, heading for the sun clutching teddy bears and dreaming of hours on the beach. The French GET fun, and appear to have no guilt whatsoever in this department.

When the first postcard was sent in the world, I would bet it was sent by a Frenchman on vacation. The custom has died down a bit in the age of computers and e-mail, but well into the 1980s it was bad form to go on vacation and NOT send a postcard to every one of your acquaintances. The mail would be shoved under the front door of our apartment and either Walter or I would sort through it. Inevitably there would be a postcard from someone we could not remember having met, but there they were, having a good time, and rubbing it in, from Africa or Martinique, Brittany or the Alps. Then when you next saw the person, etiquette required that you acknowledge the gesture, saying, "Thanks for your postcard." (To this day, chef Joël Robuchon and I have a running joke. We have never sent one another vacationgrams, but at each meeting, we'll joke, "I got your postcard.")

At flea markets all over France you'll find postcard vendors surrounded by clients patiently thumbing through thousands of old postcards, all arranged by numbers of the *départements.* Finding a postcard sent from someone on vacation from your *département* somehow puts YOU, once again, on vacation.

Then there is the matter of May! We have holidays, always, on May Day (May 1), World War II Victory Day (May 8), and the feast of Ascension a bit later in the month. And in some years, depending on when Easter falls, the feast of Pentecost might slip in there as well.

Most years, it's clear that *le Bon Dieu* intends extra-long weekends, because the holidays fall in the middle of the week. That's time to *faire le pont,* literally to make a bridge out of it, turning a single holiday into a long weekend. Talk about life screeching to a halt! As you can see from one used to working 365 days a year, all this time off becomes problematic. At one point I considered canceling my cooking classes during May because scheduling was such a problem. I have had restaurants open just for us, and one of the most renowned vineyards in Châteauneuf-du-Pape gave us the key to the cellar so I could conduct a tour and tasting. The month of May requires that one check the ever-changing opening and closing hours of every merchant to make sure one will have vegetables, meat, poultry, and fish. Thank goodness we already have a well-stocked wine cellar.

After years of living in France I've come to realize that vacation here is not official if you just stay home. In America people are more likely to say "I'm taking a few days away from the office." That means it's not official vacation, just "time off." But Parisians have now found a way to actually go on vacation while staying home. It's called *Paris Plage* (Paris Beach), and it's for those who can't leave Paris but want the Côte d'Azur and the Atlantic Coast brought to them in a single package. For several weeks each summer, the expressway along the Seine's Right Bank is loaded with sand and lounge chairs, magical outdoor showers that mimic rainfall, and striped cabanas. Kids build sand castles, music blares, and best of all, you get to buy souvenirs like T-shirts and buttons that say *Souvenir de Paris Plage*, just to prove to everyone, including yourself, that you've experienced *les vacances*.

The French obsession with vacation became particularly annoying when we began spending time in Provence, where I maintain my regular routine of writing, recipe testing, restaurant hopping, and conducting week-long cooking classes. To the locals, I guess, the Wellses seemed to be on perpetual vacation. I couldn't pass someone on the street or walk out of a shop without someone saying "*Vous êtes en vacances?*" (As if to say, "Oh, you're on vacation again?") I got so fed up with it I began to reply "*La vie c'est les vacances!*" ("Life is a vacation.") I never found anyone who would laugh at my little joke—or, for that matter, anyone who would take me seriously.

What used to shock me was the fact that many of our local merchants in Provence take time off during their busiest season—the summer—when they could be racking up their best months. Now I realize this is another way to mark the differences between us and them. Vacation and pleasure take precedence over making an extra mortgage payment or buying a new car. As much as I would like to, I can't say that I've learned very much from the French. We rarely go on an official vacation. But I feel as though we are still young enough to learn. Maybe I'll just take the rest of the day off.

WALTER:

In my (Protestant) family, there were no cousins with a lake house, no distant farm where we went to cool out. In fact, there wasn't even the knowledge that cooling out was an option, so almost everybody in my family stayed at a slow boil all the time.

A basic premise was "if you don't work, you don't eat." My parents' Depression-era farm background made that as true for their generation as it had been for the Pilgrims. For adults like my parents, whose needs had changed little over 200 years and whose values had scarcely been revisited since the colonists struggled for subsistence, that meant working all the time.

In France, and in Europe generally, society is built on roots different from those put down by the Pilgrims. The French commitment to their generous paid vacations has been cause for a lot of the sneering that hardworking Americans aim their way. How can a nation be taken seriously if its citizens don't work fifty weeks a year, or even forty-eight?

In 2003, an intense and prolonged heat wave killed 15,000 Frenchmen, many of them old and infirm and many of them simply neglected. The government came up with the idea of taking away the Pentecost holiday as a sign of "solidarity" for those who had died. The idea was that the extra day's productivity would increase the tax revenue necessary to install air-conditioning in hospitals and nursing homes.

Non, merci! The French wouldn't have it. Though the concept of social "solidarity" is as basic to the French national mythology as *liberté, égalité, fraternité*, the commitment to free time is stronger still. To protest the idea of giving up a day off, the French did what they next most like doing: they went on strike.

Patricia in her dreaded wet suit in the Red Sea:
She would rather be cooking!

~~~~~

Red Sea Squid Pasta

In all of our thirty years of marriage, Walter and I have been on a true, nonworking vacation only once. Walter has often noted that every trip we've taken over the years involved restaurant research and writing, endless moments spent reading menus, and the time came when, frankly, he wanted a break. So at the urging of friends who were avid—even professional—divers, we got our diving certification. Our one and only diving trip was to the Red Sea in 1988. We lived on a dive boat with five other couples and went on a dive two, sometimes three times a day to marvel at the glories below. While I shared with my fellow divers the beauty of schools of tuna passing overhead, I could not stop thinking that these were the freshest fish I had ever seen. By the fourth day of our trip I gave up and spent the rest of the time in the dive boat's kitchen with Netta Daiches, our thirty-two-year-old Israeli cook. This pasta dish—a sea-fresh blend of squid, walnuts, basil, and garlic—has been a family favorite ever since. I don't remember what pasta she used back then but we have found that little bow ties are perfect here.

EQUIPMENT: The small bowl of a food processor, or a blender; an 8-quart pasta pot fitted with a colander.

4 ounces whole shelled walnuts

BASIL SAUCE
4 plump, fresh garlic cloves, peeled, halved, green germ removed, minced
⅛ teaspoon fine sea salt
4 cups loosely packed fresh basil leaves, coarsely chopped
6 tablespoons extra-virgin olive oil
Coarse sea salt
1½ pounds small squid, gutted, cleaned, rinsed, and tentacles removed and reserved, tubes cut into 1/4-inch rings (you can have your fishmonger do the cleaning for you)

1 pound farfalle (bow-tie pasta)

1. Toast the walnuts: Place the nuts in a large frying pan over moderate heat. Toast, regularly shaking the pan until the nuts are fragrant and evenly browned, about 2 minutes. Watch carefully! They can burn quickly. Transfer to a large plate to cool. Set aside.
2. Prepare the basil sauce: Place the garlic, salt, and basil in the food processor and process to a paste. With the machine running, slowly pour the oil through the tube. Taste for seasoning. Place in large shallow bowl that will hold the pasta later on.
3. Cook the squid: In an 8-quart pasta pot fitted with a colander, bring 6 quarts water to a boil over high heat. Add three tablespoons of coarse salt. Add the squid rings and tentacles and cook, uncovered, for 15 seconds, counting from the time the squid

enter the water. Drain immediately. Rinse under cold running water. Set aside.

4. Rinse out the pasta pot and fill again with 6 quarts water. Bring to a boil over high heat. Add 3 tablespoons coarse salt and the pasta, stirring to prevent the pasta from sticking. Cook, uncovered, until tender but firm to the bite, about 11 minutes.

5. Drain the pasta thoroughly and transfer to the bowl with the basil sauce. Toss thoroughly to blend. Add the squid and the toasted walnuts and toss again to thoroughly distribute them. Taste for seasoning. Serve immediately.

4 main-course servings

WINE SUGGESTION: We always love this with a bright rosé wine. A favorite is the Tavel rosé from Domaine de la Mordorée.

Walter and Patricia, in her Yves Saint Laurent gown,
at a special IHT dinner in Versailles.

8

{ La Vie en Rose }

WALTER:

In our first months in Paris, our normal Sunday routine after breakfast was to clamber onto the Métro and head for the sprawling St. Ouen *marché aux puces* (flea market). There among the piles of dubious antiques and real ones, of discarded bric-a-brac and rejected heirlooms, we began choosing furniture for our apartment. One weekend we would look for armoires—there were no closets in our apartment, and the cardboard containers our clothes had arrived in had not crossed the Atlantic well. The next weekend we would look for china or for glasses. Often we found some prize we had not been searching for, and such discoveries are how the flea market habit is rewarded.

Whatever our goals, one of them was lunch at Chez Louisette, where the food was adequate and where a Piaf imitator named Emmanuelle reminded us of some of the reasons we had moved to Paris. If life at the office was not *La Vie en Rose*, Sundays at St. Ouen, with Emmanuelle's tight vibrato telling of bitter courage in the face of deceived love, gave us the Paris of our dreams. We liked the emotion of "*je ne regrette rien*," and if we weren't yet true believers I suppose we were having fewer and fewer regrets about leaving New York.

Whether heading for *les puces* or wandering in some other European city, we would think about the life we would be living if we hadn't left New York. We'd probably be climbing off the train in Reading, where we had first picked up the flea market habit. We didn't disparage that little Pennsylvania city, famous not just for acres of "collectibles" but also for the wild mushroom dishes at Joe's Restaurent. But an early tour of the St. Ouen market and then driving out into the French countryside for Sunday lunch offered more texture. On the first of those outings, to the region east of Paris that's filled with World War I graves, we had lunch with two *Trib* colleagues at the Hostellerie du Château in Fère-en-Tardenois. We dined on foie gras and drank Clos de la Mouche—and I'd never had either in Reading.

The Loire Valley was a frequent destination, even after we'd visited Chenonceaux, Villandry, and the other famous châteaux. We kept go-

Richard Reeves, Jack Harrison, Walter, and Mary Harrison
at a special IHT dinner in Versailles.

ing back for Sancerre's flinty Sauvignon Blanc as well as the delicate lactic flavors of fresh goat's cheese, still new to our palates. We hauled home big redolent Muenster rounds from Alsace; a backseat full of heady lavender from the Drôme; foamy cider and ripe Camembert from Normandy; cases of Meursault from Burgundy; and stacks of *Pierre Qui Vire* from the nearby monastery that made that richly flavored cheese. We both loved the variety of cheeses, and at one point there was so much in our kitchen larder that you got the rich odors of fermentation as soon as you opened the front door to the apartment.

Sometimes we made day trips, leaving early Saturday morning in a rented Renault 5. Sometimes we spent weekends with friends—the Marshalls in the Drôme, the Shapiros in Normandy—and sometimes we bedded down in the little hotel rooms that Patricia came to call nuns' cells when she traveled the country on assignment. We budgeted tightly in Paris so that we could go away frequently, still thinking that we had only two years to squeeze everything in. Occasionally there was an out-of-town assignment for Patricia or a professional meeting for me that let us upgrade from the cheap rooms and allow a brief taste of opulence in some of the great hotels: the Krasnapolsky in Amsterdam, the Kempinski in Berlin, the Amigo in Brussels, the Gritti Palace in Venice, the Beau Rivage in Lausanne.

After we bought our first car—the car was a Porsche, and Patricia was just beginning to develop a fear of speed—we risked longer distances in France, and as her assignments picked up we ranged farther afield. I went with her as she covered a trade fair in Cologne and again when she wrote about an endive farmer in Belgium. We flew to Venice and Florence and Rome. A conference took me to Berlin, where we crossed into the grim eastern sector for a tour with an American diplomat. We had a brush with trepidation when we crossed back through Checkpoint Charlie with no visas. Because a diplomat had driven us into the East, the guards hadn't stamped our passports. The accusatory skepticism of the guards at the return post was enough to cause shivers but nothing more.

We went to London, of course, and to Scotland for an assignment about a restaurant that had been awarded a Michelin star, one of the first in the UK. The restaurant was in the town of Gullen, not far from Edinburgh, and we took the bus, though we couldn't understand the driver's burr when he called the stop. Patricia traveled with me to Amsterdam for a trade show and wrote about coffeehouses. On a side trip to The Hague we gorged on spicy rijsttaffel. She went with me again to an international meeting of editors concerned about UNESCO's vain threats to press freedom. The meeting, wisely held in beautiful, idyllic Talloires on the Lac d'Annecy, was full of high purpose, the meal at Père Bise pure pleasure. More than once we tested the new high-speed train to Lyon by going down to have lunch at Paul Bocuse or Léon de Lyon, then back home in the early evening. We drove to Vonnas in the Bresse region to celebrate Georges Blanc's brilliance at the stove. And with friends we spent a memorable weekend in the Quercy, where Patricia had an assignment to write about a popular form of rural tourism known as "weekends on the farm." We took advantage of the proximity to Eugénie-les-Bains to schedule Saturday lunch at Michel Guérard's elegant three-star restaurant. His famous *cuisine minceur* (spa food) is not what we ate. Afterward, in the car heading back to our farm, we realized that we had failed to read through all the blah-blah in our host's letter to get to the crucial part, an invitation to dinner that night. We got back to the farm just in time to suit up for foie gras and *magret de canard*. I was still burping from the lobster at lunch and the melted butter it floated in.

For two other *weekends à la ferme* in the Dordogne we butchered a hog and fattened geese, which lined up eagerly for their stuffing, just like humans at a fast-food counter, then sat quietly in the farmwife's arms as she massaged their necks to help the thick grainy gruel pass.

Our passports grew thick with visas and extra pages. Besides our frequent trips in Europe, we went to Hong Kong and then spent two weeks with a personal handler in China; we went to Japan and

A special IHT *dinner in 1987 staged in front of the Eiffel Tower.*

Thailand and Singapore. The paper had just begun printing and distributing in Asia, and I went "to show the flag," as they said.

When we were not traveling we began entertaining at home as we added chairs from *les puces* for guests to sit on. We remember with hilarity a brunch with French acquaintances who, having never before been to a brunch, didn't seem to know when to leave. Eventually they must have gotten tired of waiting for whatever signal we didn't know to give, and pulled out around 7:00 p.m. We assumed, gratefully, that they had plans for dinner.

In the early days, while our furnishings were still sparse, we hosted a *vernissage* for our tutor, Denise Lioté, an established artist whose spare geometric pastels seem to reach into space. The pale gray walls of our empty apartment were a good backdrop for her canvases. In the week that the exhibition was up about a hundred visitors came, and I was struck by the amount of time that many of them took to write comments in the guest book.

Patricia also recalls "endless house guests," but other than our parents and a favorite aunt I don't remember their names. Whoever the guests were, her contract for the first *Food Lover's Guide* put an end to those invitations because the spare bedroom became her full-time office and the apartment turned into a workshop as she hired a series of assistants to help with her research. I worked late at the paper but she was an early riser, and for a while, when I woke up around nine, an assistant was already at work—maybe in her office; maybe in the kitchen, where I wanted my coffee and my morning fix of BBC news; and maybe at the dining room table. Our two-bedroom apartment was compact, so even the quietest assistant seemed invasive. I remember negotiating an agreement that when the assistant worked there she wouldn't start until ten, after I'd gotten up and had my first pee.

Our time for travel diminished as Patricia got her first book contract. Later, both time and means would diminish further when we began pouring resources into our farm in Provence and the new possibilities that Chanteduc offered for what a friend used to call "the high life." At a dinner there with friends many years later, my father, in one of the last of his ninety-five years, asked, "Do you always have so much fun?" And indeed we did. We always did.

FRÉDY GIRARDET'S FRESH FOIE GRAS
in VINAIGRETTE

In November of 1976, Craig Claiborne, food editor of the *New York Times*, wrote an article headlined "The World's Greatest Chef." That was Frédy Girardet, only just beginning to be discovered in his little Swiss village of Crissier, near Lausanne. Claiborne wrote of a "fantastic lobster stew, chicken with a splendid sauce of leeks and cream, an incomparable dish of sautéed duck liver, slightly crusty on the outside and melting within . . . " Claiborne quoted Girardet as saying "*La Nouvelle Cuisine* is nothing more than good taste. It is to prepare dishes to preserve their natural flavors and with the simplest of sauces." That is certainly the case here, with just the natural fat of duck, vinegar, salt, and herbs. Walter and I made our pilgrimage to Crissier in fall of 1979, experiencing the same pleasure and emotion. It seems that when we arrived in France in 1980, the streets were all but awash with foie gras. We sure ate a lot of it back then, cold as well as warm. This is one of the easiest and simplest ways to appreciate the richness of this regal ingredient.

EQUIPMENT: 4 warmed dinner plates.

> 4 slices fresh duck liver (foie gras), each about 3 ounces
> Fleur de sel
> Freshly ground black pepper
> 2 shallots, peeled and minced
> 3 tablespoons best-quality sherry wine vinegar
> Minced parsley for garnish
> Minced chives for garnish

Place several layers of paper towels on a large plate. Heat a large frying pan over high heat until hot but not smoking. Add the slices of foie gras and sear for 1 to 2 minutes on each side, or until cooked to desired doneness. Transfer to the paper towels to drain. Season with salt and pepper. Transfer to four warmed dinner plates. To the fat in the frying pan, add the shallots, shaking the pan. Add the vinegar and cook over high heat about 1 minute. Spoon the sauce over the foie gras. Garnish with parsley and chives. Serve immediately.

WINE SUGGESTION: A Sauternes is king here, the older the better.

NOTE: Fresh duck liver can be ordered online from D'Artagnan at *www.dartagnan.com*.

PART II

———

Going Native

ALMOST PARISIAN
("HAVE YOU EVER THOUGHT OF WEARING MAKEUP?")
Dried Cranberry and Apricot Bread

DANGEROUS DE-LIAISONS

A SMALL INN NEAR AVIGNON
Peach Wine

NOUVELLE CUISINE, CRITIQUE NOUVELLE
Michel Guérard's Salade Gourmande

YOU PAID TO LEARN TO DRIVE LIKE THAT?
Almond Macaroon and Fresh Berry Cake

TWO FOR THE ROAD

THE *L'Express* YEARS
La Cagouille's Salmon Tartare

MR. PATRICIA WELLS
Fettuccine with Vodka and Lemon

WEIGHTY MATTERS
Fish Cheeks with Polenta and Parmesan Crust

9

{ Almost Parisian }

("Have You Ever Thought of Wearing Makeup?")

PATRICIA:

I can remember the day clearly. It was a bright and sunny Saturday in June 1980, and Walter and I were walking along the fashionable Rue du Faubourg Saint-Honoré, home to many of the best French fashion houses. We were leaving the Christian Dior boutique where we had purchased, for me, a gorgeous pale gray linen two-button blazer, with a fine silk lining, very thin lapels, and gigantic padded shoulders. I was feeling Almost Parisian. Totally chic.

Walter turned to me and asked quietly, "Have you ever thought of wearing makeup?"

I was at first a bit stunned. True, I arrived in Paris without a tube of lipstick, a compact of blush, a wand of mascara. I didn't consider myself a Berkeley hippie sort who disdained makeup; I just had never learned the first thing about how to deal with it.

Walter never suggested I wear makeup in New York. Had Paris changed the way he looked at me? Did it change the way I looked at myself? I realized that something was shifting.

Only weeks earlier Walter had asked if I was going to get my hair cut. For some insane reason—following the trend of the time I guess—I had a permanent in New York before leaving for Paris and arrived that January with a thick crop of curly brown hair, American afro. I confessed to Walter that I had kind of let it grow out, mostly because I was SCARED. I didn't know the language, the French hairdresser lingo, the words for wash or dry or cut. I was a little girl from Milwaukee afraid of the big frightening world of Parisian chic.

Patricia posing for a publicity photo in 1984: Look, Mom, no makeup!

We had been in France for three or four months, and someone must have told me about Mod's Hair in the 6th arrondissement, giving me the name of a hairdresser who spoke English. I went through the whole scary ordeal, not understanding a word that was said. Why do they always ask, "When did you last wash your hair?" Or like a dentist, "Who did that to you?" How can a woman who is totally secure about who she is and what she does become a total wimp in the face of a hairdresser? But that's who I became each time I had to confront a French hairdresser.

I wouldn't feel really good about my hair until years later in 1992 when I called the Carita salon in Paris and gave in to having my hair—did I say the word?—dyed. Oh, yes, when I was in my twenties in Wisconsin I had my hair "frosted," a medieval process by which they put on a bathing cap that fit like a girdle with holes and then with a crochet hook pulled strands of hair out so you looked like a porcupine. Depending upon the quality of the work, you emerged from the salon as a Sort of Blonde, a bleached blond. But in my Morality Book, frosting did not translate as "Dying My Hair." So this visit to Carita marked the first step in my transformation. And there was a lot of terrain to cover.

When I moved to France, I had never had a manicure or a pedicure, had never had a massage, and probably owned one tube each of day cream and night cream.

I have never been a Hope in a Jar girl. And although I am faithful to everything else in the world—my husband, my country, my friends, my computer, my brand of lipstick, brands of pantyhose, underwear, dishwasher liquid—I am not faithful to my face cream. I have tried them all, from ultra-expensive Sisley and Chanel, Christian Dior and La Mer to inexpensive dime-store and pharmacy brands like Nivea and Roc, but none ever keep me for long. Maybe I AM a Hope in a Jar girl but just have not yet found my mate.

It took a long time for me to get into the French beauty rhythm. For me the question has always been: Is personal beauty care self-indulgence or self-improvement? The French have taught me to think of it as self-improvement. Once I was into it, I understood why French women spend so much time on daily maintenance. It's not just to fill the coffers of the salons or the beauty houses. It is because if you look good on the outside you feel good on the inside. (Walter also likes to say that the reason the French aren't fat is because there are so many mirrors everywhere: If you look at yourself often enough and don't like what you see, maybe you will do something about it!)

I look at so many of the French women I know or those I simply observe. They take care of themselves. They don't let themselves go. They don't consider a bit of pampering to be simply decadent or selfish displays of pleasure seeking.

I had my first makeup lesson from Maguy LeCoze of Le Bernardin. She and her brother Gilbert had just moved their popular fish restaurant from the Left Bank to the Right Bank. Maguy was always a fashion queen, her black hair perfectly coiffed, her makeup applied with perfection. Often she and Gilbert would sit down and dine with us, and I noticed that even after a multicourse feast, her lipstick was untouched. She revealed her secret, multiple layers of lipstick, with a good blotting after each layer, then a final fifth layer blotted with a pucker. When I have time and think of it—which is not most of the time—I follow Maguy's lipstick rule.

Patricia kneads brioche in the Rue Daru kitchen.

I especially love observing older French women, from whom I have learned so much. We have a neighbor who is about to celebrate her seventieth birthday. You wouldn't say she was a great beauty, but I admire her every time I pass her in the courtyard or on the street. Her natural gray hair is casually pulled back, but always looks impeccable. She always has on a matching outfit—shoes, skirt, sweater, jewelry—that makes sense, as though when she put it together she thought of each detail, but now the details are etched in her mind. Most of her clothes may be twenty years old or more, but she never looks dated. Just polished and what we used to call "sharp."

Today I am into maintenance big time and thank the French for it. Weekly visits to the hairdresser for upkeep and a manicure, twice a week to the massage therapist, a weekly facial, a monthly pedicure. I even multitask when I have a facial, having facial hair removed and putting my eyelashes up on rollers, so they have an even curl. If I add on the time I spend jogging, doing weight training, and just walking around town, I figure that I spend twelve hours a week on basic maintenance. In my book, time and money well spent.

The big payoff came not long ago when Walter and I passed a woman who clearly did not subscribe to the maintenance theory. Her hair was a mess, and dirty as well. She walked with difficulty, overburdened by excess weight. Her clothes were rumpled and too tight. She wore no makeup and the deep wrinkles on her face suggested she was a lifelong smoker.

Walter turned to me and said quietly "Thank you for taking care of yourself." It comes as second nature to me now, and for that I thank the women of France.

WALTER:

Not long after we settled in and went to work, an aged and bitchy colleague described an American acquaintance as "the only woman who ever moved to Paris and never learned how to dress."

Maybe I was thinking about that when I put the makeup question to Patricia. And maybe I was thinking about the line delivered by Maggie Smith as Amanda in *Private Lives*: "I've *always* been sophisticated." Or I could have been thinking nothing at all but "Ooh la la!"

Paris is a place where appearances matter, with its sweet little squares and imperial alleys of carefully pruned trees. For Parisians, and especially *parisiennes*, each trip out the door is an entrance. The *marquise* who lived upstairs in our Rue Daru apartment building—on *l'étage noble*, to be sure—never ventured out without her own version of the full monty. Coiffed, made up, and in her Chanel-inspired *tailleur* and Hermès scarf. It was her signature look, and it never changed.

That approach is sensible. Even if they are of modest means, with well-chosen makeup, jewelry, scarf, and shoes, French women achieve a "look," a *finition* that lets you know they take their good appearance seriously.

No city or country has a corner on beauty. But there's a Paris look, one that includes a reasonable and precise use of makeup, and it's as becoming to Patricia as to anyone. It's true that you get used to what you see every day, and my own eye had adapted to the very appealing way that French women put themselves together. Her new clothes were a sign that Patricia was settling into life in Paris and moving on beyond the anxieties that surrounded her loneliness. But she wasn't completely over the hump on that Saturday morning when I suggested some makeup, and I thought some encouragement for playing her new role of *parisienne* might help.

Despite what Grandmother said whenever she saw my sister primping, beauty really is more than skin deep. Patricia's interior beauty is greatest, though the skin deep part is okay, too. But curled eyelashes? Now I know why she comes home from the hairdresser sometimes looking like Betty Boop.

DRIED CRANBERRY
and APRICOT BREAD

Quick breads have long been a staple in our kitchen. Walter and I both grew up with mothers who were deft bakers, and this bread, along with our standard date and nut bread, are in our lineup of comfort food. We slice these breads and have them with cheese in lieu of dessert. And we enjoy them even when I'm not wearing any makeup.

EQUIPMENT: A nonstick 1-quart rectangular bread pan.

1 teaspoon best-quality walnut oil
½ cup quick-cooking oatmeal
1¼ cups 1% milk
1½ cups whole-wheat flour
1 tablespoon baking powder
½ teaspoon fine sea salt
1 cup dried organic cranberries
½ cup coarsely chopped dried organic apricots,
   or dried blackberries
½ cup honey
1 teaspoon ground cinnamon
1 large egg, lightly beaten
1 teaspoon pure vanilla extract

1. Preheat the oven to 375°F. Coat the pan with the walnut oil. Set aside.
2. In a large bowl combine the oatmeal and milk. Stir to blend. Set aside for 10 minutes.
3. Add the flour, baking powder, salt, dried fruit, honey, cinnamon, egg, and vanilla. Stir to blend. The batter will be quite thin.
4. Pour the batter into the pan, evening out the top with the back of a spatula. Place in the center of the oven and bake until a toothpick inserted into the center of the bread comes out clean, 40 to 50 minutes.

5. Remove the pan from the oven. Let cool for 5 minutes. Turn the loaf out and place it on a rack to cool. Do not slice the bread for at least 1 hour, for it will continue to bake as it cools. The bread can be stored for up to three days, tightly wrapped in plastic. Serve in very thin slices.

1 loaf, 24 thin slices

A portrait for a New York magazine: Note the shoulder pads!

10

{ Dangerous De-Liaisons }

WALTER:

Early in our interlude, returning to Paris started to feel like coming home and landing in New York felt like a trip to another country. Even those big Citroëns no longer looked strange whereas a stretch Town Car did. One day, turning through the newspaper, looking for the latest news on expatriate taxation, it dawned on me that I had become an expat. (Now, there's frequently a typo when the word is used—it comes out "expatriot," which must mean something like pretreasonous. That would give any loyalist a moment's hesitation about the identity, as it did me.)

Yet inevitably, it became not just acceptable but worn in and comfortable. After all, it was born of simple familiarity and not some wrenching choice between conflicting values. It was a sense of knowing not just the local language but of learning the local code and how to make it work.

But as the comfort factor grew, so did the self-examination. When posted abroad, a correspondent is warned by his editors not to "go native," not to let the charms and exoticism of new surroundings cause him to lose perspective. The job is to report on his new surroundings, not to be changed by them. That suggests that perspective is something fragile or a consequence of your tribe rather than the attribute of observing competently and reporting fairly. In truth, perspective is too often tied to a passport, though it isn't fragile—it is enhanced by maturity and experience, not jeopardized by them. Just as learning a second language gives you a sharper understanding of your first one, learning a new cultural set gives you insight into your own values.

Questions of allegiance might not occur at all and certainly wouldn't be worth pondering if we had wound up living in England or in Singapore. The time would come, in an era poisoned by George Bush's foreign policy, that having a French address seemed to raise issues of loyalty that not even Sweden or Canada had a generation earlier, when both countries welcomed young American dissidents. But that wasn't the atmosphere back in 1980.

When we moved to France it was during a brief period of détente in the long and complicated relationship between our two great republics. The French recall better than we do the importance of Lafayette and Rochambeau—and French loans and munitions—to American independence, and Americans remember the bloody sacrifice on Normandy's beaches. Both sides oversimplify: French support for American independence had many motivations that didn't involve the rights of man, and America alone did not put an end to Hitler's Reich. The liberation of France (which, lest we forget, was joyously celebrated in the United States) eventually became a catalyst for Americans' anger at their beholden ally, chiefly perhaps because the ally didn't recognize just how beholden it was supposed to feel. There was considerable feeling back then that America had come to the aid of democratic values and not just the French tricolor. Though some level of bad feeling has existed forever between France and America, it is since De Gaulle's time that official recriminations have flowed and good will has ebbed.

As France reconstructed itself after World War II, it did so with more apparent hauteur than gratitude. De Gaulle's memorable *"certaine idée de la France"* included no supplicant's role.

Beyond international politics, there's all that other stuff. A French-bashing riff can go on and on, but most of the substance seems to come down to "they think they're something special." That different kind of special relationship would also include:

They smoke too much. The sidewalks are smeared with dog shit. They stand too close to you when they talk and they shake hands too often. Lunch lasts for three hours and the rest of the time they're on vacation. They are always all alone in the world, blocking escalators or sidewalks with blithe unawareness. They are scary drivers. They take their dogs to restaurants and feed them off the table. They are arrogant and ungrateful. And have you noticed that the women are getting fatter? My personal favorite was an attack on the basil found in a farmers' market: The leaves are too tiny.

Turn about: What's the French take on us? Well, it's equally stereotyped. Americans are children, aggressive and unrestrained. Wherever we are, we push to the front and assume we're in charge. We talk too loud and our clothes are sloppy. (Though you will note that the casual American style is totally worth adopting.) We shout at each other across the street or across restaurants. We brag about how much we make and the value of our real estate. We speculate loudly about what a watch or a ring at the next table might cost. We want the antismoking laws expanded to include the sidewalks. We're immature—ours is not the land of liberty, but of puberty. We are self-involved and self-engaged and otherwise alarmingly incurious. We threaten the climate with our greenhouse gases and pollute the world with our crass pop culture. And in business, like sports, we can be so successful because we cheat.

Inevitably, America will bash France. Inevitably, France will point out that Uncle Sam has come to resemble Major Hoople, a comics-page character of my youth who was full of bluster and spittle. Except that Major Hoople didn't have nukes. The Franco-American relationship is like a bad marriage that can't quite come to an end, no matter how tiresome it has become for everybody who hears about it.

Our differing insults derive from different birthrights. We really are very different peoples. The paradox is that the source of the differences is a single great parallel—we are both natively Cartesian: We are, ergo we by God *are*. The American variant is that we by God are the greatest. The French have certain reservations about that, because though the sun has set on empire, the Sun King's glory still renders France unmatched for shimmer.

Now, had I given all this any thought before my expatriate's identity became my chief one? Of course not. Who would bother, from the comfort and security of home, to do more than vaguely acknowledge the differences, as some comedian did by saying "those French have a different word for just about everything." Well, yes, and then some.

For all our differences, a big similarity screams out. On both sides of the Atlantic we confuse our national myths with reality. "Freedom and justice for all," for example, or "*liberté, égalité, fraternité.*" Those are slogans but they are not reality. They may not even express our true core values anymore.

America thinks it's always right, and the French mistake as true grandeur what is merely their "storied pomp" (in the poetically dismissive words of Emma Lazarus chiseled on the base of the Statue of Liberty). France is a wonderful, admirable country. France once competed to run the world. That was a long time ago, and now France is fourth in rankings of the nuclear powerful, or sixth in economic terms. In other words, American words, France is a welterweight. And American eyes are usually closed to the fact that France so often punches above its weight.

It is ironic that France's overreach is so resented in America. In the land where anybody can make himself up, where your reach is supposed to exceed your grasp, France is dismissed as arrogant and pretentious.

And the subject of arrogance introduces another area of paradoxical similarity and difference. Americans tend to think that their country is the greatest in the world, and with religious fervor don't admit to any doubts about that. Whereas the French are relentless in how hard they are on France. Whatever goes awry, the French reaction will be a disgusted, "That's France for you." And they expect that you'll agree. There's plenty of criticism of America, but in my experience it's never delivered as personal. It's not about Americans but about policy. Bush is detested, Clint Eastwood is loved.

Besides our birthrights, our differences are developed through our training. Whereas Americans are taught that there is a state called "nice" and we're supposed to mask everything behind niceness, the French are taught that there are rules and that the rules must always be followed. One of those, of course, is to be polite, but it's not the first one. Rather, well ahead of politeness are the "*normale*," the "*moyen*," and the "*logique*," or simply convention—*ça ne se fait pas* (it's just not done). Following the rules is the chief end. We allow ourselves to break the rules as long as we're nice about it (and don't get caught). When someone else isn't nice, that entitles you to stop being nice too, so we have never been particularly nice with each other, we and the French.

With all that, what do we like about each other, the French and the Americans? Well, why does it matter so much? Why, when we're so different, do we pay so much attention to what the other thinks? What's wrong with thinking "*vive la différence*" as well as saying it?

I'm not sure that in our long interlude we cracked the code to that difference, but one thing we came to understand helped persuade us to stay. In France, pleasure is okay. We Americans have famously and formally declared our right to pursue happiness (which sends us in droves to Las Vegas or across the border). But we tend to talk about pleasure in terms of sin. The French are entitled to pleasure without guilt. In fact, except in a legal sense, my observation is that guilt is rarely discussed in France—unless you don't follow the rules. If you follow the rules, there's no reason to feel guilty. That's a reason to love rules.

Patricia and I never fled the United States, of course, nor have we ever thought of ourselves as exiles. We chose new jobs, not a new country. In the best traditions of the American frontier we were look-ing for adventure and opportunity. And though we learned a new language and a new code and gained perspective, neither of us ever traded in our basic values, the ones we call "American" but that we might instead simply call "humanist."

So, back to that problematic identity: expatriate? I would rather think of myself as just someone who, like Benjamin Franklin in Paris, was accused of going native, and, like Jefferson, loves both his coun-tries.

11

{ A Small Inn Near Avignon }

PATRICIA:

It was, in truth, a dark and stormy night. The Provençal skies had opened and unleashed torrents of rain. But we were nevertheless on our way to dinner. Winemaker friends had raved about a restaurant they had been to just outside of Avignon and the place was on my "To Try" list. Good friends from California, Missy and Lee Isgur, were staying at l'Oustau de Beaumanière in Les Baux, and the restaurant served as a perfect place for meeting halfway.

When I called to reserve the day before, the chef answered with a cheery shout, "Jean-Marc *à l'appareil*" (Jean-Marc on the line). Stupidly assuming he didn't know who I was, I had reserved under the name of Wells.

His instant response was "*C'est PATRICIA Wells?*" I responded yes, and he shouted "*Je vous adore!*" (I adore you!)

Stupid me, I thought, I always reserve under a different name. What got into me?

As we drove down the hill the following night, the rain pounded the windshield as well as our spirits. We thought of turning back, but those were the days before everybody carried a cell phone and we were sure that Lee and Missy were already en route. We always lose our way when driving around the outskirts of Avignon, so the certainty of getting lost at night, in winter, in a downpour did nothing to boost our spirits. On top of it, this was a vacation weekend—Armistice Day—so the *autoroute*, shrunken by an enormous amount of road construction, was crammed with vacationers.

As we neared our destination there was nothing of the village charm I had counted on. It was all suburban sprawl, with strip malls, chain stores, and fast-food joints. "This is going to be a mistake," I said to myself, my anticipation of an unforgettable country meal suddenly washed away in the downpour.

At last, with the pelting rain and wind reducing visibility to almost zero, we found the restaurant. Though the restaurant was ablaze with lights, its gate was locked and there was a sheltered chalkboard announcing "*Fermé à cause de deuil douloureuse*" (the restaurant was closed due to painful bereavement).

We felt bereft for the chef. Certainly a close family member had died and he had had no way to get in touch with us. As we waited for Lee and Missy to arrive, we began to feel equally sorry for ourselves. I just wanted to be in front of a cozy fire with a sip of red wine. Or two.

It seemed as though we waited for hours. Cars kept driving up and it was impossible to see who was inside the cars. So as each car drove into the parking lot, I left our car to see if it might be Lee and Missy. Finally, they arrived. As I got out of the car to announce the bad news, a man arrived with an umbrella and called out "Patricia?" He kissed me. I offered my condolences, and he laughed.

"Get inside. It's a joke. I'll explain later," said the stranger. We quickly surmised that this was the chef. We all breathed a rather hesitant sigh of relief and were ushered indoors.

The restaurant was gorgeous, a personal dream. It was furnished with Provençal antiques and decorated with the sort of old food objects I love to collect myself. There was a roaring fire with a rocking chair set in front of the fireplace. The tables were all in white, with the charm of mix and match silverware, and arranged all around were comforting jars of colorful jams. I breathed a second sigh of relief, but was still wary because of the sign out front.

We were led to a cozy table by the fire, and just then a tiny X-ray of a woman hobbled hesitantly down the stairs, coughing with every step. She introduced herself and explained—with no minor anger in her voice—that her husband made her get out of bed to serve Patricia Wells.

The chef was clearly overexcited, even manic. He was a bald man, with big round glasses on a round face and smooth, taut skin. His eyes were almost bulging from his face. He walked over to a silver Bose CD player mounted on the wall, with five disks lined up, playing Petula Clark recordings exclusively. He pumped up the volume, and in the background his wife muttered, "He's the president of the Petula Clark fan club."

We were disoriented. We were confused. And we were chilled to the bone despite the warming fire. The chef was babbling in our faces. Telling us how wonderful he was. His wife told us his life history, how he made pastry in Lyon that was like works of art, like the trompe l'oeil pottery known as *Barbotines*. She worked at a medical laboratory by day and by night she wrote pastry labels by hand using a miner's headlight to focus clearly on her delicate work.

She said that one day in Lyon someone announced that Patricia Wells was coming. "But she never came." It was said wistfully, though without recrimination.

I had no recollection of changing plans about a pastry shop in Lyon. It was hard to concentrate on anything other than the cold and the discomfort of being the only people in the restaurant. At one point, with both husband and wife in the kitchen, the door opened and six people came in the door. I recognized the blonde as someone who was in one of the cars I had approached earlier. Obviously it was a group who had reserved. They were confused. We knew they would be turned away. I realized that, for sure, the chef was nuts, and that he clearly wanted to cook only for me.

The owners approached the group at the door, explaining that they were too sad to cook, and had closed for the evening. We tried to look sad, too. As the chef passed our table, he mumbled under his breath, "One more group and we can lock the door."

I was thinking of Buñuel's sustained and harmless madness in "*Le Charme Discret de le Bourgeoisie*" with the coffin sitting in the other room. I knew we were locked in for the night. I counted on the madness being harmless, and on having a story to tell when we got out.

Finally the wife came to take our orders. Dressed all in black, not a gram of fat on her body, she was clearly not a happy lady. And that wracking cough continued. And continued.

We were offered homemade orange wine, a delicious brew fragrant with the aromas and flavor of cinnamon and cantaloupe. It was explosive, and one of the best things I tasted that evening.

We ordered. The second group of diners was turned away and the doors were locked.

We waited and we waited. We heard shouts in the kitchen.

The chef came out and proudly presented a platter of baby *oursins*, some of the tiniest sea urchins I have ever seen, each topped with a giant mound of whipped cream and a few grains of caviar. The rim of the plate was sprinkled with green, which we later learned was the chef's fetish, green tea.

We picked the sea urchins up with our hands, and waited for a spoon to scoop out the briny, dark sea creatures. The couple rummaged around and finally found demitasse spoons. The whipped cream stayed on the platter, as we devoured the Mediterranean delicacies with passion.

But the chef would not leave us in peace. He pulled up a chair next to me, and his face all but touched mine as he raved. All the famous guides were bad, he said, and their authors corrupt. An honest guide to restaurants in France, the one he would write, might include twelve addresses. They were all bad and all journalists were bad. The assumption was that his was the only sacred place in France. We were not yet convinced.

Another platter of sea urchins arrived. These were topped with white blobs of *brandade*, the popular Provençal purée of salt cod, garlic, and potatoes. ("Do you know what this is? It's local!") The rim of the platter was showered with a sprinkling of the lesser known Mediterranean delicacy, *poutargue*, or pungent salted and dried mullet roe. ("Do you know what this is? It's local!") And to prove it there was a whole piece of *poutargue* on the plate, looking like a fossil in wax.

We ate it. And we kept quiet. Conversation was not something we wanted more of.

The chef went back to his kitchen, and Madame came out and continued to recite the story of their lives. But she was soon cut short. Talking clearly interested the chef more than his stove, so he came out and told the story himself. Tales of no parents, being raised by grandparents, of changing his name over and over again.

He slid back into the kitchen just long enough to get the next course ready for the table.

Madame X-ray delivered lovely antique bowls from nearby Nîmes, filled with a truly weird combination of poached fish, sautéed scallops, some nicely cooked mushrooms and frogs' legs the chef claimed to have gone all the way to Nîmes (46 kilometers/29 miles away) to secure.

The evening was getting to me. I couldn't eat and could barely breathe: Someone was always in my face, and Petula Clark blared away. Whenever he came into the room, he increased the volume on the CD player. As soon as he disappeared into the kitchen, Madame turned the blaring music down. (*"Petula Clark, c'est une artiste. Comme moi,"* he said, *"une vraie."* I knew I would never listen to her again in the same way. And I haven't.)

We were lucky that Missy and Lee were good friends. Despite the strangeness of evening, we were already laughing about the bizarreness of it all. At one point I got up to go to the ladies' room and announced to our group that if there was a window in there, I'd climb out. (In retrospect, I am not sure where I would have gone, once liberated. It was still pouring buckets outside.)

Near the end of the evening the chef came into the dining room again, but carrying his pet duck. He put the bird on the floor and let it wander around the empty restaurant. The duck of course pooped on the floor. "*C'est rien!*" (It's nothing!) he said. I decided then that no one would ever believe this story.

Clearly, we never returned, but have dined out on the story for years.

WALTER:

As Patricia's driver and frequent accomplice, I have shared rare and memorable experiences. Farmers have invited us to stay for lunch and fishermen have shown us secret spots. Winemakers have opened a last remaining bottle from a historic vintage. Once, in Saint Emilion, returning very late from a festive dinner, we had to find a ladder and climb into an upstairs window at our hotel.

But nothing else has ever matched that rainy evening near Avignon. My sharpest memory of the meal, an embarrassing one, is that I ate every absurd bite. Blame it on nervousness, but as the chef's mouth moved, so did mine, his to talk and mine to chew.

We heard later that the chef had been arrested after head-butting a client, a wealthy Avignon woman. That part of the story is too good to check out. A fact that doesn't need to be checked is that I no longer drink the wine made by the guy who recommended the restaurant.

PEACH WINE

Whenever I make this fruity wine, it brings back memories of that wacky night in Avignon. Then Walter and I get to laugh about that meal all over again.

EQUIPMENT: A food mill fitted with the finest screen; 4 clean clear wine bottles.

> 18 ripe peaches
> Six 750-ml bottles white wine
> 3 cups sugar
> 750-ml bottle vodka

1. Prepare a large bowl of ice water. Set aside.
2. With a small, sharp knife, cut a cross at the stem end of the peach. (This will make them easier to peel.) Bring a large pot of water to a boil. Plunge the peaches into the boiling water and boil until the skins begin to peel away from the flesh, about 2 minutes. With a large, slotted spoon, remove the peaches from the boiling water. Immediately plunge them into the ice water. As soon as they are cool enough to handle, peel them. Cut them in half. Remove and discard the pits.
3. In a large casserole, combine the peaches and the wine and simmer gently for 25 minutes.
4. Pass the mixture through the finest screen of a food mill. Stir in the sugar and the vodka. Place in clean clear wine bottles, seal with corks, and store in a cool place. Serve as an apéritif or with a peach dessert.

Makes 4 bottles

12

{ Nouvelle Cuisine, Critique Nouvelle }

PATRICIA:

When Walter and I left New York and the *Times* for Paris and the *IHT*, there was no twofer deal. We both quit, he was hired by the *Trib*, I was off on a new and frightening freelance career.

It was 1980, and the wave of *nouvelle cuisine* was growing, leading French food away from the overly rich, overly sauced cuisine that Fernand Point had gloriously refined decades before.

By the fall of that year the former restaurant critic had left, leaving an opening. The *Trib* paid almost nothing, but the expense account was adequate. And I had the luxury of time, which allowed me to research my subjects in exacting detail. For each of my biweekly pieces I visited restaurants many times, usually once with female friends at lunch, another time on a weeknight with Walter, then on a weekend evening with a group of six or eight. I also had the luxury of not writing about many places that were simply not worth the ink—the *IHT* wanted me to tell visitors about places they would enjoy, not about places they wouldn't.

Once I made up my mind about a restaurant and decided to write about it, I usually introduced myself to the chef and interviewed him or her. More often than not, I would then go to the market with the chef and spend a day or more in the restaurant kitchen, getting under the skin of the place, helping me to fully understand the chef's practices and goals. This research also allowed me to begin gathering recipes for my future books as well as spy a bit, learning things—good and bad—that I couldn't have found out by simply staying put in the dining room.

Often I would test many of the recipes from the restaurant before writing a review, so that I could understand the cooking, the concepts, and the technique (as well as gauge how easy or how difficult it was to execute each recipe). As I always do, I plunged in and devoted myself 1,000 percent to the challenge. I even took the pictures that ran with my regular *IHT* columns.

The French chefs all responded positively to this methodical approach to restaurant criticism, since they were used to the rather slapdash approach of French critics, who then rarely paid for a meal and expected to be treated as stars in their own right.

(The French food critics, of course, hated me. For years, each time I was introduced to critic Claude Jolly [Jolly was Claude Lebey's pen name at the time] he acted as though he had never met me before. I finally told him this was the twenty-fifth time we'd met and his only response was "Oh, you changed your hairdo." Critic Christian Millau once took my fork out of my hand at a major dinner, and shouted "Here, this is the way you eat!")

But what a time it was! It seemed as though we willingly, even eagerly, dined out on foie gras, cassoulet, cream-rich potato gratin, and duck confit at every other meal. The most prominent cuisine at the time came from France's southwest, one based on fattened duck and goose, beans, and rich desserts.

All of this feasting took place in smoke-filled dining rooms where dogs sipped and dined at their master's feet, fed from special bowls.

Many a night I would return home and hang my clothes to air out in front of a high open window in our *buanderie* (laundry room). More than once I had to step into the shower before going to bed, my hair and entire body reeking of stale cigar and cigarette smoke, grease, and pungent food odors.

It was not uncommon to finish such Rabelaisian wine-filled meals with a glass (or two) of rare Cognac or Armagnac. And that was just for weeknight *grande bouffe*! (The words "French Paradox" had not yet become a catchphrase, and our bodies were still young enough to withstand the calorie onslaught.)

At many of these restaurants, vegetables and greens were considered a waste of good space. We had not yet heard of the Mediterranean Diet.

In those days in Paris, revered culinary institutions were already a big part of the dining scene, as Madame Allard served up her famous duck with olives; owner Michel Petit trotted out his wondrous display of hors d'oeuvres at the landmark Chez Benoit; Antoine Magnin, with his long white beard and slow, aging gait, was filling his coal-burning stove at L'Ami Louis, where he amazed us all with his simple but assured culinary gestures—deftly pan-fried scallops, giant golden potato cakes, and incomparable roasted leg of baby spring lamb. Alain Dutournier and his wife, Nicole, turned diners away every night at their new Belle Époque, out-of-the-way Au Trou Gascon on the city's eastern edge; and the aging Madame Cartet, there near the Place de la République since 1932, assuaged our gluttonous ways with giant servings of herring and the silken codfish purée known as *brandade de morue*, her meaty terrines, and classic bacon-drenched *salade au lard*. We sipped Beaujolais at the famed wine bar, Les Rubis, and devoured the Poilâne open-faced sandwiches at the tiny *bistrot à vin* Au Sauvignon, and laughed out loud with mustachioed *bistrotier* and winemaker Jacques Melac.

I arrived in Paris as the revolutionary culinary movement known as *nouvelle cuisine* was in its heyday. It was also the very early days of many of the top chefs working in Paris today. It took me years to realize, but we were all about the same age, at the same fledgling period of our careers. We all felt we were on the wave of something new, brave, and challenging.

The politics of France's dramatic 1968 riots had done more than change the face of the nation. It had shaken up the kitchens and dining rooms as well. The world was waking up to the realization that although foie gras, cassoulet, and eau de vie may have been delicious, the diet was doing nothing for our general health. Likewise, food follows fashion. It was no longer fashionable in France to dine out in the old-fashioned way. There needed to be a revolution. Any revolution. Out of that wave, *nouvelle cuisine* was born.

In 1973 the critics Gault and Millau had published the ten commandments of *nouvelle cuisine* in their magazine. The rules went like this:

- Do not overcook things.
- You will use fresh, high-quality products.
- You will make your menus lighter.
- You will not be systematically modernistic.
- You will nevertheless look into what the new techniques have to offer you.
- You will avoid marinades, hanging game for too long, fermentation processes.
- You will eliminate white and brown sauces.
- You will not ignore health.
- You will not rig your presentations.
- You will be inventive.

As someone who had been dining out four or five nights a week on heartier, old-fashioned fare, some of these guidelines appeared as a breath of fresh air. Yet *nouvelle cuisine* committed many a sin. One of my favorite anecdotes is of a visit at the time to a New York City restau-

Patricia and chef Joël Robuchon at a banquet for the
Paris Opera: Socks in red, white, and blue—
as a joke, as well as a gift—for Joël.

rant called *Coup de Fusil*, which translates literally as "a gun shot" but in French slang means a rip-off. The name was no doubt intentionally chosen for a pricey place that New York critics had pronounced the ne plus ultra. They also made up explanations about what the name meant, though no one offered "the emperor's new clothes." We went on a Saturday night, and the restaurant was filled. As the *cloches* came off at the next table, and a diner saw her plate carefully arranged with half a dozen peas and a single scallop, she wailed, "Don't we get no potatoes, or nothin'?" (I was appalled. Clearly this diner had not gotten the message, was not about to play the new game.)

At its worst, *nouvelle cuisine* was known for its gigantic, oversized plates with undersized portions, too often delivered with haughtiness and a silly silver *cloche*. At its best, it allowed for a new surprise with each meal, as we oohed and aahed with each unveiling.

But doesn't every revolution have to go through its "silly" phase before it settles down to create true change? Out of the ashes of the revolution came many riches, mostly in the name of a new band of young and energetic chefs freed from the rituals and rules of classic cuisine, all the while intent upon preserving the techniques and the discipline.

Bernard Pacaud had just opened L'Ambroisie on the Left Bank, Gilbert and Maguy LeCoze were wooing everyone with their fresh take on fish and shellfish at Le Bernardin on the Left Bank Quai de la Tournelle, Guy Savoy was cooking alone in a cramped, tiny kitchen on the Rue Duret in the 16th arrondissement, and chef Alain Senderens on the Rue de Varenne was amazing everyone with such audacious dishes as his spicy roast duck served with sweet Banyuls wine. We tasted our first kiwi and Granny Smith apple and began to rediscover the modest potato, and giant mixed green salads—known as *mesclun*—began arriving at the best of the city's tables.

But if I look at my reviews from the early 1980s, the food was far from light, or healthy. It was the era of the rolling dessert cart laden with dozens of irresistible sweets, and the waiters egged us on, and on. At Michel Rostang's I noted that diners took "three or four tarts per person, along with a plateful of smooth sweet mousses, including a stunning caramel concoction . . ."

Elsewhere, we were thrilled at the arrival of warm salads (who knew?), greens that topped warm, saffron-scented mussels, or calves brains garnished with chervil.

One of the trendiest *nouvelle* restaurants of the day was Chiberta, then considered ultimately modern with its black décor and lush Art Deco motif. Chef Jean-Michel Bédier was the most talked about chef of the moment, with a rule that food should be both *bon et beau*, good as well as beautiful. In one review I raved about his play of colors: "thin slices of sunset-orange salmon with multiple shades of green—a touch of forest green gherkins, of fawn-green capers, and grass-green chives." I loved that each plate resembled an Oriental painting and "like most nouvelle restaurants, Chiberta's menu favored fish and shellfish over meat and poultry." He also had a raw duck salad (it was in fact a *carpaccio*, though we didn't use that word in France back then) that was the talk of the town.

When Gilbert and Maguy LeCoze moved their popular Left Bank bistro, Le Bernardin, to a larger Right Bank space in January of 1981, it was near the Arc de Triomphe—and near our Rue Daru apartment. The restaurant became our *cantine*. Again, what Gilbert brought from the kitchen was totally new to us, "a simple and personal cuisine, mixing fish and shellfish with little more than a dash of herbs, butter, or oil, and a shower of tomatoes or sorrel." He also served "slivers of raw salmon dressed with olive oil, minced fresh tomatoes, coriander, and lemon juice." Likewise, though this was essentially a *carpaccio* or a *ceviche*, Gilbert called it *émincé de saumon*, or little bits of salmon. Diners still smoked excessively in those days, and one of my criticisms of Le Bernardin was that "ashtrays were left to overflow . . ." (As an aside, I remember back then that Gilbert had a reputation as a womanizer, and one who found special attraction to female food writers. I never knew whether to be complimented or insulted by the fact that he never made a pass at me, even when we would visit the Rungis fish market in the middle of the night.)

Then, I needed to do a lot of translating for readers, noting that sushi was raw fish. I suggested that the new wave of Japanese restaurants were easy to understand, since "some of the training has already been provided by nouvelle cuisine, with its emphasis on artistry and smaller portions . . ."

By March of 1981, everyone had HAD IT with *nouvelle cuisine*. In an interview with chef Michel Guérard, who was one of the first to popularize the idea of a simpler, less rich style of French cooking, the Michelin three-star chef noted that "today, too many dishes lack dignity, nobility, pride, and nuance."

*Mickey and Patricia: On location for a freelance job
in Orlando with Disney.*

The cuisine that was intended to become a breath of fresh air had become claustrophobic. The cuisine that was designed to rescue chefs and diners from sameness and boredom had, indeed, become repetitive and tedious. There was more emphasis on looks than flavor.

After my interview appeared in the *New York Times*, the paper ran an editorial noting: "The new cooking was . . . a worthy revolt . . . there were brilliant moments: extraordinary vegetables, veritable haikus of fish, miraculous sauces of vinegar instead of fat. But it went too far, and it grew solemn."

WALTER:

When Patricia told me in Paris that she was applying for the job of restaurant critic, I said: "You're on your own, kid." My desk in the *Times* newsroom had been less than a whisper away from James Greenfield's and every time the subject of Patricia's work came up I couldn't help overhearing. It was an uncomfortable time for me. As the *Trib*'s number-two editor I didn't want to be hiring my wife, making her assignments, editing her copy, or approving her expense accounts.

But I did love our evenings in restaurants, both the sparkling temples (Taillevent, Guy Savoy, the ever-glorious Robuchon . . .) and the ones that were temples of another sort. Chez l'Ami Louis, less well known a generation ago, was more accessible than it became but

Patricia's portrait of the period.

nearly as expensive. "Lammy Looey" many of our countrymen called it; the place looked grungy—and its cellar toilet truly was a hole in the floor, reached while clinging to a rope strung along the steep and well-worn stairs. Besides the mounds of food at L'Ami Louis, there was the show of the limousines lining up out front and the long minks and sables of the chic clientele tossed onto the racks above the tables.

Chez Allard was another of those Old Paris institutions that deserved periodic visits just to show gratitude that it survived. Likewise Cartet, where there was nothing forced about the abundant feeding.

It takes more than great food to make a great restaurant. The grunge at L'Ami Louis was turned into charm. The alarmingly copious spread that Monsieur Petit put on at Chez Benoit was memorable, but the way his waiters bantered to loosen you up was just as important.

Loosened up, and fattened up, and then eventually fed up. But not yet. Many restaurants were special destinations and would be for a long time.

Patricia, those shoulder pads, and homemade sourdough bread.

MICHEL GUÉRARD'S SALADE GOURMANDE

In the early 1980s, almost every serious restaurant in Paris offered some version of Michel Guérard's *Salade Gourmande*, a very simple and sublime first course that always included a slab of rich duck foie gras and steamed or blanched green beans. The original recipe also included asparagus tips. The dressing included walnut oil, an ingredient that was brand new to most of us back then.

EQUIPMENT: A 6-quart pasta pot fitted with a colander.

> 6 tablespoons coarse sea salt
> 1 pound very fresh green beans, rinsed and trimmed at both ends
> 24 asparagus tips

VINAIGRETTE
> 2 teaspoons freshly squeezed lemon juice
> 4 teaspoons extra-virgin olive oil
> 4 teaspoons walnut oil
> 2 teaspoons red wine vinegar
> 2 teaspoons minced fresh parsley leaves
> 2 teaspoons minced fresh chives
> Fine sea salt
> Freshly ground black pepper

> 8 large lettuce leaves, preferably red trévise, washed and dried
> 1 shallot, finely minced
> 4 ounces foie gras, fresh or mi-cuit from a jar
> 1 black truffle (about 1½ ounces), canned or fresh, cut into very thin slices (optional)

1. Prepare two large bowls of ice water. Set aside.
2. Fill the pasta pot, fitted with a colander, with 5 quarts of water and bring to a boil over high heat. Add 3 tablespoons coarse salt and the beans and cook until crisp-tender, about 5 minutes. (Cooking time will vary, according to the size and freshness of the beans.)

Immediately remove the colander from the water, allow the water to drain from the beans, and plunge the colander with the beans in it into the ice water so they cool down as quickly as possible. (The beans will cool in 1 to 2 minutes. If you leave them longer, they will become soggy and begin to lose flavor.) Transfer the beans to a strainer, drain, and wrap in a thick towel to dry. (The beans can be cooked up to 4 hours in advance. Keep them wrapped in the towel and refrigerate.)

3. Rinse out the pasta pot and fill again with 5 quarts of water. Bring to a boil over high heat. Add 3 tablespoons course salt and the asparagus tips and cook until crisp tender, just 2 to 3 minutes. Immediately remove the colander from the water, allow the water to drain from the asparagus tips, and plunge the colander with the asparagus into the ice water so they cool down as quickly as possible. (The asparagus will cool in 1 to 2 minutes. If you leave them longer, they will become soggy and begin to lose flavor.) Transfer the asparagus to a strainer, drain, and wrap in a thick towel to dry. (The asparagus can be cooked up to 4 hours in advance. Keep them wrapped in the towel and refrigerate, if desired.)

4. Prepare the vinaigrette: In a small jar, combine the lemon juice, oils, vinegar, and herbs. Cover securely and shake to blend. Season to taste with salt and pepper.

5. Place the lettuce in a large bowl and toss with just enough vinaigrette to coat the lettuce. Do the same for the green beans and the asparagus.

6. Arrange two lettuce leaves on each of four salad plates. Arrange a mound of green beans on top. Arrange the asparagus tips on top of the beans. Decorate the salad with the foie gras and the truffle slices, if using. Serve.

4 servings

13

{ You Paid to Learn to Drive Like That? }

*Patricia and her first VW convertible in 1987: Red with
white interior, stolen on Rue Daru on New Year's Eve
when it was only a few months old.*

PATRICIA:

Like most Americans of my era, I received my driver's
license on or about my sixteenth birthday. My dad taught
me to drive in our spiffy 1957 green and white hardtop Desoto, an
automatic of course, with push-button drive. I don't remember any
scars or scares of the era. For me, driving has always has been a way to
get around, nothing more.

The first car I ever bought on my own was a 1969 red Porsche. It was 1975 and I was newly divorced. At the time, I decided that the little bundle of extra money that I had set aside would either go to pay for therapy to deal with the shock of divorce, or to acquire the sports car that had somehow been offered to me. The red car seemed like more fun, and maybe even a better psychic cure.

When Walter and I moved to Paris in 1980, we had no car for the first year or so, so I rarely drove. Back then France accepted an American license as evidence that you could drive. All you had to do was take your American driver's license to the French prefecture and trade it for a French one. But there was no reciprocity—only a few states in the U.S. would make a parallel trade, so France stopped its easy exchange.

I wasn't driving much, and was not in a hurry to drive, so I never bothered to trade in my U.S. permit. When it came time to get on the road to research *The Food Lover's Guide to France*, I matter-of-factly took on the driving role, since my assistant, Jane Sigal, did not drive. Although Walter bugged me about getting my French license, I ignored his pleas, figuring that we had insurance, and nothing was going to happen to me anyway. I was a safe and sound driver.

On one of the first of dozens of trips into the French countryside, Jane and I left Rue Daru in our gray VW Golf. Within two blocks, I had hit another car. I don't remember now whether or not we continued on our journey, but I do know that from then on, we took a train to a city in the region we were researching, and rented a car at the train station. This meant I did not have to drive in Paris or in any major cities.

But our troubles were not over. Those were the days before strict limits on speed. My budget was severely limited, and we usually were given a tin can of a car, a Fiat Uno or its equivalent, cars that would rarely go more than 90 kilometers (55 miles) an hour, no matter how you pushed it.

We researched winter and summer, spring and fall, driving the mountains of the Basque region and along the shores of Brittany, through the snow-capped roads of the Jura and the narrow roads of the Alps. As I drove, the ever-serene and unflappable Jane served as navigator, Michelin maps and itinerary neatly posed on her lap.

More than once we landed in a ditch, and in time became experts at perfecting the back-and-forth rocking motion that rescued us from my embarrassment. On more evenings than I like to count, our after-dinner drives from restaurant to hotel (we could rarely afford to sleep in the three-star inns where we ate) were along crowded two-lane roads, being tailgated bumper-to-bumper by double-long semis beeping endlessly and often passing us slowpokes in dangerously close quarters.

We can laugh now, but one of the most harrowing drives took place in the French Alps in winter. We had visited a sausage maker and were on our way back to our hotel. There was lots of snow, but as a Wisconsin girl, I had plenty of experience in that department, and so was unfazed until the single-lane road stopped. Dead. Nowhere to turn around, no way to move ahead. I asked Jane to examine the Michelin map, and tell me what the legend on that road meant.

She looked me coolly in the eye and muttered, "I won't tell you. I can't . . ." After a lot of begging on my part, she relented, and explained that the markings meant that the road was "*difficile et dangereuse.*" I don't remember exactly what came next, but somehow we got ourselves out of the fix, and found our way home again.

In time, Walter wore me down with his repeated requests to "go legal" and I agreed to get my French driver's license. By this time, the law had changed. I could no longer just go down to the French traffic bureau and trade in my American permit. At the age of forty-eight, I had to go to driver's school! Worst of all, I had to PAY to learn to drive like the French!

Our friends Maggie and Al Shapiro had a friend with a driving school on the outskirts of Paris and we were all certain that as a gesture of friendship to them—and as one who had driven for more than thirty years without so much as a ticket or serious moving violation—I would get some special handling. Little did I know.

On the first day the instructor took me out in his tiny Peugeot 204 for a test drive. In France you must learn to drive with a stick shift, which was never a problem for me, especially since the red Porsche. And the rule was that you had to take lessons in the instructor's car, not your own. He took me out around the 19th arrondissement, onto the *périphérique* near Charles de Gaulle airport, then directed me to a quiet parking lot. He put his hand on my thigh, patting it, then squeezing it tight. Clearly, he expected more than his fee in exchange for "teaching" me to drive.

I was struck dumb. I removed his hand and scowled at him. With no more words exchanged, I drove back to the driving school, got back on the Métro, and went home.

That night, I burst into tears explaining to Walter what had happened. But I needed that license and was not going to let this guy get to me. Ever since the day I rejected the driving instructor's advances, he was on my case. I used the clutch too much, I was too timid, he didn't understand why Americans got out of the right lane on a freeway to let in an entering car. He was going to do everything to see that I did not pass.

It took months: I had to study for the written test and when the day came I was the only person older than sixteen and not in jeans in the huge auditorium testing room. Once the test was over, the hundreds of hopeful drivers had to sit and wait until all the exams had been corrected. Then they called us up to the front of the room and announced to all present whether it was a yes or no! There were a lot of tears that day, but mine were tears of joy. True, my driving instructor had given me a handwritten cheat sheet of questions, all of them regulations that seemed to date from the 1960s. When I asked him about the more up-to-date issues that were covered in the *Code de la Route*, he explained that the exam had not been updated in decades.

My two favorite French driving rules include the exceptions as to when you can blow your horn. There are only two situations allowed: one is when your car approaches two bicyclists riding side by side on the side of the road. The other is when you see a ball roll in front of your vehicle: It's a sure sign that a child will follow, running into the street.

After passing the written test, you can take the road test, but the instructor decides when you are ready. Because the schools profit from each class you take with them, they keep suggesting that you are "not quite ready" and certainly need "another class or driving lesson or two."

Patricia and her 1995 white VW convertible with red leather interior.
Still running like a top!

The day of the driving exam another student and myself—along with the grumpy driving instructor, and a well-groomed female driving examiner—crowded into the instructor's Peugeot. The instructor drove to a parking lot nearby, where I was ordered to get behind the wheel. The examiner directed me to drive out of the parking lot, make a left turn, then a right turn, then drive back into the parking lot.

The second student took her turn, and was visibly so nervous that she nearly hit another car, more than once. Back in the parking lot, Madame Wells was told she passed, the second student, eyes welling up with tears, was told she needed "a bit more time in school."

I was elated. It was a gold-letter day. To this day, one of my most precious documents is that pink French driver's license, mine for life!

Somewhere along the line I developed a true aversion to driving, and the driving school experience didn't help me get over it. I am probably the only person who, at age eighty-nine, will be happy to be told, "Patricia, we really don't think that it is safe for you to drive anymore."

My current car is a 1995 white Volkswagen convertible with red leather interior. It has carried me no more than 35,000 kilometers in the past twelve years, meaning an average of less than 2,000 miles a year. I think that my car ought to go into the book of Guinness world records, since on most years, I fill up the tank only once throughout the year. I hope to keep that car—the one we call "Flash"—for the rest of my life. Or at least until at eighty-nine I am told that I can't drive anymore.

Almond Macaroon
and Fresh Berry Cake

I feel fortunate that I inherited neither the shoe gene nor the sugar gene. Think of all the money and calories saved over the years! I rarely engage in stress eating, but during those first few days of taking driving lessons in Paris, sugar seemed to offer a touch of solace. I can usually pass on dessert, but there is something about this cake—sort of Miss Almond Macaroon meets Mister Angel Food Cake—that makes one want to EAT THE WHOLE THING! Use any kind of berries in season, or in off months, use frozen berries. Note that since the quantity of egg whites is important here, go by the liquid measure of the whites, not the number of egg whites.

EQUIPMENT: A 9½-inch springform pan; a heavy-duty electric mixer fitted with a whisk.

> 1 teaspoon almond oil or vegetable oil for preparing the pan
> 1 cup egg whites (6 to 8 large)
> 1 cup raw sugar
> A scant 2 cups almond powder
> Grated zest of 2 lemons, preferably organic
> 3 tablespoons cornstarch
> ¼ teaspoon fine sea salt
> 2 cups fresh raspberries or other small berries
> Fresh fruit and seasonal sorbet for serving

1. Preheat the oven to 375°F.
2. Brush the springform pan with the oil. Set aside.
3. Place the egg whites in the bowl of a mixer fitted with a whisk. Beat at low speed until frothy. Gradually increase the speed to high, slowly adding the sugar, and whisking until the egg whites are stiff but not dry. At low speed, carefully add the ground almonds, lemon zest, cornstarch, and salt and mix until blended.
4. Spoon the mixture into the prepared pan. Sprinkle the berries

on top. Place the pan in the center of the oven and bake until the cake is firm and golden, and begins to pull away from the side of the pan, 35 to 40 minutes.

5. Remove from the oven and transfer to a rack to cool. After 10 minutes, run a knife along the side of the pan. Release and remove the side of the springform pan, leaving the cake on the pan base. Serve warm or at room temperature, cut into wedges. Serve with additional fresh fruit and a favorite seasonal sorbet.

8 servings

14

{ Two for the Road }

WALTER:

Driving in Paris is not so hard when you understand that the basic traffic rule is simple displacement: Where my car is, yours cannot be. What proved hard wasn't the traffic, but owning a car in France's capital. In fact, it was an Everest-size challenge.

We learned that the first time when our Porsche was stolen from a locked garage, then again when thieves drove off in our new VW convertible on New Year's Eve. Even an old yellow Fiat station wagon that a repatriating friend left behind to assuage our loss of the Porsche disappeared from the spot by the Avignon train station where we left it. Good luck has abounded in our lives, but so has bad car karma.

That 1975 911S Porsche came into my life in 1982 with a past that included 90,000 kilometers and one change of paint, from the blue of a troubled sky to the hard edge of anthracite. I should have read the colors as portentous symbols.

In a large sense, the car was found in the first place. I say that because Patricia secretly put together the money to buy it through several years of tightfisted bookkeeping. When she surprised me with

Walter and his 1977 Porsche. Later stolen!

the news I was touched, even dumbfounded, and also comprehending of why we had been so broke. But mostly I was just eager to get on the road.

For nearly two years the Porsche brought great pleasure, like any object of envy, passion, and obsession. It carried us across the manicured European countryside, through dizzying Alpine switchbacks, and along the smooth straightaways of our heady first years in France.

I loved learning to drive like a European—the speed limit of 130 kph (80 mph), was not seriously enforced in those days, and those smooth, well-engineered *autoroutes* would allow comfortable cruising at 160 kph (100 mph). However, I never drove like a Formula 1 pilot, unlike the young drivers I encountered in the French provinces. Their driving was fueled by their hormones, and they probably screwed just as recklessly.

Like a lot of other things about France, the way the speed limits were enforced would change. While Nicolas Sarkozy was in charge of the national police as interior minister he placed hundreds of cameras strategically along major roadways. He also armed the police with special binoculars that register a driver's speed, and in urban areas it is now routine to see the police hiding along the road and aiming their binoculars at the cars whizzing by. Over a month-long period I was "flashed" twice by the cameras on the *autoroute* between Paris and Provence. I paid the fines and, just like nearly every other French driver, I slowed down. Not surprisingly, fatalities in auto accidents dropped by 40 percent.

Wayne Marshall and Walter: posing with their twin beat-up Peugeot 504s.

One of my sharpest memories from our three-week tour of the country in 1979, driving around much of the country in our boxy little rental Renault 5, was cruising along at 90 kph (a sedate 55 mph) and having horns blaring behind us. More than our red temporary tags, our pokey speed gave us away as tourists. That didn't happen when I got the Porsche because the issue wasn't speed. The issue was the nagging disquiet I felt because the car was not insured against theft.

Explaining why there was no insurance is still complicated. Why would anyone keep a Porsche, of any vintage, and not insure it? Even if he didn't know—and I didn't then—that he was living in one of the world's principal auto-theft capitals. Well, as I have said often enough, trying each time to catch my breath and not speak too rapidly, I had tried to buy insurance with a half-dozen companies and none of them would touch it. Wanting the car more than I wanted to get the message, I plunged ahead with my own protection plan, a state-of-the-art alarm system and a locked cubicle in a locked garage.

I also used the car infrequently. Cars are stolen from the street, I thought. If mine wasn't on the street, the thieves would take one of the many that were.

One morning, only weeks after paying a body shop a large amount of money to take out all the dings and repaint the car, I went into my garage, took the elevator to the second basement, and found a very large empty space.

I had no car and no recourse. My heart was heavy, and not so much with longing for the pleasures the car had given me or even the financial loss. It was mostly heavy with embarrassment. Admitting the lack of insurance, no matter how many times I practiced the story, always sent listeners away in bewilderment if not sniggers. (Years later I learned that my staff at the *Trib* preferred its own explanation: I was too cheap to pay for it. I guess they had reason to believe that.)

Six years went by, and spectacularly the car was found again. In a telephone call from a very excited Paris policeman, I learned that the Porsche had turned up—in an altered state, of course. Not just another color (fire-engine red, naturally), but with a different gearbox, a more powerful engine, a rear fender lift, and a forged registration card.

That didn't sound or look like my car, but the serial number said it was. The cop was pleased and convincing. "There's not the slightest doubt that you'll get it back." He proposed that to celebrate the recovery I could maybe get him and his colleagues tickets for the next Formula 1 race.

The lawyer I hired was not really necessary, the policeman advised, but good insurance. The lawyer was so confident that we even decided on the restaurant where we would celebrate the recovery.

Apparently only one guy had been tooling around in my car since it disappeared. He was caught through a fluke: Since buying the car from a chop shop for an appreciably discounted price, he had had it serviced at the same garage. Then the place suddenly closed—the mechanic had been locked up for auto theft. So the owner brought the car to a Porsche dealer for servicing. Much to Porsche's credit, it spotted the altered identification and alerted the police.

The man was arrested and charged with three offenses: receiving stolen goods, forgery, and use of the forged documents (the registration card plus a bill of sale, nonexistent until he had created it), and verbal abuse of the police officers who picked him up.

At trial, three impatient, stern-faced jurists listened to everyone's stories, conferred among themselves for two minutes, then pronounced him guilty of two of the charges, but not of receiving stolen goods. His argument that he was a victim was the version they accepted. Because that charge was the basis of my claim, the claim was adjudged *irrecevable*—that is, inadmissible, though the translation that I preferred was that the case was beyond the court's competence.

"So we'll win on appeal," said my lawyer. Since France is a country where, it is said, things can be "arranged," I looked for extra juridical help. A friend had a friend, a high-ranking official, who could be approached. We weren't talking bribery, simply a whispered good word on the merits of my case.

"Tell your friend not to worry," word came back. "I've looked at the dossier and it's clear. The car is his and he'll get it back."

But I didn't. It turned out that correct court procedure had not been followed. As though Johnnie Cochran had been in charge of the chain of evidence, the dossier was no longer solid. Papers had gone missing. The defense, claiming it had additional evidence, threatened action against me if I didn't drop the case. Back to the friend of my friend.

Now his certainty about the outcome went in the other direction. "You should drop the case," he messaged back. "You have no chance."

Once again, I didn't have the right insurance.

If no more Porsche, I had a consolation prize, that Fiat station wagon. It was no Porsche, but it would serve us well when we bought our farm in Provence. We called the car *le Bourdon*, meaning bumblebee, because it roared and it was sluggish. When the car disappeared from an Avignon parking lot, I made no effort to track it down.

The Fiat was followed by a number of other cars, even another 1977 Porsche 911S. It was insured against theft, and its chirpy alarm system was the one most recommended to frustrate thieves. Supplementary antitheft devices were installed, special ones. I was covered, I thought, for every exigency. Except that the car was a lemon.

Now, more modestly, and more reliably, there is still Patricia's 1995 white VW convertible, with red leather seats. It's getting on in years, but carries itself well enough for one young gas station attendant to comment recently, "*Ça fait flash, Madame.*" Flashy or not, it hasn't been stolen.

Walter and another 1977 Porsche, jubilee edition.

15

{ The *L'Express* Years }

PATRICIA:

It was close to midnight on a sweaty, humid Friday night in August of 1988. I had returned to our Rue Daru apartment after several days in Amsterdam, there to promote the new Dutch edition of *The Food Lover's Guide to France*, entitled *Reisboek Frankrijk voor Finjnproevers*.

I was flat out exhausted, and Walter greeted me at the door with a glass of chilled, bubbling Champagne.

"Sit down," Walter said, ushering me to one of the cozy blue love seats in our living room, a part of the apartment we rarely used. "I have something important to tell you."

It's strange what runs through one's head in a situation like that. Walter was uncharacteristically solemn, and the only thing that I could think of was that he was about to announce that he was having a torrid clandestine affair, though I noticed that the Champagne was Grande Dame, which we opened to celebrate important occasions.

"*L'Express* wants you to be their restaurant critic," he blurted out, barely containing his own excitement.

My immediate thought was that this was some kind of joke. My written French was worthless: I couldn't even write a proper note to the *concierge* to say that I would be away for the weekend. And I was way too tired for a joke at this moment. Why would the country's leading newsweekly allow a "country" girl from Milwaukee to have the power to hand down judgments and even criticize an essential part of France's patrimony? And not for Anglophones but for the French?

"No," Walter insisted, kindly refilling my Champagne flute. "Guy Lagorce, the features editor at *L'Express,* called and he wants you to call him on Monday morning."

I called Guy Lagorce first thing Monday, being quick to say thank you very much but to warn him that he had the wrong girl.

"I am very flattered, but I can't write proper French," I explained apologetically, and not without a touch of embarrassment.

"That's okay," replied Lagorce. "We are a liberal publication, but not so liberal that we will run your column in English." he laughed. "We'll translate you."

I was frightened, scared even. This was more than I had ever bargained for. But at that moment I drew out of my soul the mantra that I created in the 1970s while living in Washington, DC. It was the first time I had ever been asked to speak in public, and I was scared to death. But as I accepted the engagement I created this rule of life: "Being afraid is not enough reason to say no."

Once I decided that I HAD to say yes, I also realized that I couldn't believe my good fortune. It had been quite a summer. *La France Gourmande*, the French edition of *The Food Lover's Guide to France*, had appeared in the stores in July and was such a hit that I was invited to appear on the country's most popular television show, *Apostrophe*. At the time, the Friday night book-and-author show, hosted by French national treasure Bernard Pivot, was the best thing that could happen to any author, anywhere.

It was a coup. But it came with no guarantee. The publicity direc-

July 1988: Patricia on the set of Apostrophe.

tor of the book's publisher, Flammarion, gently warned me not to get my hopes up. You are only being invited as *"un petit côté pétillant"* (a bubbly little aside), she cautioned, a trinket of amusement to counter all the other truly serious French authors. (I had visions of those poor guests on the old Johnny Carson show, the ones who sat down at his side just seconds before the show went off the air, getting a simple introduction and nothing more.)

The evening came for the live show and I was the only female and only foreigner among six guests. The others included a man who had just written his hundredth mystery novel; a psychoanalyst who had just retranslated all of the works of Freud (and who also happened to have a vineyard in Burgundy, Pivot's home region); the still-famed French novelist Philippe Sollers, and the now deceased author-*provocateur* Jean-Edern Hallier.

Cameras rolled, the show began, and Pivot started introducing the other authors one by one. It was taking so long that I just figured he would simply forget about me and go on with the show. Then he held up *La France Gourmande*, began interviewing me, and didn't stop for a full fifteen minutes of the hour-long show. I was on first! I remember both wanting these moments to last forever as well as wanting the whole show to just be over with.

Sporting a curly brown bouffant hairdo, and wearing my bright turquoise Louis Féraud designer jacket with exaggerated shoulder pads (the look of the moment), I felt as though I had just been chosen Queen for a Day. Pivot was in love with the book and I was in love with him. He quizzed me on many details in the book, and was most thrilled about my discovery of a quaint (and now defunct) bistro in Lyon, called Chez Tante Paulette. The owner of the 1930s-style restaurant was in her seventies at the time, and famed for her garlic-laden fare, including chicken with garlic; salads of greens, bacon, and more garlic; and an amazing bouillabaisse of chicken, with the poultry stewed in olive oil and pastis and served with—of course—a garlic sauce. Pivot loved that sort of rustic French fare and it sure helped put me in a better light, especially with the French intellectuals sitting at my left and my right.

The TV appearance helped sell books, for sure, but also was the impetus for the call from *L'Express*. The stable of French food critics—still all male—was remarkably stale at the time, and each writer seemed to be wed to one publication or another. The news magazine's choice of a female and a foreigner was clearly a liberal statement as well as a slap in the face to all the other critics. (At the time chef Joël Robuchon once told me that he could never repeat what the other French critics were saying about me. I could imagine, but didn't really want to know.)

I had pretty much *carte blanche* for my weekly reviews, and the datelines varied, from Lille in the north to Perpignan in the south, and included reports from trips to San Francisco, New York, Los Angeles, and Florence. I took the job on one condition: that I got to choose my translator. Sylvie Girard, a food writer in her own right, is also a professional translator. She had translated both my France and Paris guides from English to French and I loved her work. When I read myself in French it sounded like me! (As a pleasant aside, Sylvie and my *L'Express* editor Guy Lagorce met over my translations and fell in love, married, and now live in France's southwest, where Guy writes novels and Sylvie continues her food writing and translating.)

My first thought about the job was, how was I going to write for the French? Should I change my style? Take a different approach? As I went about my work, I realized that I had only one way to write, and that nothing would change.

In retrospect, I had to be both young and crazy at the time. I don't think I could have the stamina for such a life today. For as I jetted off to Perpignan for lunch or raced off to the Sologne for a wintry game dinner, I continued my twice-monthly reviews for the *International Herald Tribune*. By choice, I never wrote about the same restaurants for the two publications, meaning I had to double up on meals.

My column, called *Les Étapes Gourmandes*, ran for more than three years, until the summer of 1991, when the direction of the magazine changed and the editors felt they no longer needed a national food critic. I was, in fact, relieved.

But the opportunity allowed me to continue to cover all of the most important trends in contemporary dining, from tiny village *winstubs* in Alsace (where we all but bathed in sauerkraut and sausages, washed down with crisp white Sylvaner) to eleven-table bistros in the heart of the Auvergne in central France (where at La Reine Margot we devoured crêpes stuffed with hearty Cantal cheese, and green salads garnished with thick slabs of country ham and melted Cantal).

Grand tables were put to scrutiny as well. Alain Passard (now a Michelin-starred chef in Paris) was just coming to maturity in June 1989, when he moved to Paris from the suburb of Duc d'Enghien. Tuna was rarely seen on Paris restaurant menus in those days, and Passard's thick tuna steaks topped with a highly seasoned butter sauce and a salad made up of nothing but herbs took the city by storm. Today such food would be mundane, old hat even, but then it sent shockwaves through the nation's educated palates. The combination was considered truly original, even explosive.

Bernard Pacaud (now a Michelin three-star chef) had just moved to the elegant Place de Vosges from a bistro-like spot on the Left Bank. His food was austere and pure; I called it *cuisine moderne* and praised the demise of *nouvelle cuisine*, saying that his cooking took the best qualities of traditional classic fare with a totally new and wise understanding of how we really wanted to eat today.

I commented that the new emphasis on flavor, ingredients, and healthy simplicity was beginning to win out over an "excessively decorative style." The review noted: "It is as though Pacaud has taken all the weight out of food, leaving behind only the purest of flavors."

I wasn't always kind or favorable. Les Trois Marches in Versailles caught my wrath for its "bland lamb chops soaking in sickeningly sweet sauce," and I dismissed the restaurant as nothing but "clichés with culinary ideas way past their prime." I found Marc Veyrat's (now a Michelin three-star chef) food shockingly minimalist; and wrote that the ideas of Jacques Maximin of Nice (now retired from his restaurant in Vence in the south of France) with his cooking on stage in a defunct movie theater, were simply silly.

Trends have always been slow to come in France. This was and still is a land of tradition, despite the revolution of *nouvelle cuisine*. At the time, Portuguese chef Jose Lampreia was a trendsetter, first at his restaurant La Maison Blanche in the 15th arrondissement, and later at 15 Avenue Montaigne. We couldn't get enough of his revolutionary looks and flavors, a bright, sunny cuisine laced with figs, Moroccan spices, ginger, fresh coriander, and preserved lemons, and his famed mashed potatoes seasoned with fruity olive oil in place of butter.

Fresh vegetables, simply prepared, were new then. The most famed was the *salade à la maraîchère*, named for the market gardeners who supplied fresh and wholesome lettuces and vegetables. I found it at its best at Auberge du Templiers in the center of France, describing it as a first course of my dreams: "perfectly tender lettuces, green beans, tomatoes, baby carrots, onions, and snow peas, nothing fancy, just simple perfection."

High points during the period included the discovery of Didier Oudill's short-lived Pain, Adour et Fantaisie in France's southwest. I can still see and taste his intense dish of a double lamb chop coated with tiny cubes of zucchini, garlic, basil, and bacon, wrapped in caul fat and gently seared, then served with a sweet eggplant purée.

From the beginning, my dream in all of my work was to make three people happy. The goal was to find authentic, real, hard workers, serious people whom I could bring to the public eye. The object of my affection was happy, for she or he had found a new audience. The reader was

Patricia's portrait ran each week with her
restaurant reviews in L'Express, the French custom.

happy, for he or she found a new restaurant, *boulangerie*, cheesemonger, or market to explore. And I was happy to have met my goal.

My portrait, in color, appeared each week alongside my column in *L'Express*, a very non-American food critic's custom, but one the French stood by. They can never understand the American custom of a food writer's anonymity. But as I continued to reserve under another name, it was rare that anyone recognized me along the trail. Readers did recognize me in the streets, though, and years later I would be stopped—usually by male gastronomes—to thank me for an article, disagree with my judgment, or suggest a new place I might try. But the most amazing reader letter ever came from a male inmate in a national French prison. He wrote that he was there because of fraud (mostly padding his expense account with lavish restaurant meals) and after his dinner of soggy green beans and fatty meat consisting of nothing but gristle, he would retire to his prison cell to read my *L'Express* columns and satisfy his gastronomic longings, filling himself up on chapters from *La France Gourmande*!

WALTER:

Patricia said the *L'Express* job was the best she was ever offered and the one she was happiest to leave, and her feelings mirrored my own. It's because of Patricia that the successful people I admire most are the ones who have invented themselves, and her *L'Express* gig confirmed that she had done a pretty good job of it. By the time it started in 1988, she had published two books in the United States, both of them translated into French. But it was her copious freelance work that demonstrated her competence and confirmed her determination to show that colleague back at the *Times* that she could indeed earn her keep writing about food in France. She filed regularly for the *Times* daily sections, for weekend Travel, and for the Sunday magazine. She was on the masthead as a contributing editor at both *Food & Wine* and *Travel + Leisure* and wrote for a welter of other food publications: *Bon Appétit, Cuisine, European Travel & Life, Departures*, the

Telegraph in the UK, and others that I don't remember. It seemed that she had more deadlines than even my three-a-day at the *Trib*.

She was happy about the workload, and that made me happy. Doing the taxes after our first year in Paris, she had told me with a heavy heart that she earned only $1,500 that year. "Give yourself a break" would have been my response, though the frequent overdrafts made me keenly aware of our financial shortfall. By that tax time, in fact, things were picking up, including the twice-monthly *IHT* restaurant reviews. And even when the assignments had been slow in coming, they allowed for a few weekend trips.

More than money, her two *Food Lover's* guides, their translation into French, and then the call from *L'Express* showed that she was no longer "some twinkie freelancer" (her words). It was, in fact, a culmination of our original "go for it" moment back on Forty-fourth Street. Since then she had trudged through snow in lost Alpine villages and checked out breezy oyster shacks on the Atlantic coast. Most often I was not along on those trips, but we did have some nights together in fussy hotels in central France. And I remember an outrageously disappointing Sunday lunch on a restaurant terrace in Châteauroux as the waiter studiously ignored a dog's ample dump nearby.

The weekly *L'Express* columns gave me boundless pride—I loved having a famous wife and felt no jealousy of her success. In journalism, a field famous for huge, bruising egos, my own has a different dimension. I take more satisfaction in coming up with a good idea for a story than in seeing my byline on one, and that was true at home as well.

To avoid special treatment in restaurants, her policy was always anonymity—she used her maiden name to reserve, and had a bank card in that name to settle the bills. In conversation we avoided subjects that might give her away. But when she was recognized, I admit that I loved the extra attention the table got—the glass of Champagne, the treats the chef wanted her to try.

In time the pace wore both of us down. Meals became a series of assignments, and not always welcome ones when they meant daybreak

Tante Paulette, a favorite chef in Lyon.

flights to remote destinations, or long drives back to some minimalist hotel after dinner. Deconstructing dishes and analyzing each bite was fun at first but it soon detracted from the pleasures of the table. "It's only food," I began saying, much too often.

We had celebrated with Champagne when *L'Express* offered her the job, and we popped a cork again when new owners ended the magazine's national restaurant criticism. "Been there done that," she said. Quiet evenings at home were a welcome change of pace.

La Cagouille's
Salmon Tartare

La Cagouille, a casual fish restaurant in Paris's 14th arrondissement has been a favorite for decades, and I've reviewed this popular spot many times. Chef-owner Gérard Allemandou all but seems to have fins, he loves fish so much! This recipe is a personal favorite, and like so many great and simple things, the hardest part is to keep from embellishing. The fish can be cut a few hours in advance and kept well chilled. At the very last minute, drizzle the lemon and oil mixture on a chilled plate, arrange the salmon, then add a final drizzle and seasoning. I like to vary the final seasoning, sometimes cutting Japanese seaweed sheets (nori) into a fine julienne, or simply topping the salmon with sprigs of fresh chervil.

EQUIPMENT: A small jar with a lid; 4 chilled salad plates.

> 1 pound very fresh skinless salmon fillets
> 6 tablespoons freshly squeezed lemon juice
> Fleur de sel
> 6 tablespoons best-quality extra-virgin olive oil
> Freshly ground black pepper to taste
> A fine julienne of dried Japanese seaweed (nori)
>   or fresh chervil sprigs for garnish
> Toasted country bread for serving

1. Up to 5 hours before serving the salmon, carefully cut the fish into small rectangles, about 3 by ½ inches. Arrange on a plate, cover with plastic wrap, and chill until serving time.
2. In a small jar, combine the lemon juice and ¼ teaspoon fleur de sel and shake to dissolve the salt. Add the olive oil and shake to blend.
3. At serving time, drizzle each of the four chilled salad plates with a light coating of the lemon and oil dressing. Arrange the rectangles of salmon on each plate. Drizzle with another light coating of dressing. Season generously with fleur de sel and

freshly ground black pepper. Garnish with a fine julienne of seaweed or with sprigs of fresh chervil. Serve with plenty of freshly toasted country bread.

4 servings

WINE SUGGESTION: A fine, flinty Sauvignon Blanc would be my choice here, a wine with enough zest to stand up to the salmon but not smother it.

16

{ Mr. Patricia Wells }

WALTER:

It's not that the sandwich was bad. Smoked turkey on a sesame bun with tomatoes and lettuce and, *bien sûr*, Dijon mustard. A submarine, or a hoagie, as they say in Philadelphia. Nor was it that the table was bad, at least no worse than any other table in any other fast-food joint along the crowded, noisy international departure concourse. But sitting in the E terminal at the Philadelphia airport, my laptop on my knees, the Dijon mustard dripping onto the keyboard, and neighboring tables all swarming with cranky children, I sure didn't feel like *Mister* Patricia Wells.

And just then she called. When either of us is traveling we telephone often and our conversations frequently touch on food—on what she has tested at home or had in a restaurant—as well as the usual foundations of a happy marriage: how much we miss each other, pledges of undying love, and (when it's me who's on the road) all the light switches and equipment that don't work. The maintenance man, I'm responsible for logistics and equipment in our life.

With each list, I know once again that I'm needed; when I get back home in a week the job jar will be reassuringly full.

The news in this call is about a polenta dish that she had been working on and now declares perfect. I think of it as refried polenta and it *is* perfect. The delicious corn meal is cooked with Parmesan and spread in a shallow round dish to cool. Then Patricia slices it like pie and browns the wedges in olive oil and serves them with a tomato chutney that is again spiced with the delicate peppers from Espelette, down near the Spanish border.

I tell her about my sandwich, but fail to engage her even when I mention the crispness of the iceberg lettuce and those remarkable Styrofoam tomatoes. Food is fuel, at least some of the time, and toward that purpose my airport sandwich has been, well, heroic. But hearing about the polenta makes me frown and think about retracting my rejoinder to Stéphane, the headwaiter at Cap Vernet near the Place de l'Étoile in Paris.

"Nobody feels sorry for Madame Wells," he had said as Patricia sighed and rolled her eyes when yet another unordered dish was set in front of her. "It's *Monsieur* Wells no one should feel sorry for," I replied. "I only have to savor it, and she has to write about it."

Patricia's writing is obviously solitary, so the part of her job as critic that I was closest to was *à table*. For a quarter-century, at tiny French bistros, at trattorias in Italy, at wondrous sushi bars in Tokyo, and at one endless banquet in Chengdu, where they served all the sea slugs from all seven seas (or so it seemed), I have been the man on the other side of the table who doesn't always know exactly what we are eating and certainly can't tell you exactly how it was made.

Though no longer a critic for hire, Patricia approaches every new restaurant with unfailing optimism that the meal will be great. "Uh-oh" is how I prepare myself. "Even if it's not just fuel, it's only food," I say. "How good can it be?" Yes, sometimes it's exquisite, but often it isn't. Francophile that I am, I love to correct people who say, "You just can't get a bad meal in France." But oh yes you can. You can get a bad meal absolutely anywhere in the world.

And at one of those bad meals, when Patricia drops her fork on the plate in exasperation, her disappointment having grown with each bite, what builds in me is the regret that we're not in our own kitchen sharing a large salad of fresh, and freshly washed, spinach. Nobody feels sorry for Madame Wells, but it took a lot of ordinary or even disappointing meals to come up with restaurants that merited her endorsement.

At the *Trib*, Patricia's luxury was to be able to send readers to restaurants, not tell them what to stay away from. But her occasional slams—delivered with relish when she felt that a restaurant had had elaborate undeserved praise—were the ones that chefs remembered.

When Patricia wrote for *L'Express* (and she is still as far as I know the only foreigner and only woman ever to review restaurants for a national French publication), we spent two years flying to some provincial capital for Saturday lunch, then driving a couple of hours for dinner in another town. The next day there was another meal somewhere else, then we flew back to Paris on Sunday evening. Sounds like fun, doesn't it? And indeed it was, for the first six months.

Enthusiastic and conscientious as ever, Patricia tried to get to all sides of the country that calls itself the Hexagon. Her reviews were often critical, and chefs were often outraged. One famous up-market chain of hotels and restaurants threatened to pull its ads from *L'Express* after a coincidental series of negative critiques of restaurants in the group.

As she did for the *IHT*, Patricia took an American journalist's approach and wrote like an outsider about how the chef cooked and how the restaurant served. For *L'Express*, it was a novel and refreshing approach, one that other critics at other magazines subsequently adopted. She had great support from her editors and readers there, but the deviation from the norm wounded feelings and sometimes provoked vituperative reaction from the restaurant fraternity. After a severe review of one well-known Paris chef, whose pricey restaurant was the "must" of the moment, he went on television and attacked her. "What can she know?" he asked as he prepared his own answer: "She was raised on hamburgers and Coca-Cola." In reality, she wasn't. Growing up in Milwaukee she savored all the ethnic cuisines that that little melting-pot city offered. And her mother kept an excellent, earthy Italian kitchen.

Being an American was an effective disguise—no chef ever seemed to catch on to it. They were offended, in fact, that she didn't announce herself and give them a chance to show her how well they could cook. Again, that's against the rules that strive for fairness for other diners, not just for the critic.

The reductio ad absurdum of the issue, in the mind of one television interviewer who maybe saw cracks in his own Villeroy & Boch rice bowl, was that a good critic was one who paid the check. It wasn't possible to lead him beyond that and to the principle of independence.

Over the years, most of the time her dining companion was been someone other than me. Close friends went with her, and so did two different assistants on the *Food Lover's Guide*s who later launched their own careers in food journalism. But some trips have been unforgettable, including a series of weekend visits to Italy that pushed me to records on the scale. We would fly to one of the major cities for a three- or four-day weekend and eat two big meals every day we were there. There were platters of antipasti, two or three pastas, primi, secondi, and extra servings before we got to those rich gooey Italian desserts. A friend asks how I survived, but by the looks of me I thrived.

But much beyond frequent overeating, the stupidest thing I ever did in my life was drive like a fool to get back to Paris in a snowstorm on a Sunday afternoon during the first Gulf war. Her gig at *L'Express* seemed to require that through rain and fog and slipperiest snow Patricia had to get her review though in fairness it wasn't snowing when we headed out that morning for a restaurant in the Sologne, some hundred kilometers south of Paris in a region known for its game.

We arrived at noon, hoping to be through with the meal and back on the road by two-thirty or three, and if I drove as fast as I liked to drive, that would get me back to the office by the four-thirty news meeting. But the ritual of Sunday lunch in the French countryside cannot be hurried. Families gather for celebratory meals, and the pace of the service is as relaxed as the conversation. High chairs and wheelchairs intermingle as three or four generations take pleasure in each other's company, or seem to. It's a wonderful thing to observe.

But that's not why we were there. The pace of a before-theater dinner is what I had hoped for. Telling the waiter that we were really pressed was not convincing—why would we have driven out from Paris on a cold and dreary Sunday if we were pressed for time? With effort, we convinced the waiter to eliminate courses and skip dessert. And as the snowfall began looking significant, I even pushed my wineglass aside. But we couldn't wrap it up and get out of there before three-thirty.

Snow was falling, and the *autoroute* hadn't been plowed or salted. It was one of the times when I chanted under my breath: "I can do this I can do this I can do this." And I did. In reality, the car never weaved or wobbled. There was no close call, and I was not the only driver in the left lane pushing above the foul-weather limit of 110 kph. We arrived back in Paris in time for me to put together another war front page. But the safe arrival was not what I thought we deserved. To this day I do not know what I could have been thinking, or why I thought I couldn't take the day off. Or why that restaurant was so important on that weekend.

No other restaurant would ever be again, not if I was driving.

Over time, the meals together became really important to our relationship, to who we were and how we knew each other. We met most evenings around nine in the restaurant she had chosen to review. And with food as the only distraction, we talked comfortably of our day but more importantly of what we were thinking about. Often it was the book she was working on or construction projects, current or future, at Chanteduc. But it was also us as a couple and the constant negotiation that marriage requires. I think that the conviviality of dining helped us step over a lot of potential problems.

I valued that, but I regret that I grew jaded about all but a few favorites and some of the great tables, like Taillevent and Joël Robuchon. At heart I am what the French call a *pantouflard*, a stay-at-home. (*Pantoufles* are bedroom slippers.)

At Robuchon's table, at Taillevent, in the gastronomic company of other great chefs like Pierre Gagnaire and Guy Savoy, there have been epiphanies and raptures. But the meal I have most enjoyed remembering was at another of those great restaurants—Paul Bocuse's digs. Patricia and an assistant had been traveling in the Lyon region working on the *Food Lover's Guide to France*, and I joined them for a weekend in the French city that is best known for its hearty food. They had interviewed Bocuse, one of the seminal influences in contemporary French dining, before I got there, and I joined them for dinner. Patricia had said she was tired, but at one point in the meal I looked over and saw more than fatigue. She had literally turned black. Some malaise had settled in and she was close to swooning. Bocuse kept coming to the table to see how we were doing and even sat with us from time to time. We developed a routine—as soon as he walked away, Patricia got up and went to the ladies' room and I swapped her plate and mine and ate for us both. When she returned to the table, so did Bocuse, and both our plates reflected capacity for his famously butter-rich dishes. In time her color returned and we went back to our hotel. Rich food, rich memories. And I enjoyed the evening not because Patricia was visibly ill, but because I got in two Bocuse meals at a single seating.

Besides trying to get phrases into Patricia's reviews, I was also the guy who carried the plastic, which meant I was the one who had to get the check. Interestingly, though chefs may have hired PR agents to lure Patricia to their restaurants, she was rarely recognized once she went. We used a different name to make reservations, and unless you announce yourself beforehand as Very Important, it's likely that you won't be recognized as anything other than an American who happens to speak French. If you do announce yourself, the understanding is that you expect your meal to be free. And that's not how she worked.

But if she was recognized, then getting the check required a lot of effort. The conversation would go something like this:

"You are our guests, Mr. Wells."

"Thank you for your hospitality, but we must pay. It's the rule."

"No, the chef insists. And he's my boss."

"Please thank the boss. He is very generous. But there has to be a bill. If there's no bill Madame Wells will be fired."

"That's all right. She works too much."

"No, it's not all right. She has to work, so someday I won't have to. We'll sit right here until there's a check."

"That's fine—okay. You look comfortable, and wouldn't you like a Cognac? Compliments of the chef?"

Finally, after feints and shuffles, the check would usually come. But sometimes it was the chef who won in the mano-a-mano, and the only solutions we found was to leave a large cash tip or send flowers to the chef's wife the next day.

Joël Robuchon argued that theater critics don't pay to see the shows they review. "Oh yes they do in the United States," I responded. "And book critics?" he asked. And there he had me, since I had known of a few who not only didn't buy the books but sold their free review copies. Nonetheless we settled the bill if not the argument.

PATRICIA:

For more than a good quarter of a century, Walter has been a willing and supportive table mate. I knew that there were many days—after long and intense days at the office—when he would rather look forward to sitting on a stool in our kitchen having the simplest of fare, surrounded by the fragrance of a roasted organic chicken, accompanied by green beans, mushroom salad, and a bottle of our house Clos Chanteduc. But he rarely, if ever, complained about our dining out four or five nights a week, and since he has a very discerning palate he was the ideal companion.

The only question he ever asked me was, "What kind of restaurant are we going to, tonight?" this as he carefully laid out his costume for the day. Walter pays attention to his clothes, always has, and he needed to know if the restaurant allowed Friday casual or demanded what he really wanted to wear: a Hong Kong tailored suit, a custom-made monogrammed shirt, and perhaps a red Charvet tie, the gift I most love to offer.

Most often, by that time in the morning, I hadn't yet figured out where we would dine. It was too early to know what I would be in the mood for that night. One luxury I had was deciding on my own where to go, whether it be a new spot from my huge To Try list, or a return visit to favorite bistro or grand table. I always selected with care—often making a detour to pass the restaurant before I reserved, to see if it looked okay from the outside—for I am not good about bad meals. I get cranky, even angry at myself for having chosen badly. I think that many people think that restaurant critics secretly love to hate a place. Not me. Why waste calories, time, and the chance of a great meal just to be grumpy?

I remember as though it was yesterday. We were in a taxi on our way to a first visit to Le Petit Marguery in the 13th arrondissement at the southern edge of Paris, far from our apartment and even farther from his office in Neuilly, west of the city. Walter said to me, "Is this going to be one of the places that, when we get there, we are all alone?" In my memory that never happened, but I think it was his way of saying that he'd rather be dining at home that evening. When we got to the door of the brasserie, the place was bustling, crowded, jovial, and the restaurant became a favorite for more than twenty-five years.

FETTUCCINE
with VODKA and LEMON

For weeknight dinners, our lineup sounds like airline choices: chicken or pasta? But in truth, who can resist a glorious, golden farm chicken turning on the spit in the oven, or a bowl full of lovingly dressed pasta? As often as we can, we make dinner together, Walter deftly chopping and slicing (he is much more exacting than I am) and me acting as producer. We open a bottle of wine, turn on some music by our friend and crooner Todd Murray, and count the seconds until we'll be sitting on our stools lingering over our home-cooked dinner. We always have dried pasta in the pantry, and light cream, lemons, and cheese for grating in the refrigerator, so this is a common last-minute dish.

EQUIPMENT: A large nonstick frying pan with a cover; an 8-quart pasta pot fitted with a colander; 6 warmed shallow soup bowls.

> 3 tablespoons coarse sea salt
> 1 pound fresh or dried fettuccine
> ¼ cup freshly squeezed lemon juice
> ¼ cup lemon-flavored vodka
> 1 cup light cream
> ½ cup freshly grated black pepper pecorino cheese
> About 1 cup pasta cooking water
> Grated zest of 2 lemons, preferably organic
> Freshly ground black pepper

1. In the pasta pot fitted with a colander, bring 6 quarts water to a rolling boil over high heat. Add the salt and the pasta, stirring to prevent the pasta from sticking. Cook until tender but firm to the bite, 2 to 3 minutes. Remove from the heat. Remove the colander and drain over a sink, shaking to remove excess water. Reserve some of the cooking water for the sauce.
2. In a large nonstick frying pan, warm the lemon juice, vodka, and cream. Add the drained fettuccine and toss to evenly coat. Add the pasta cooking water, tablespoon by tablespoon, until the pasta

stops absorbing the liquid. Add half of the cheese and toss once more. Taste for seasoning. Cover and let rest for 1 to 2 minutes to allow the pasta to thoroughly absorb the sauce. Toss again. Taste for seasoning.

3. Transfer to individual warmed shallow soup bowls. Season with the lemon zest and freshly ground pepper. Serve immediately, passing the remaining cheese and the pepper mill at the table.

6 servings

WINE SUGGESTION: We like the zest and minerality of a good Pinot Grigio here.

17

{ Weighty Matters }

PATRICIA:

When I was growing up in the American Midwest in the 1950s, girls did not sweat. We couldn't even dream of being jocks or playing on a team. Girls could swim, they could ice skate, and they could be cheerleaders. There were no other options.

In high school, "gym" happened about once a week and was limited to wimpy calisthenics, a trampoline, or volleyball, all supervised by ill-tempered, unattractive, overweight women. So much for role models.

But in 1968 I bought a pair of high-top boy's basketball shoes (no Reeboks, no Nikes back then, especially not for girls) and began to jog. Over the years I ran a few 10k races (they wrongly called them mini-marathons back then), working my way up to an easy, hour-long run several times a week. Most of the time, I loved every minute of it, even looking forward to the quiet time with myself, my thoughts, my goals. I always looked upon the runs as a time to solve problems. And if there was nothing special bothering me that morning, I would offer to solve some of Walter's worries!

Patricia in August 2000, still harboring hopes for a marathon.

But as happens with age, what worked for me in my twenties, thir-ties, and forties did not work in my fifties. It was as if the hour-long runs counted not at all. I tried running longer and more often, but the numbers on the scale went up and my spirits went down.

By the time I was fifty-three, I had almost reached the point where a decision had to be made about continuing my career as a food writer.

I fretted about my weight a lot—the scales read 180 pounds by the end of 1999—and although I was running greater distances, and more often, I was getting nowhere. I began to believe that my size-sixteen frame was simply inevitable, part and parcel of my age and my work as a cookbook author, cooking teacher, and restaurant critic.

Then a friend talked me into a week at the legendary Golden Door north of San Diego, California, known for transforming bodies of the stars and putting the words "spa cuisine" into our mouths.

For most of my life the very idea of a spa (remember when we called them fat farms and weight-loss clinics?) appealed to me about as much as a quadruple root canal. At that point in my life, I was not into fluff and pampering, wasn't interested in looking at two naked carrots on my plate for lunch, surrounded by snotty people who all looked like Cindy Crawford in spandex. I had never been into massages, body wraps, facials, or, God forbid, aerobics classes.

But there was one detail that did appeal: For seven full days no famous chef would present me with a well-meaning glass of Champagne, an "extra" tasting of foie gras, a third or fourth chocolate dessert, another pour of bubbly, a final sip of eau de vie.

Those naked carrots were beginning to look good.

As it turns out, there were no Cindy Crawfords, just forty incredible females, ranging in age from twenty-three to eighty, lawyers and corporate presidents, mothers and daughters, a woman chef, a New York agent, a mom whose kids asked if she was going to have all her fat taken out of her, and, yes, a dentist who specialized in root canals.

The reality of it all is that in a given day at the Japanese garden–filled spa, I spent a good six hours exercising, beginning with strenuous sunrise mountain hikes, followed by private tennis, swimming, and jogging lessons, multiple meetings with Mike Bee, my personal trainer and new best friend, grueling workouts on every kind of machine designed to strengthen every body part, stretch classes and back-care and posture classes, strength training and aqua dumbbells, body sculpting and slide-and-tone. After that, the gal who used to turn her nose up at massages now craved her daily hour-long rub, those soothing facials, hair treatments, manicures, pedicures, and the best of all, an almond oil–sea salt "glow." I felt as though I was in the fitness supermarket and I, the novice, was filling up my shopping cart.

Fitted with a heartbeat monitor to see just how hard I was working and how hard I had to work to be truly fit, I quickly learned what most other women also discover. We women think we work harder than we really do. So all those hour-long runs counted for little: They were not intense enough, long enough, or frequent enough to offset those extra portions of foie gras, chocolate cake, and Champagne.

At the spa, I also learned a good deal about portion control and found that I could be totally satisfied on a lot less food than I was used to.

So Mike took me aside and set up a personal program, with realistic goals and endless encouragement for getting and staying as fit and healthy as possible. On my return to Paris, a treadmill was in order (to fill in on all those endlessly dark and frequent rainy days when jogging outdoors is simply not a reality) as well as a gym membership for twice-weekly stretch sessions to balance the cardio training on the track and the machine.

Back at the Door, when our bodies weren't in constant motion, we were eating.

At snack, lunch, and dinner time, sheeplike behavior took over, and we lunged for the gloriously arranged bowls of fresh fruits and vegetables set before us. (When you check into the Golden Door you meet with a fitness instructor and together determine how intensely you want to work out and how much or little you want to eat. I voted for a lot of workout and a little bit of food.)

Even with the lightest food allotment, I felt I was eating all day long. Upon return from our hikes, breakfast appeared on a lovely tray delivered to our spacious private rooms. Overlooking a bubbling Japanese fountain and with the *New York Times* in hand, I feasted (on various days) on a single poached egg with a thin slice of whole-wheat toast, mixed fruit with low-fat cottage cheese sprinkled with almond granola and raisins, a bagel topped with sprouts and pineapple ricotta cheese. And there was fruit, fruit, fruit. I think in one week I ate more raw fruit than I had in the previous year, and rediscovered the perfect fast food, the banana.

Each day we were allowed to choose from two or three entrées for lunch and dinner, and were truly amazed by Belgian chef Michel Stroot's ability to transform all those good and healthy and wholesome ingredients into dishes that were beautiful, delicious, and most of all, satisfying. From the Golden Door's organic vegetable garden and surrounding groves of kiwis, avocados, oranges, and lemons, we were served up food that was pure, unfussy, and nourishing to body and soul. At appetizer time, we had chef Stroot's ingenious baked pita chips dipped into a spicy, lightened hummus spread. Marvelous frittatas were filled with an appealing mixture of spinach and artichokes, potatoes and basil, tomatoes and feta cheese. Chicken breasts were baked and topped with a tangy mustard sauce, paired with garden-fresh green beans and garlic mashed potatoes. Even welcome slices of duck breast arrived in a fine raspberry sauce.

I lost six and a half pounds during that first week of my new life and began to feel crisp and upright, younger, more flexible. I returned to Paris determined to maintain the established habits, determined to make them true lifelong habits.

I once thought attaining complete fitness and maintaining my job were mutually exclusive. Now I knew that they were not. I learned to always leave a little bit of food on my plate, whether at home or in restaurants, simply to cut back on portion sizes. Although I never counted calories, I was more aware of the protein/fat/carbohydrate balance in my daily diet.

Within two months I was feeling thirty-five, not fifty-three, and had lost a total of eighteen pounds. Within seven and a half months I had lost thirty-six pounds. My body was firmer and more taut than it had been in my thirties. I, the woman of boundless energy, now had even more to spare.

Most of this was achieved with nothing more complicated than thirty-minute daily sessions of very doable cardiovascular training, either jogging or on the treadmill. About four months into my program, I added strength training, to build upper-body muscle that helped me be a better and stronger runner (and also build stronger bones to guard against osteoporosis).

I don't think any one thing made the difference, but the entire package—the combination of daily aerobic exercise, regular weight training, and greater attention to portion size and nutritional balance—became my recipe for a lifetime of fitness.

Throughout, I kept up an almost daily e-mail correspondence with Mike, my personal trainer, who continued to offer cheerleader-like support, encouragement, and warnings as I sprinted from goal to goal.

The weight was lost without pills or diet aids, only simple common sense and healthy eating.

I sat down and examined my eating patterns more closely and worked out a very livable routine: Where I had total control, I took total control! I came to the realization that it was not my job, but my non-job (my at-home eating) that was getting me into trouble.

It was those seemingly day-to-day habits that needed to change. A single nibbling of cheese that turned into three or four nibbles around five in the afternoon. That extra glass of wine at the end of the day. So I changed the way I ate at home, when I was not recipe testing. During the day, I cut as much fat from my diet as possible, so I that I could do my job and thoroughly enjoy my restaurant meals at night. My at-home diet is to this day made up of low-fat yogurts and cheeses, lots of raw vegetables, healthy vegetable soups and broths, whole-grain crackers, and lean protein such as chicken or tuna. I also paid close attention to how much water I drank, making sure I downed at least ten glasses a day. (Remember, water is a nutrient!)

In restaurants, I ate normally (though what is normal to me may seem excessive or even decadent to others), always ordering the foods I crave most. Fortunately, the foods I crave most are also the foods that are best for me. I drank wine in moderation. But most important of all, I gave up nothing I really love and never intend to.

My palate rewarded me right away: Flavors were more intense, I enjoyed food more than ever, and trained myself to be satisfied with

Patricia with her trainer Mike Bee in May 2001 at our first Fitness Week.

less. Since then, I never count calories, but I do count the number of minutes I exercise each day.

I am a salt person, not a sugar person, but strangely enough my desire for sugar went from minimal to nonexistent. As I built muscle from longer and more frequent runs and from weight training, my desire (and actual need) for protein increased. Fortunately, I have always been a lean protein gal, loving all manner of fish, and I devour the immense array of delicious, low-fat dairy products that France has to offer.

Somewhere along the line I realized that what personal trainer Mike and I were talking about could be of interest to many others. So in 2001 we added a Fitness Week to our roster of cooking classes in Provence, with five-mile hike and vigorous pool classes added to the regular schedule of cooking and touring.

Today, I still weigh thirty pounds less than I did in January of 2000. I no longer shop for clothes that will fit me when I am ten pounds lighter, thus everything in my closet fits, summer and winter, and has since the fall of 2000. My weight fluctuates from five to eight pounds each year, and I weigh myself each and every morning. (Usually three times, allowing myself the bonus of writing down the lowest of the three!)

So the future lies ahead and I am not afraid that my weight will ever again surge out of control. I still splurge at times, but much of the time I do not. That has made all the difference. I have found the key to what works for me, and my job is no longer in jeopardy.

WALTER:

One by one, the pounds packed on. Each year when the *Trib's* official doctor gave me the cursory physical that French labor law requires she scolded me for the kilo I had gained in the last twelve months. "It's beginning to add up," she would say in the early years. And then she started saying that my weight was a matter of concern.

The French are not all thin, but as a culture they are the thinnest in well-fed Western Europe. There are many explanations, many of them paradoxical, but my own is simply mirrors. There are big mirrors everywhere, in hallways and entrances, in elevators and in dressing rooms, and the French are not shy about looking at themselves.

Even with mirrors my challenge was obvious. To borrow words that John McPhee once used in writing in the *New Yorker* about a couple of chefs, I was never falling-down fat, but there was plenty of evidence of having eaten too well and too often. As I liked to say, my corpulence was built by the greatest chefs in the world and I wanted to treat it with respect.

But when a journalist writing about Patricia described me as "a teddy bear of a man," I vowed to take off the thirty-five excess pounds. They didn't come off easily, but they did come off, and for a long time in the early 1990s I was so thin that I took to thinking I had made the ultimate transition to life in France.

FISH CHEEKS with POLENTA and PARMESAN CRUST

Once I had lost weight, I concentrated on creating a healthy series of low-fat, high-protein recipes. This is one of them. One Saturday morning our fishmonger in Vaison, Eliane Béranger, went back to her cooler, handed me a little bag of goodies, and said, "Try these." She said they were rare skate cheeks, a delicacy sent by her fish supplier in Brittany. At first I turned up my nose. What could they taste like? I took them home, cooked them according to her suggestion, and became an instant convert. Fish cheeks are extremely tender, tasty morsels. They are light and have a fine, firm texture. In fact, many people consider the cheeks the best part of the fish because of their concentrated sweetness. The flavor is delicate, and so a minimum of embellishment is called for here. If fish cheeks are not available the same method can be used with fish fillets cut into three-inch squares or with fresh scallops.

EQUIPMENT: 4 warmed dinner plates.

> 2 egg whites
> ¼ cup instant polenta
> ¼ cup freshly grated Parmigiano-Reggiano cheese
> ¼ teaspoon ground Espelette pepper
> 8 fish cheeks (halibut, monkfish, or skate)
>   about 1 pound total
> 2 tablespoons extra-virgin olive oil
> Fleur de sel
> Fresh lemon wedges for garnish

1. Place the egg whites in a shallow bowl. Combine the polenta and cheese in another shallow bowl. Season the polenta mixture with the pepper.
2. Dredge the fish in the egg whites. Dredge them in the polenta mixture. Place on a large plate.
3. In a large shallow frying pan, heat the oil over moderate heat. When hot but not smoking, add the coated fish cheeks, cooking

them until golden and cooked through, about 2 minutes per side. Season with fleur de sel. Serve immediately, with fresh lemon wedges for garnish.

4 servings

NOTE: Alaskan halibut cheeks can be ordered online from Great Alaska Seafood, www.great-alaska-seafood.com or by phone, 866-262-8846. They arrive frozen in one-pound vacuum-sealed packages.

PART III

―――――

Our Private Universe

A Farmhouse in Provence
Rolando's Eggplant

Making a House a Home

Chantier-Duc
Colette's Vinaigrette

Grow, Garden, Grow
Just Tomatoes!
Fig Chutney
Eggplant in Spicy Tomato Sauce

All About Yves
Scrambled Eggs with Truffles

Vineyard Tales
Grape Harvest Cake

Our 1984 Christmas card, taken on our first Thanksgiving at Chanteduc.

18

{ A Farmhouse in Provence }

WALTER:

There was a point in our negotiations to buy a farmhouse in Provence when I said to the owner: "How do you keep your skin so smooth and so beautiful?" And at that moment Patricia looked stricken. She said later that she had almost gagged. I didn't think my comment would make her choke, though I'm not proud to recount it, but a lot was at stake. Lust, even for a house, can drive men to say outrageous things.

The seller, Régine Boissarie, sixty-five years old and twice widowed, called Chanteduc her "*haut lieu privilégié,*" but "private universe" was the description we came to favor. Patricia loves to tell visitors that the name is not something we made up, but an ancient *lieu dit,* a place name that means "song of the owl."

The house is a *mas,* a farmhouse that is modest in its size but whose hillside site is grander than a château's. Surrounded by vineyards and woodland, Chanteduc is only a few minute's drive from the center of town but it's hidden, like an enchanted clearing in the forest. (A friend calls it "En-Chanteduc.") Trails follow two of the property lines, and in mild weather we can hear the hikers making their way along or trail bikers squeezing hard on their brakes as they coast down the steep hillside. But when you're at Chanteduc, you have the impression that you are alone in the world, and securely on top of it. More than one friend has remarked on how the earth seems to give off a profound sense of security and well-being in that spot.

We bought the property in 1984 from Madame Boissarie, a native of the Dordogne who had married the son of Vaison's most important industrialist. As a young student Régine had mastered English well enough to do business with Americans who wanted to rent the house. "Provençal farmhouse furnished in antiques with swimming pool" was how she described it in tiny ads in the *Saturday Review* in the 1970s, and though brief, the description was very appealing. Régine worked at making her aristocratic pedigree appealing, too. Many of her American renters knew her as "a baroness, or something." We called her *La Comtesse*, and it was not necessarily out of fondness.

Because Régine had rented the house to vacationing Americans for many years in the 1970s, there were many *amis de Chanteduc*, two of whom were our friends too, Rita and Yale Kramer. The Kramers were neighbors in the same building in New York, half a generation older and light-years wiser. In time they became our closest friends. But it was before we knew them and before we moved to France in 1980 that they first responded to that ad and rented Chanteduc. In 1981 they got in touch with Madame Boissarie again and invited us to spend two weeks with them. We had traveled very little in France at that time. My new job kept me at the office, and Patricia's freelance assignments then were less likely to take her to Provence than to Germany to a sausage makers' school, or to Belgium to interview an endive farmer. We had had a tiny glimpse of the region the summer before on a weekend visit with other old New York friends, Lydie and Wayne Marshall, in a remote village in the Drôme, and we were not the first humans to be preternaturally drawn to the sunshine and the dramatic landscapes—hillsides dotted with vineyards, olive groves, sunflowers, and smears of lavender even more brilliant than Cézanne has rendered them.

But Chanteduc was different. The views were expansive, but it was the house and the site itself that captivated us. Viewed from the top of the stony vineyard that rises in four terraces above, the house appears dwarfed by parasol pines. There's a softness about it, almost a cuddliness as it hugs the earth like something growing there, marked by an uncomplicated coherence and aesthetic. When you drive up, you first confront the austere back of the house. Seriously unprepossessing, with mismatched and odd-shaped windows, the façade projects a sense of "so what's the big deal?" But when you walk from the parking lot to the other side the impact is wondrous. As more than one French visitor has said, "*Ah, mais vous êtes bien ici*"—sort of "Nice place you got here." First, there is a terrace on a lower level, with a shady pergola and a big stone table. Next, the eye falls on an even more impressive live oak tree whose age has been estimated at three centuries. The oak is believed to give off extraordinary strength. (Régine's electrician, who later became our electrician, recounted how Régine's husband, as his health declined, used to stand for what seemed like hours hugging the immense trunk, hoping to draw life from it.) Near the gate that opens onto to the courtyard, a single cypress tree exclaims over the scene.

A fantasy? Well, isn't life?

The *mas* had been built over several centuries, room by room, as different generations had a new baby or a good crop from the olive trees that provided the only regular cash revenue at an earlier time (before hard freezes in two consecutive years in the 1950s ended olive production for a generation). We loved the way the house spilled up and down with entrances on different levels. The gate opened onto a central courtyard, with different-sized windows all around, sort of like an Advent calendar. Though small, the house allows a surprising sense of privacy inside as well as out because it lets everyone who wants to claim a spot as his or hers alone. We loved the view over Chanteduc's

Spring 1985.

stubby Grenache vines and on to Mont Ventoux and the other *pré-Alpes* in the distance. And we loved the trees.

We also liked the village. The centuries-old Roman ruins attract enough tourists to keep the town animated, but the farmers and wine growers give Vaison its gritty year-round authenticity.

In her first marriage, as Régine Fabre, Madame Boissarie had bought Chanteduc from the Reynaud family who had lived there for generations. It was, she said, "a pile of rocks," with pigs and chickens in the courtyard and no indoor plumbing.

We supposed that Chanteduc had been for Régine what Le

Hameau was for Marie Antoinette, both a project and a playhouse to be in charge of. As the daughter-in-law, living with *maman* in the big Fabre house in the village, it was said that Régine had a conflictual life because her mother-in-law still controlled everything. And that did not sit well with Régine, who, we came to find out, knew something about control.

Whatever role Chanteduc played for Régine, her restoration was respectful and therefore inspired. She started, of course, by installing a bathroom. After buying Chanteduc, for several years every time that I encountered Monsieur Jullien, who owned the old-fashioned hardware store on the Place Montfort in the center of Vaison, he told me the story of Régine's bathtub. The story went like this—and as I type his rich, gravelly baritone and Provençal twang resonate in my mind:

"Madame Fabre was a very grand lady. She had traveled all over the world and entertained ambassadors and senators in Paris and at her mother-in-law's big house in town. It wasn't thinkable that she not have a bathroom with a proper tub. There were two wells on the property, and when he sold her the place Monsieur Reynaud had told her there was plenty of water. She thought that meant there was enough water for her baths. So she had the bathtub carried up the steep, winding half-mile track on someone's back.

"But the first time she tried to take a bath, she got *pfft*—a few centimeters of water in the tub, then nothing else."

His eyes would always shut at this point and he would say "*pfft*" again, hold up his fingers inches apart and chuckle before going on.

"For Monsieur Reynaud, his two little wells were plenty. But Monsieur Reynaud, he only needed a little water for his goats. Sometimes he took a bath on Saturday night. And he never, ever put water in his wine."

Always in the telling, Mr. Jullien would then squeeze his eyes into tight crinkles, knock his knuckles together twice, and laugh with unburdened delight.

Our negotiations to buy Chanteduc lasted for two years, and the price was never the issue—it was more basic than money. Régine was going to sell, Régine wasn't going to sell. Régine was going to give Chanteduc to her sons. Her sons didn't deserve it. She had another buyer willing to pay more. She had decided to live there permanently.

In the meantime, we dangled on the hook. We visited Vaison and the region on our own, staying in hotels in town or nearby. We stayed at Chanteduc as "paying guests," sometimes when she was in residence and sometimes not. As her "guests" we had to provide our own food, of course, as well as bring our towels and toilet paper, too. We also had to take the sheets to the laundry and leave behind a sixty-two-centime rental fee per sheet. When she was there, she expected us to take her to dinner. Once when I suggested we just go to the pizzeria, she said she would like a real meal, so off we went, as usual, to the closest Michelin-starred restaurant. And once Patricia had dinner ready when Régine drove up in her little blue Renault 4L. When we owned the place and were sorting through the boxes of papers she had left behind, we found a note saying the dinner was "*gentil*" but the gratin dish had new stains on it. Apparently she had thought better of sending it.

What we were trying to do on those trips was due diligence. We scarcely knew Vaison, and we knew no other house prices except Chanteduc's. So we began making appointments with real estate brokers to discuss what we were looking for—that is, to describe Chanteduc: an old *mas*, well restored, with some land and even a little vineyard, near the center of the town but set apart, with a lot of privacy. The agents would invariably react as if to a loony. "What you describe simply doesn't exist anymore. You should have come twenty-five years ago."

There was one agent in Vaison who said: "There is a house exactly like that, but the owner will never, ever sell." We felt reassured by the reactions, though troubled by that degree of absolute certainty about the chances of a sale.

We spent a lot of time with *La Comtesse* in our two-year courtship, enough time to grow weary with the repetitious *vieille France* stories that had charmed us in the beginning. We had also lost patience with her on-again, off-again salesmanship. Finally, when she announced to us once more that the property was off the market, I wrote her a letter saying it was just as well because I had found other less emotion-laden investments. Practically overnight she called to say she would sell after all and would accept my offer. We went to dinner in Paris, and I made a great show of shaking her hand over the deal and saying repeatedly that I always kept my word. She was as coquettish as ever, but we exchanged the names of notaries and set an approximate timetable for the sale.

But her capriciousness was not finished. The night before the signing, Régine called very late to accuse me of something—I don't remember the conversation, except that she was very emotional and said the deal was off. We went to bed depleted, and resigned. But early the next morning, she called and, as though the previous conversation had never happened, she said, "Come pick me up, and we'll go to the notary's."

It had been a long negotiation, and we felt buffeted by Régine's whims. The signing was tense, too. It was a long, formulaic ceremony in which the many pages of the sales agreement, the *acte de vente*, were

In 1985 with our best friends Yale and Rita Kramer, who "found" Chanteduc for us.

read aloud. I focused on watching *La Comtesse* and hiding my nervous tics. We had heard that at a previous signing ceremony Régine announced halfway through that she had changed her mind and would not sell after all. With white knuckles on the big Louis XII chairs arranged around the notary's conference table, we feared a final *coup de folie*, but it never came. She interrupted the notary's drone several times but for nothing that affected the deal. (I remember that she wanted him to correct the order of her given names—like many old aristocrats, she had four or five.) After the papers were all signed, each change and each page initialed by all of us, with a *"lu et approuvé"* and a *"bon pour accord"* handwritten by each of us at the end, we left the notary's office and set off to our bank.

The notary already had the money from our bank, but there was another matter to be resolved. Throughout the two-year ordeal, as Régine played us on her line, I had naïvely held firm about two things: We had agreed on a price at the outset—her asking price—and I insisted that we honor that. And I was not going to pay anything under the table for the property. The practice is common in French property transfers, but it is illegal and it is not in the buyer's interest to have a falsely low acquisition value on a property he'll probably sell someday.

But we did agree to pay for the contents of the house in cash. We had gone to meet Régine at Chanteduc, to talk about buying several of her antique armoires and commodes. She welcomed us into the room she called the *salle blanche*, sat on the sofa. and motioned for me to sit in a chair arranged diagonally from her. I did, but first I nudged the chair closer. It's a bad habit I can't shake, a bit of nervousness, to move the furniture before sitting down.

"Why are you moving the chair?" she asked. "To be closer to you, my dear," I replied. Like wonderment at her skin—which was exceptionally unlined—the comment was shameless. But I had long ago realized that her weakness was for attention to her beauty. If ever there were a time to exploit it, this was it.

But my ploy was nothing compared with her own. She had invited the antiques dealer from the next village to join in the price discussion. "To be sure the prices are fair," she said. "To be sure," I thought.

But instead of several pieces of furniture, we wound up with all the contents. In the end, the price wasn't all that high, and in fact, over the years, we more than recovered the money by selling pieces ourselves.

On the day we closed I withdrew the cash for the furniture from my account and a friendly banker left us alone in a private room to count out the money. Then we drove *La Comtesse* to her bank. She gave each of us a kiss on both cheeks, then went inside presumably to put the cash in her safety deposit box.

Walter is always waving his magic wand around Chanteduc. Here he poses with a broken lawn chair and a metal carcass: He will make them new again!

Thanksgiving 1985 in the snow: Catherine O'Neill, Fiona Reeves,
Richard Reeves, Patricia, Amanda Urban, Kate Auletta, Ken Auletta.

And it was over. We never saw Régine again. She called and wrote from time to time with suggestions that she was available for a visit, but we always dodged. The relationship had been spent by her capriciousness, and we did not want her ghost to return.

ROLANDO'S EGGPLANT

One evening in late June, my friend Rolando Beramendi—expert in all things Italian—created this stacked eggplant dish from our garden. This recipe is simply a blueprint: Use the eggplant as a starting point, but stack all manner of vegetables, cheese, and herbs and most of all, enjoy!

EQUIPMENT: A nonstick baking sheet.

> 2 small, firm fresh eggplant, washed but not peeled (each about 8 ounces)
> Extra-virgin olive oil
> Coarse sea salt to taste
> 2 to 3 large ripe tomatoes, cut into thick crosswise slices for 24 slices
> About 4 ounces soft goat cheese
> Several tablespoons tapenade
> 32 large fresh basil leaves
> Fleur de sel

1. Preheat the oven to 475°F.
2. Trim and discard the ends of the eggplant. Cut the eggplant crosswise into slices about ¼ inch thick. You should have 16 slices. Place them side by side on a nonstick baking sheet. Brush lightly with oil and season lightly with salt. Place on a rack in the center of the oven and roast for about 5 minutes. Turn and season the other side with oil and salt. Small eggplant should cook in 10 minutes. Larger eggplant will take a little longer.
3. Remove the eggplant from the oven. Arrange a slice of eggplant on each of 8 salad plates. Place a slice of tomato on top of the eggplant. Top with cheese. Brush the cheese with tapenade. Place two basil leaves on top of the tapenade. Repeat for another layer. Top the final tower with a slice of tomato and two more basil leaves. Drizzle with olive oil and season with fleur de sel.

8 servings

19

{ Making a House
a Home }

PATRICIA:

It is very difficult for one woman to replace another in a house, especially when that house is imbued with centuries of history, and every inch of space is flooded with someone else's spirit and taste. Régine was a hard act to follow. She was an elegant, educated woman whose slimness and jet-black pageboy haircut made her appear years younger than her age. She was proud, and just a bit officious. And I really didn't agree with most aspects of her taste.

Those first two weeks we spent as guests at Chanteduc made up our first true experience with Provence. But even back then I knew, somehow, that much of what I saw there was out of whack, not native, more a holdover from someone who had not completely bonded with Provence, its soil, its people.

The color of the shutters—a drab dark brown—seemed out of kilter with the light, playful Provençal spirit. And the furniture—lots of Louis this and Louis that—made me think that she really wanted a château and this modest farmhouse was somehow all her budget would allow.

It was months, maybe years, before I felt I had exorcised Régine from the house. And for years I had a recurring dream. That she came back and said it was all a mistake. She was taking the house back again.

A house transform one's life? I wouldn't have believed it, but almost from the day we first saw Chanteduc our life was altered forever. Ever since it became ours, Walter and I have looked differently at the world. And certainly at one another.

Christmas 1985 with our new bread oven.

I distinctly remember a scene very early on. We were alone (a rare occasion) and I had just come up from the garden, picking baskets full of cherries ready for the copper jam pot. Walter was on his tractor, looking like the happiest man in the world. I thought then, here we are, two American adults who feel we are fiercely independent, don't let ourselves get stuck in role playing. Well, we could have been a classic couple from centuries ago, the male playing his role, the woman hers. And to tell the truth, we both love it!

I may have been a woman's libber of the 1960s and always insisted on paying my part at a restaurant meal, but even to this day I call Walter when I can't open a jar or figure out how to tear into those crazy plastic packages. (I call myself packaging-impaired.) I love it when Walter waves his extraordinary magic handyman wand: Seemingly out of nowhere, little wooden drawer separators appear just as I am organizing a spice drawer, or he surprises me with a handmade wooden paddle just as I am ready to nudge a fresh pizza into the oven.

Chanteduc was a certainly a major factor in turning what was to have been a Paris interlude into a permanent sojourn in France. And what was to have been a weekend refuge from the city became a home, a lifestyle, an obsession, an extension of our very personalities.

Almost before we unpacked our bags in Provence, we had more French friends than we had made in all our time in Paris. Within a year, we could no longer even remember life before Provence. For us, it symbolized all the essential elements of the happiness we sought in life: friends, family, food, and feasts. The experience opened our eyes, our ears, our sensibilities to the rituals of French daily life in the countryside. Before, we had only read about this life, and finally we were witnesses, participants; we were making it happen. Was it just the sun, or did this place have a magic way of magnifying ordinary pleasures?

Before long, we could not go to the village for a morsel of goat cheese or a sack of nails without the errand turning into a social event. Conversation is central to Provençal life, so there was always talk of the sun (or lack of it); talk of the raging local wind known as the mistral, talk of the tourists (or lack of them); talk of the latest scandal or outrage in faraway Paris.

From the very beginning, Walter and I did not know that Chanteduc was a place where we could be alone. Each weekend every guestroom was filled to overflowing. At table, we were always eight, or ten, and occasionally even twenty. The guest list was often unconventional, as we routinely invited the local mayor, the plumber, winemaker, our banker, and the neighborhood poacher for long festive meals beneath the giant oak tree, with lively games of *boules* along the vineyard path afterward.

We gave Chanteduc what the French would call a *relooking*: Dull, harsh brown shutters that seemed to pull one emotionally down, rather than uplift, were painted a warm celadon green, a more natural and traditional color from Provence, a color that seems to come to life beneath the crisp and eternally brilliant blue skies of Provence. We chose a tone that most closely matches the underside of an olive leaf, more luminescent and finer than the darker top leaf.

Indoors, the natural look came easy. We banished all the Louis stuff, as well as Régine's hideous collection of owls: Exposed stone walls, sturdy wooden beams, stucco walls stained the color of ochre from natural dies found in stones up on nearby Mont Ventoux, all create an even, warming backdrop to a collection of old and still useful objects. I collect little things, like tiny scissors that I use to ceremoniously cut the raffia ties that bind the dried chestnuts leaves that envelop one of my favorite cheeses, a goat-sheep's milk combination found in the nearby village of Banon. Old linens are a favorite, and sometimes I wonder just who all these people were, with the initials emblazoned on my sheets and pillowcases, napkins and tablecloths. Just who was WS, or JR, or JJ, or GG, or AS? Man or woman, young or old, rich or poor, happy or unhappy?

And as to the overall décor, color changes were in order as well. No more bright oranges, dark browns, tacky patchwork prints. We turned to natural ochres, changed smooth walls to rough, prints to solids, hard fabrics to soft.

As I look back at our years there, I realize that we did not have a master plan but we had passion and we had dreams. We nurtured those enthusiasms and visions season by season, visit after visit. As we formed the character of the house, it formed ours. Soon the house became a scrapbook of our life together, of our life in France. I have never believed that a house had a soul or could give off vibrations, but we quickly found that it was difficult to be unhappy at Chanteduc.

I have always had a love affair with bread, and after touring community ovens all over France, I was determined to someday tuck a round of sourdough into my own wood-fired oven. A chance conver-

Patricia and pizza in the oven.

sation with our young mason turned that into a reality, and soon our courtyard sported a domed, brick-lined oven with an ancient sandstone door.

Eventually, I realized that I had my own living food encyclopedia just beyond the courtyard door. When I needed to know the true life of an olive, the exact shape of a fig leaf, the manner in which apricots let you know they are ripe (they simply fall from the tree), the time it takes a cherry to go from blossom to ripe fruit (six weeks), I didn't turn to my library but observed nature to find out.

And of course over time my cooking changed. Naturally and un-self-consciously I began to develop a style of cooking that I could call my own. It's a method that clearly reflects my philosophy of cuisine: Keep it fresh, keep it simple, respect the seasons, and allow the integrity of the ingredient to shine through. Follow the elementary rule: "What grows together goes together," meaning the lamb that grazes in fields of wild herbs will naturally taste best enhanced with local rosemary, thyme, and summer savory, and served not with a Bordeaux but a spicy Côtes-du-Rhône. The rabbits from the land love wild fennel, so why not put them together? The basil plants that grow between my tomato plants are perfect partners on the plate, too, as are the artichokes and fava beans that grow next to one another in symbiotic bliss.

My cuisine is one of whole foods, meaning I prefer to roast a fish whole—head, bones, and everything but the guts—to maintain maximum flavor and moistness, to take advantage of the flavorful gelatins that are there naturally, the texture, its very freshness. Leg of lamb is simply roasted on the bone, except when I do it with a special marinade of rich olive oil and fresh herbs. Poultry is almost always cooked whole, carefully trussed, so that its character and flavor are maximized. My uncomplicated desserts—most often fruits or little cakes—follow the seasons, from the first cherries in late May to the last figs in early October, and on to the final grapes left on the vine in November.

It is a cuisine that is accessible, created for the way we live today. By natural evolution, it is mainly Provençal, with extra-virgin olive oil as the fat of choice, with menus that follow what is in the market and what is in season. Home-cured olives, homemade apéritif, multigreen salads, homemade breads filled with grains and seeds, bountiful platters of local goat, sheep, and cow's milk cheese are present at almost every meal. In time, I had a trademark, a Patricia trademark, one I carry on to this day.

When we acquired Chanteduc, my postage-stamp-sized kitchen window faced north, and as I cooked or did the dishes, I looked out over a gravel parking lot. I would stand at the stained stainless-steel kitchen sink each morning as the postman came up the hill and hand me the day's news through that pathetic slit of light onto this world of sunshine. That was the only convenient thing about that window. (Actually, in the old days, there would have been no window at all, since in Provence the north-facing wall of the farm was always windowless, as protection against the elements, most of all the chilling north wind known as the mistral.)

Many mornings I left the kitchen and walked to the adjacent room. I guess you could have called it a family room, but then it was just a spare bedroom that was totally out of place in this rambling farmhouse of small rooms, spaces that had once served to house goats or rabbits, the family mule, to dry figs or linden blossoms, or just to store stuff.

This room, the one that the previous owner called *la salle blanche*, because it was all white, had the window of my dreams. The top of my head just brushed the top of its frame, and though I had to stoop a bit, the mountain view was majestic. The window faced due west, so each evening as the sun set in a ball of reddish-orange fire, I would be drawn to that spot, watching as the day said goodbye over Mont Théos. I was determined that someday I would peel carrots at that window. This room HAD to become my kitchen!

We saved our centimes and made the conversion, installing the kitchen of our dreams, and now I sit writing at the big ochre-tiled kitchen counter, looking right out that window, examining the pine and oak forest in the distance and the pine-covered Théos beyond, a sea of green growth beneath blue skies. We arched the window a bit, so that now even I, at five feet four inches, do not have to stoop to watch nature's passing show. And instead of that old stained sink, I

Our dream kitchen, with a cooking fireplace.

have a massive white marble one, the exact width of my forty-six-inch kitchen window.

The first thing I do when I get up each morning is turn on our trusty espresso coffee machine. The second thing I do is open the window, and hook it with the brass marine latches that Walter installed to keep the windows from banging in the wind. Most mornings the sky is a riotous swirling array of pink, reflecting the sun that is coming up over our bedroom window on the opposite end of the house. Some days I spend almost the entire day in the kitchen, yet my window to my world makes me feel as though I am outdoors all day long.

For me, that window has come to symbolize all that is right about the world, about my kitchen, about our Provençal farmhouse and life in general. If I ever bought another house, the kitchen would face due west, preferably with a view of a mountain or the sea.

It's funny how one can create an element in a home without thinking of the consequences. And the consequences turn out to be better than you might have dreamed. I can make a long list of all the things that that window has added to our lives. To get to the front door of our farmhouse you must pass in front of that window, so the postman, the pool man, the gardener, the FedEx man, our friends, or strangers coming up the hill can't just sneak past. Since I spend almost every waking moment in my kitchen, either cooking, or cleaning, or writing, I have a front-row seat on the farm's activity. I am Chanteduc's gatekeeper.

Right now, the ochre-tiled windowsill is filled with plump basil plants, there not only for their fragrance and beauty and flavor, but also to keep away flies. (I can't swear that the old Provençal custom really works, but I can tell you that we rarely have flies.) I have to add here that the window, like all doors and windows in our farmhouse, is screenless except during the worst wasp attacks in late summer. Although you will occasionally see a screened window or door in Provence, they are not very common. This is much to the amazement of most of our American visitors. You can see better out of screenless windows. To go with the sunset view, we planted a small garden, a sunset terrace filled with plants that don't shed their leaves in winter, so that all year long I can look out upon a sea of green: lavender and rosemary, olives and boxwood and bay leaf. We did plant a butterfly bush, a buddleia, that we cut back in winter. From spring until late autumn its brilliant purple flowers attract white and purple and yellow butterflies that dance around over the terrace. One day the Three Tenors were singing loud and clear from the speakers in the corners of my kitchen, and I would swear that the butterflies were dancing to the music. It made me cry with happiness.

Every Tuesday for centuries there has been a market in our village. Not just any old market, but rather a full-blown village fair where merchants sell everything from fruits and vegetables to farm machinery to pantyhose and this season's fashions. The farm wife who lived here until the 1960s used to walk down the steep hill to town, taking with her homemade goat cheese and live rabbits to sell. Sometimes I stand at that window on Tuesday morning and think about all the farm wives who also may have looked at the view with anticipation of another successful Tuesday morning.

The same farm wife who carted her rabbits and goat cheese down the hill also did her laundry in a *bassin* (small pool) that once sat in the center of what is now our sunset terrace. I wonder if she ever stood and stared at Théos as I do, grateful for the kind of clean open space that seems to rinse your mind and open it to new thoughts.

There was a cat—a very fat tabby cat—that visited us for years. She usually arrived soon after we did late Friday night, and always came at dinnertime. If it was winter and the window was closed, she let me know she was there by hurling her body against the window and quietly meowing. I know that she had been coming at least since 1991 when we began building the kitchen, and she tasted just about everything I have tested since then, recipes for *Trattoria* and *Simply French*, *At Home in Provence*, as well as *The Paris Cookbook*. She devoured *panna cotta* and beef *daube*, she lapped up bits of rabbit with lemon *confit*, and she never turned her nose up at leftover bits of tarte Tatin. I am sure that she even tasted fresh black truffles and foie gras. She got fatter and fatter, and then she disappeared. Someday, if ever we live at Chanteduc full time, I hope to find her soul mate.

One Christmas it began to snow flakes the size of goose-down

Patricia and Maggie Shapiro in the snow on Christmas Day.

feathers at nine in the morning. We were a group of eight, all busy in the kitchen, roasting a stuffed turkey on the spit in the kitchen fireplace and creating numerous side dishes. We marveled at that rare Provençal snow as it began to smother Théos in white. Everyone went outside and stood in front of the window for a group photo. Once again, the window served as the prettiest frame I could have imagined. This house had become my home.

20

{ Chantier-Duc }

*Once the kitchen was finished, we threw a celebratory feast
with our plumber, mason, electrician, painter, and their families.*

WALTER:

Throughout the fits and starts of our efforts to buy Chanteduc—to enhance the fantasy as well as sign up for a new level
of debt—we reassured ourselves that the house was completely livable.
Yes, the bathrooms were inadequate, the windows didn't shut out the
wind, and those tangles of wires in the cellar meant that the electricity
needed some attention, too. But not that much had to be done—like a
great many renters over the years, we could move right in.

Then we found that it wasn't enough to hold the title. We wanted ownership, the kind that only a makeover can give. The French word for "jobsite" is *chantier*, so it was inevitable that over the years I frequently thought of our place not as "the owl's song" but as *Chantier-Duc*.

But before any other home improvements, before rewiring, before shoring up porous foundations or putting in new windows, there was the matter of the water supply. Water problems in Provence can have near-biblical dimension, like the frequent droughts and the devastating flash floods that can carry away villages and vineyards. Our own crises are less dramatic, but I nevertheless think of them as alpha and omega, existing before everything else, and certainly long after everything else, too. I also think of them as routine.

But there is a hero to our story and he's known as Vivi. For besides selling us the house, *La Comtesse*'s greatest contribution to our well-being was introducing us to Jean-Claude and Colette Viviani. Nominally the plumber, Vivi has been our technical adviser in all domains. Also at times our social adviser, our political adviser, and on certain occasions our *gentil organisateur*, as Club Med would identify him. That's when he leads a gang of his friends to the Rouge Gorge, the Avignon nightclub he favors.

Vivi is jocular and jovial. His presence fills rooms and his booming laugh dominates a scene like the Rouge Gorge, and his voice cuts across Mr. Bricolage or any other French version of Home Depot to get you refocused on the project you have asked him to focus on.

Sometimes Vivi worked magic, and sometimes I thought he was magical himself. As I was in the middle of more than one faltering handyman project Vivi arrived, deus ex machina, to pull my chestnuts out of the fire, or something else. One time I decided that in order to paint an enormous radiator, I needed to take it out of the house. In disconnecting the pipes I stripped a valve and gallons of antifreeze in the heating system started pouring onto the floor. Miraculously, Vivi drove up unexpectedly as I stood there like the little Dutch boy trying to hold back the flood and not having any idea of what to do except run.

From that moment on I believed in Vivi's magic. Colette's open kindness and generosity reflect another kind of magic. Far more than the plumber and his wife, they are the kind of friends who teach you what friendship means.

Like *La Comtesse* before us installing her tub, bathrooms were the first changes we made in the house, and Vivi was in his element. The main house had two bathrooms, but only one was upstairs serving four bedrooms, and it was a first-generation indoor-plumbing basic. We determined to redo it and turn one of the small bedrooms into a second upstairs bathroom.

Bathrooms need water, and in Provence water means complications. There are two wells on the property, but neither of them yields enough water to fill a bathtub, as Mr. Jullien liked to recall. But seventy meters lower on the mountainside, there's an ancient waterline that since Roman times has brought water from an artesian well several kilometers away to supply Vaison's fountains. (And as you might deduce, that's why the road is called *le Chemin des Fontaines*, the Road of the Fountains.)

After buying Chanteduc, *La Comtesse* took Vivi's suggestion and had a waterline put in from that source. But the system requires two pumps. Double trouble, in other words, because pumps fail, and it became clear that the failures would go on and on and on. The first problem came early, in our first winter. Freaky temperatures of minus-fifteen degrees Celsius (minus-five degrees Fahrenheit) froze one of the pumps and it literally fell into pieces. We replaced it, and we also accepted Vivi's suggestion of putting a small electric radiator in each pump house to avoid that problem in the future.

It didn't, of course. Wise though it may have been, the suggestion could not anticipate a rare heavy snowfall that broke tree limbs, which fell on power lines. Without electricity, the radiator wasn't working, but frigid temperatures were.

There have been more routine malfunctions—a part wears out, the pressure tank explodes—and others that were less routine, as when

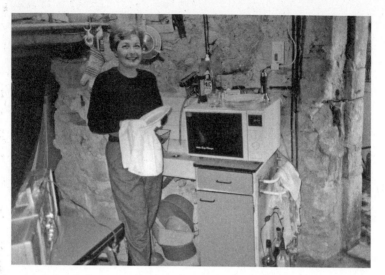

Patricia in her temporary kitchen in 1991, with microwave and boom box.

ants ate away the electrical insulation so the whole thing shorted out. Or a summer storm knocks out power, but the simple matter of flipping the circuit breaker isn't so simple if hornets have built a nest in the pump house. When that happens, you first call the fire department, and after sundown that day or the next a couple of twenty-year-olds drive up, don Darth Vader costumes, and destroy the nest.

Besides trying to solve the water problems, the goal of making Chanteduc our own involved a long series of restoration projects. Among the archives that Régine Boissarie left behind were various remodeling plans, some of them for turning the house into just another neo villa. Luckily for us she had not carried through on any of them but had left the house intact, with its harmonious exterior and little square rooms. Chanteduc had housed generations of peasants subsisting on their hardscrabble farm, and respect for their lives persuaded us that it should stay that way.

Provençal farmhouses have traditionally grown room by room, and that was the way we went about restoring the interior. In the beginning as we set out on annual improvement projects, Jean-Claude and

Colette Tricart, our young mason and his wife, coached us in authenticity. Jean-Claude spent a month lying on his back atop scaffolding in the *séjour* replacing the ceiling. Though small, the room was once truly the "living room." The peasant family cooked, ate, and slept within its close walls. The floor was earthen, the fireplace a sandstone slab with a conduit above it. But that was typical of Provençal farmhouses, as were the essential furnishings: a *fausse armoire*, set into one of the two-foot-thick walls; a *panetière*, or fancy carved cage for storing the bread that was baked weekly; a clock set into the wall near the *fausse armoire*; and the *pétrin*, where flour was kept and bread kneaded. The oven for baking the bread was in a tiny adjoining room but had been demolished long before our arrival. The *fausse armoire* is still there, though the other essentials are long gone.

A fifth essential in the legends of peasants, a cache of gold coins, never turned up. The lore was that a mason had found and stolen it years before.

The ceiling in the room was a scant six feet above the floor, held up by five blackened beams, logs that had been felled centuries ago. And because they were still solid, it was evident they had been felled during "*la bonne lune.*" As we were told over and over, work involving planting and harvesting had to be done according to the moon's phases, and wood that had not been cut and cured in the right phase simply wouldn't last. (The relationship between wood and the moon is thought to be so enduring that exposure to moonlight can cause furniture to deteriorate. That's reason enough for keeping shutters closed firmly at night.)

Our beams had lasted just fine, but stuffed between them, though hidden by a thin sheet of plaster, was the jumble that Jean-Claude discovered. Twigs and sticks, straw and even rocks were used as filler. The beautiful Provençal ceiling we had fantasized about finding—big beams supporting smaller ones with cement filling the space between the little ones—had never existed in our modest little house. Undaunted, Jean-Claude said he would build the ceiling we fantasized

Walter repairing worn shutters.

about, though it meant he had to build it without disturbing the floor above.

It took a long time, but he pulled it off, and in the process he discovered that two of the five beams bore no weight. Out they came, leaving the room feeling a little less enclosed.

The kitchen, the biggest project of all, was our last with the Tricarts. As it moved slowly forward, Patricia was finishing her first book with Joël Robuchon, who with his wife, Janine, had come to spend a weekend with us. Three food memories from the weekend stand out. We boarded the TGV (*Train à Grande Vitesse*) in Paris at nine in the evening, all of us expecting to get a sandwich on the train. But the bar car stewards were on strike, and there was no food on board, nothing at all. Throughout the trip Joël kept saying: "I'm starving, I'm really starving!" I could just imagine what delectables he might have been fantasizing about, and even more, what his kitchen could have packed for the trip.

Once we got to Chanteduc, about one in the morning, we made popcorn as a quickie snack. That mainstay of the American late-night

Walter cleaning the pool, the hard way.

---

diet was not a hit. "So this is popcorn," Joël kept saying. Nothing more, except for his little giggle.

The second memory is of Joël, the world's greatest chef, cooking in the cellar. While the real kitchen was ripped up, we had set up a rudimentary gas flame in the jumble of a cellar, where an unused toilet sat stored in a corner. As he cooked, Joël said it was the first time he had ever cooked in a kitchen with a crapper. He laughed and I did too, but I was mortified. Luckily Joël returned to cook in our real kitchen, and that made memory number three a much better experience.

Throughout the remodeling projects with the Tricarts, we amazed our friends, and ourselves, too, by recounting our good fortune with workmen. But in the building trades luck comes in all varieties, and it can change. The Tricarts moved on to other careers and eventually

The dining room, in transition.

Walter begins the demolition for the new kitchen and living room.

ended their marriage. Both were bittersweet evolutions for us, but we found another for the next project. Let's call him Pierre, and while that's not his real name, his talent as a mason was very real. In the walls that he built, each stone seemed to have been chosen with an exacting eye, then placed with precision. You could go to him with an idea and he would tell you how to adjust it to fit into the Provençal aesthetic. When we had a job under way or an idea to work through, Pierre would come by late Saturday afternoon and we'd talk it through. After a little discussion I would offer a drink and he would accept. I drank more whiskey with Pierre than with anyone else in my mature life—he loved single malt Scotch and I kept it on hand for his visits.

And then in the middle of a job he fired us. He had been enthusiastic about the project, converting an outbuilding into a gym, then something happened and he stopped coming. We were patient at first, then beseeching, then finally insistent. "I don't accept ultimatums," he said, and he came and hauled his tools away. I still don't know what set off the dispute, but I do know that being abandoned by a workman in the middle of a job is as crippling as being abandoned by a lover. And it may be harder to find a replacement.

I still see Pierre from time to time, either at the building supplier or passing on the highway. We always wave and when we stop to chat we still address each other as though we were friends, with the informal "*tu*." Occasionally, I wonder if he'd undertake a new project, but then remember past anger and my gratitude that it is past. As our neighbors say about things you can't control, "*C'est comme ça.*" But there aren't many days when one of us doesn't comment on something he did—a wall, a window, a doorway—and we pause to praise his skill.

COLETTE'S VINAIGRETTE

Our friend and Provençal neighbor Colette Viviani makes the very best vinaigrette. Like most home cooks, she never uses a recipe and just creates meals by feel. I finally insisted that she make this dressing in front of me, so I could write down the proportions. I was surprised at the small amount of vinegar she used. This is so delicious, I am a convert!

> 1 teaspoon French mustard
> Fine sea salt
> Freshly ground black pepper
> 1¼ teaspoons best-quality red wine vinegar
> ½ cup extra-virgin olive oil

Place the mustard in the bottom of the salad bowl. Season generously with salt and pepper. With a fork, whisk to blend. Add the vinegar and mix again. Add the oil and mix. Taste for seasoning.

About ½ cup vinaigrette

VARIATIONS: Depending upon the salad greens, add minced garlic, onions, or shallots. Herb variations include parsley, chives, cilantro, mint, or basil.

21

{ Grow, Garden, Grow }

PATRICIA:

I am convinced that people don't find houses, houses find people. And it's as if our eighteenth-century French farmhouse on a rock-strewn, chalky hilltop in northern Provence had been waiting for us for centuries. In my mystical thinking, the property somehow knew that we would not only discover its specialness and appreciate it, but also try to help it reach its potential while we were its brief caretakers.

When the property "found us" in 1984, it had a certain charm, but an organic horticultural wonder it was not. The garden was a horror show planted in harsh-colored annuals that seemed ill-suited for the rugged soil and bright, clean light of Provence. There were bright pink and shocking red begonias that wilted in the summer sun and demanded extraordinary care yielding minimal results. Spiky red flowers that resemble firecrackers made me feel dizzy and agitated just looking at them, and I am now convinced that all these bright colors only attracted the swarms of *guêpes* (nasty wasps) that never left our sight from spring to late fall.

And then there was the vineyard. It was ill-tended and sprayed with chemicals, and worst of all, row after row of vines were infested with mildew. Not only dreaded by winegrowers, mildew turned out to be a super breeding ground for mosquitoes. They swarmed into our bedroom and threatened to drive me from my own home. One July—my body covered with hundreds of bites—I told Walter that the place was a living hell, and I would have to return to Paris. I didn't, of course. *Huile de citronnelle* (lemon balm oil) kept the mosquitos away, as it has forever.

In fact, it is hard to believe today that it was love at first sight. In the first place, we were not looking for a country house. And we hardly knew our way around Paris in those days, let alone the rest of France. But we did buy the house and, from the very first weekend, it began to change our lives in the most positive, unimaginable ways. Weather—be it sunshine, rain, or drought—became a preoccupation, for whatever happened in the sky affected our day, our garden, our crops, and the mood of the farmers and merchants around us. When the half-dozen gnarled old cherry trees in the orchard began to bear, we dropped everything to pick the shiny, purple-red fruit and set about putting that bounty to work, making *clafoutis*, ice creams, *confitures*, and homemade liqueurs. The unfurling of every leaf—lettuce, grapes, figs, and irises—became the object of our weekly concentration. We eagerly turned our attention to a fledgling vegetable garden, only to find that about all this parched, chalky, stony soil could promise were vegetables that tasted of struggle. The growth of nearly every olive in our small grove of trees was following throughout the season, though more than once we arrived at harvest time to find the trees picked bare by passersby.

We learned about spotting the property's edible wild mushrooms, but only after years of listening to the neighbors boast of discoveries on our land. An invitation to join us on a hunt, with the promise of a multimushroom feast to follow, was the key to uncovering the secret gardens hidden among the scrub oaks and pines. (Fortunately, in France pharmacists are trained in mycology, and if I ever have a question about the safety of eating a mushroom I collect in the pine woods, I simply have it verified in town.)

We also learned about unearthing the rare black truffles that hid beneath the soil of our vines, not far from the rows of scrub oak that enclosed the vineyards, but knew secretly that most years the poachers' bounty far exceeded our meager findings.

Slowly, we began to make changes that not only flattered the property but made it an organic whole, an authentic Provençal patch of paradise. Sometimes good things happened unconsciously, without our planning. We ourselves planted row upon row of lavender, of thyme, and of rosemary, not because we wisely thought it would change the ecology of the land, but because we loved the scent, the color, the ease of care. Only years later, when the wasps appeared to have lost interest and the lavender-, thyme-, and rosemary-loving bees seemed to have the rule of the roost, did we realize that WE were making a difference on this land.

Walter and our friend Maggie Shapiro, planting bulbs.

Early on, we made a decision to plant a new kind of fruit tree each year, adding to the tiny orchard of ancient and production cherry trees, the plump, sweet, full-flavored variety the French call Bigarreaux.

We planted a trio of espaliered pear trees (Pear Williams, Comice, and Beurre Hardy); a tiny shoot of a quince given to us by a neighbor; two varieties of plump and delicious apricots; and a very special fig tree, a deep purple variety known as St. Jean, and chosen for its flavor and productivity (in a good year it produces two full crops). But one of our most prized fruit trees actually was born on a balcony in Paris. Our good friend Maggie Shapiro had purchased a loquat (what the French call a *néflier*) in a Paris street market and planted the giant seed in a pot on her balcony. Before long it grew a foot high. In 1984, she brought it down on the high-speed TGV train, we planted the seedling, and it is now at least twenty feet tall, producing regular harvests of nutritious fruit, the color of apricots and tasting much like a sweet, juicy mango.

One plant that also loves our land is *millepertuis*, a green-leafed, yellow-flowered plant that we call St. John's Wort. Here in Provence it is said that the red pigment from the crushed flowers signifies the blood of Saint John, for the herb is in full flower on June 24, St. John's Day. Local folklore says you must pick the flowers at exactly noon on the twenty-fourth, macerating them with oil and white wine to create an oil used to calm burns and bites. (I've never had the patience to try making it. We find Betadine quite adequate.)

But it was our love for the peach tree that helped us create rules and regulations for just what we could (and would) grow and could not and would not. Committed from the beginning to a thoroughly natural and organic way of life, we shunned chemical fertilizers and turned to natural organic fertilizers and our compost pile to nourish the poor, rocky soil. Peaches, we soon learned, are subject to multiple diseases and did not enjoy life on our land on our terms. After trying for three years and finding ourselves with leafless, almost peachless trees, we inaugurated the Three-Year Rule. If a plant gives us trouble, is not happy with an organic life, it gets three years to show its stuff. If not, we rip it out and find room for something more naturally compatible.

That became the case of my coveted espaliered pear trees. It seems that no one—including myself—ever figured out how to prune them properly and so rather than resembling the regal trees of Luxembourg Gardens, Versailles, or the châteaux of the Loire, they looked like Looney Tune cartoon characters instead. Although the pear trees thrived and produced, so did the hornets who loved their sweet nectar and always managed to get to the fruit before I did. What was I thinking, anyway? Provence is not pear land! Out they came and in their place we have more locally compatible berries.

Patricia in 1985 with her first cherry crop.

Other plants that have not lived through the Three-Year Rule include all root vegetables (they end up tasting of struggle, not what I want to put on my plate) and artichokes (they flourish for a bit, then wither).

What does thrive is sorrel (like a weed, and thank goodness I adore it and find myriad uses for it in the kitchen), tomatoes (we plant local as well as several dozen heirloom varieties), chives, salad burnet (*pim-prenelle*), lemon verbena, borage, lovage, lemon balm, hyssop, purslane, summer savory, and sage. I have an annual patch of varied pumpkins, what the French also call butternut as well as the tiny bright orange *potimarron* for cutting into cubes and adding to a summer's *soupe au pistou*; and the giant *muscade*, with its pale orange skin and faint flavor of nutmeg, perfect for roasting and pureeing for soups and desserts.

Patricia and an abundance of herbs.

We also live in fig land! Pierre Baud, a neighbor not more than ten minutes away, is one of the world's leading fig experts, with dozens of varieties for sale in his thriving nursery. One year he invited us to a fig tasting—we sampled no less than thirty varieties—and from that tasting selected the nine varieties that caught our attention. Now, the property is ringed with all manner of figs.

My greatest pleasure in the summer months is to stroll to the garden just after awakening, a steaming cup of espresso in my hand. I "make the rounds" and see what has come up (or what has not) since my last tour. Sometimes I begin harvesting—tiny zucchini, baby cucumbers, baskets full of golden zucchini and squash blossoms—and on days that I am pressed for time I make a mental note to return later to pick what is ripe.

There are some fruits and vegetables that are left to Walter. I don't know how the practice began, but he somehow has a knack for finding all those tiny green beans that need a meticulous eye and utter patience, two traits I can't really claim. So Walter takes care of the green beans, along with our ever-expanding crop of berries: fat, almost mutant-sized blackberries, golden gooseberries, delicate tayberries, and

Heirloom treasures from our garden.

several varieties of strawberries, which seem to give us pleasure as well as bowls full from May through October. Almost every summer morning—before or after his morning swim—Walter approaches me in the kitchen with a basketful of multiple berries. Better than a diamond ring or store-bought roses any day! What a lucky gal I am!

Now, wisely, we are learning to encourage what grows easily and naturally, without undue intervention: I am the proud owner of thriving herb gardens filled with dozens of varieties of mint, basil, and thyme. My most prized possession is my caper bush, a sprawling plant that—on a good day in the heat of summer—will produce a tiny jar filled with tight green buds. I tried curing them in coarse Mediterranean sea salt, but they just sat there and did nothing. I then learned to simply cure them in distilled white vinegar and they now prize our table on pizzas, in potato salads, and anything that might need the vinegary bite they invoke. (Amazingly, the project almost came to a screeching halt one September, when a wild boar made regular forays into the herb garden, destroying stone walls in the process. He finally

Spring irises.

went away and I am wondering whether he did not show up on a neighbor's table in the form of a tasty wild boar terrine.)

In the flower garden, plants became pastel-colored as I banished harsh and bright reds and oranges in favor of white, pale pink, lavender, and purple, colors I found made me calmer and more relaxed beneath the always-brilliant Provençal sun and bright blue skies. Nothing gives me greater pleasure, nothing calms me more than picking baskets full of pale purple agapanthus, pure white roses, freshly opened lavender, and anointing every room of the house with natural bouquets.

Season after season, we work hard to make a mark on our Chanteduc, a positive mark that will uphold its integrity. We also have to make sure that it will work with our modern life, but why would anyone look for an electric or gas oven when our mason can build us a wood-fired oven built of stone and heated by the year's vine clippings? Why would one install a stainless-steel sink when our local supplier of old recuperated materials offers us models fashioned of sandstone or marble?

At Chanteduc we awake to the morning sun from the east and sip Champagne at sunset facing west, watching the golden ball fall behind the mountain known as Théos. A few years ago we cut back dozens of scrub oaks, opening up that 360-degree view, letting the house know that it is at the center of the Chanteduc private universe, and we the caretakers can turn our gaze to all sides of this world.

Just Tomatoes!

Our friend Fabrice Langlois is the sommelier at the well-known Châteauneuf-du-Pape estate Château de Beaucastel. When he describes the simplicity of wine making and emphasis on purity, he takes a tomato as an example. As he notes, if you take a cardboard supermarket tomato to make a sauce, you need to add olive oil, tomato paste, garlic, onions, salt, pepper, basil, celery, bay leaves, fennel, and more. "Anything to hide the misery," he likes to say. But if you take a ripe, garden-fresh tomato, all you need is salt and maybe a single herb. Here is my Just Tomatoes! liquid, a cross between a juice and a sauce. Tomatoes are simply cored, quartered, and cooked over low heat with salt and a bit of fresh bay leaf. I pass the mixture through a food mill and either reserve it to be reduced for a sauce or drink it as a healthy, full-flavored juice that tastes of absolutely nothing but pure tomato. No misery to hide here!

I make this in three colors: For a yellow sauce I use a combination of Yellow Stuffer, Banana Legs, and Saint Vincent Jaune. For an orange sauce I use varieties called Valencia and Coeur de Boeuf (in America I think that it is the equivalent of Herman's Yellow), an impressive heart-shaped variety that is actually a deep golden orange. The flavor is almost creamy. For red sauce, my all-time favorite is what we simply call La Russe, which I believe is Russian No. 117, a huge, dense, meaty tomato that grows to two pounds. But if they are not yet ripe, I'll go for Paola or Coeur de Boeuf. In France, I grow very fresh, delicately flavored bay leaves that I use with abandon. In America, it's best to grow your own or make sure that the variety you use is not overly assertive.

EQUIPMENT: A large heavy-duty casserole; a food mill fitted with the finest screen.

> 5 pounds garden-fresh tomatoes of a single color, rinsed, cored, and quartered
> 1 tablespoon coarse sea salt
> Several fresh bay leaves

1. In a large heavy-duty casserole, combine the tomatoes, salt, and bay leaves. Cover, and cook over low heat until the tomatoes begin to give up their juices, about 3 minutes. Uncover and let simmer, stirring frequently, for about 25 minutes. Cook longer if you want a thicker sauce. Taste for seasoning. Remove and discard the bay leaves.

2. Place the food mill over a large bowl. Using a large ladle, transfer the sauce to the food mill and puree into the bowl. The quantity will vary according to the juiciness of the tomatoes. (Store, covered, in the refrigerator for up to 1 day, or the freezer up to 2 weeks.)

About 1½ quarts liquid

~⊙~

Fig Chutney

Unable to choose among the many colors, sizes, textures, and flavors found at Pierre Baud's nursery, we planted nine varieties of figs, including the Grise de Saint Jean (intensely flavored and an early producer), Madeleine des Deux Saisons (huge green figs with an intense strawberry flavor), and Ronde de Bordeaux, my favorite (small, deep purple, dense, and delicious). For this chutney I combine the varieties depending on the harvest so each batch of chutney has its own wonderful and unique flavor.

> 2 pounds whole fresh figs, rinsed
> 6 tablespoons dry white wine
> 6 tablespoons best-quality red wine or sherry vinegar
> 2 whole sticks cinnamon
> 4 whole cloves
> ½ teaspoon ground cayenne pepper or Espelette pepper
> 1 cup raw sugar
> 2 tablespoons olive oil
> 2 teaspoons coarse salt

In large saucepan, combine all the ingredients. Bring to a boil over high heat. Reduce to a simmer and simmer for 1½ hours, stirring from time to time. Taste for seasoning. Ladle into the sterilized jars. Seal. Stores indefinitely in the refrigerator.

Makes 5 12-ounce jars

⁓☙⁓

EGGPLANT IN SPICY TOMATO SAUCE

During a good year, I can have a hundred long, lean, glistening eggplants hanging from their elegant vines. I panic, for I hate to see anything from the garden go to waste. I distribute the vegetables to our friends the merchants around town, and try to find ways to be able to profit from their proliferation all winter long. This recipe fits the bill: The eggplants are halved and baked until meltingly tender, then buried in a thick, spicy tomato sauce. This dish is delicious hot or cold, and leftovers can be pureed to make a delectable pasta sauce. It also freezes well, so in December I can enjoy the flavors of summer.

EQUIPMENT: A large deep frying pan with a cover.

> 4 small, firm, fresh eggplant, washed but not peeled (each about 8 ounces)
> 3 tablespoons extra-virgin olive oil
> Fine sea salt
> 2 onions, peeled, halved, and thinly sliced
> 2 tablespoons thin slivers fresh ginger
> 6 plump garlic cloves, peeled, halved, green germ removed
> 1 small fresh chile pepper, minced, or 1 teaspoon ground dried chile
> 1 tablespoon ground cumin
> 1½ cups tomato sauce
> 2 cups chicken stock

1. Preheat the oven to 425°F.
2. Halve the eggplants lengthwise. Brush the flesh lightly with 1 tablespoon of the oil and season with salt. Place the eggplant

halves cut side down on a baking sheet. Place on a rack in the center of the oven and bake until soft and golden, about 30 minutes.

3. While the eggplant cooks, prepare the sauce: In a large deep frying pan, combine the onion, the remaining 2 tablespoons oil, and about ½ teaspoon fine sea salt. Toss to thoroughly coat the onions with the oil and cook, covered, over low heat until soft and translucent, about 5 minutes. Add the ginger, garlic, chile, and cumin and toss again to evenly coat the onions with the spices. Add the tomato sauce and chicken stock and simmer, covered, for about 5 minutes. Add the roasted eggplant halves, burying them in the sauce. Cook until the eggplant is very tender and has absorbed the sauce, about 20 minutes more.

8 servings

VARIATION: As a main-dish vegetarian offering, add about 1 cup cubed feta cheese, warming it slightly so it begins to melt.

Yves sniffs a freshly unearthed truffle.

22

{ *All About Yves* }

WALTER:

As we quickly learned, Chanteduc had many friends, but its one true child was Yves Reynaud, who was born next to the fireplace in the room he called the *séjour*. When he was a young man and away doing his military service, an obligation in those days, his father sold the place to Régine Boissarie to settle his debts. Yves never forgave his old man. After 1962, he didn't live there anymore, but he really never left either. He roamed the woods, shot the game, and found the truffles, constantly renewing his claim on the land if not his title to it.

Both rustic and *rusé*, Yves seemed the consummate *paysan*. For us Anglophones, the word "peasant" is weighted with snobbish disdain, but in France a *paysan* is simply a countryman, usually a farmer or, as in Yves's case, a hunter and trapper. That's not how he made his living, but it was certainly what he lived for. When he died in 2006, the tribute to him in the local weekly newspaper was headlined, "The hunter has gone away."

Classically, the *paysan*'s greatest attribute is wiliness, and Yves did his best to live up to the reputation. Not a landowner, he was closer to the earth than most and knew every tree and every rock on our five hectares (12 acres). "*Vous êtes chez vous*," he would say in the course of nearly every conversation we had. We took it as sort of "your home is your castle" declaration, then came to understand the further regretful implication that except for his father it would have been his.

It was easy to know when Yves was pooching around in the woods. Friends would correct me. "You mean 'poaching,' " they would say. But I really did mean "pooching" because his nine dogs each had a tiny bell at its neck. With Yves's pack jingling through the forests, his presence seemed both constant and reassuring. We first knew about Yves from Régine, and we heard the tinkling of his dog pack before we saw Yves. Régine's disapproving description was built around her new discovery that Yves was regularly taking truffles from the property without telling her there were any there. Tiny second-quality truffles grow in the edge of the vineyard, and for a long time now it has been not Yves but some other *paysan* who ferrets them out, sometimes sharing but more often not.

If Yves felt some failed claim on the house, it was nothing compared with his attachment to the woods, and because of that he was the de facto *vigile*. "Caretaker" would suggest a more activist role in maintenance than Yves would ever sign on for, but he was often around Chanteduc and always watchful. That was a fit, because his wife Suzanne was the housekeeper we inherited from Régine. After claiming possession of the house on an early October weekend, our first act was to take Suzanne a bouquet of roses from the garden and ask her to give us a chance. The gesture worked for a while, until her health declined or our exoticism wore off and she passed the job along to her daughter Annick.

Yves worked for *la mairie* (the town hall). Without any further detail, that could have suggested he was the deputy mayor, but he wasn't. A classic "*homme à tout faire*," he helped set up the market every Tuesday, then cleaned up afterward. He did whatever else was necessary, including digging graves and driving the garbage truck. But what Yves mostly did was wander the forests and, in season, he hunted. He had learned a butcher's skills, but the story was that a weakness in his lungs meant that he couldn't stand being in cold storage lockers, so he began looking for other things to do. The mayor, an old hunting chum, saved him with a patronage job. But Yves kept his hand in meat cutting by butchering hogs for farmers in the winter months. His *boudin noir* was delicious—when I tasted the rich black coils, cut into chunks and panned in olive oil, I thought I could eat "*des kilomètres*," as he said he himself had done.

But hunting was his passion, and we profited from his keen aim and woodsman's knowledge. Rabbits, thrush, and even one pheasant all found their way to our table, or we found our way to Suzanne's when Yves's quarry was being served.

On a fall Saturday afternoon, the dogs' jingling bells would announce Yves's arrival, dressed in *bleus de travail*, the ubiquitous bright blue uniform of the French working class. Often he brought something for us and often it was a rabbit he had freshly killed. Spotting us as city slickers at best, Yves would take the rabbit behind the garage, skin and gut it and throw the innards to his dogs, all of them yelping, jingling, and manifestly ravenous. We followed him the first time, not again.

One Saturday he drove up in his classic little Citroën *Deux-Chevaux* truck and dropped off two rabbits, dressed and ready for the pot, that he had shot that morning. We had gone down to the village and weren't there when he stopped by, so our dinner was left hanging in a plastic supermarket bag at the front gate.

There was a note that said "*Merci pour le fusil*," and signed with a Gallic flourish. The gun, an aged blunderbuss, had hung over the fireplace at Chanteduc when we took possession, and I assumed it had belonged to the Reynaud family and made plans to give it to Yves. It wasn't useable, and I felt mild apprehension that the gift would be misunderstood. In French custom, one must never give anyone a

Yves Reynaud and pal, with truffles, dog, wine, and cigarettes.

knife without asking for a symbolic payment—a centime or two—because otherwise the knife "cuts the friendship." God knows what a gun might do.

But Yves seemed truly pleased on that Christmas Eve when I gave him the shotgun. "I killed many a rabbit with this one," he said, holding it to his shoulder and sighting along the barrel. His whole family was there and the presents for the others were less successful. A second gift for Yves, a box of shotgun shells, was not huge but it was heavy, and Suzanne was impressed by the weight. But she wasn't impressed by the contents when she ripped off the paper. I'll never forget the look of disappointment on her face when she saw what it was, but Yves was happy, and the two dressed rabbits soon followed.

A pack of dogs scrambling over the rabbit guts was a Squire Worthy scene, almost literary. But for literal earthiness, nothing matched truffle hunting with Yves. The association of French truffles is with the Périgord, of course, on the other side of the country from Provence. But in reality, more *truffes du Périgord* are produced in our region of

Provence than in the Périgord. The practice in our region is to hunt with dogs, not pigs. You don't have to fight the dog for the truffle, as you do with the pig. And pigs are carnivores, remember? They don't distinguish fingers from sausages. But the explanation I like is that if you're wandering around on somebody else's property, it's harder to explain why you're walking a pig than a dog. To say nothing of driving around with a pig in the car.

A keen-eyed expert can also find truffles "*à la mouche*," by sighting a tiny golden fly that lays its eggs on the soil just over where a truffle is growing. The fly truffler walks slowly along holding a small branch close to the ground. When disturbed by the branch, the fly hops straight up, thus revealing where to dig for the truffle, which is growing there eight inches or so below the surface.

When Régine sold Chanteduc to us she had only just learned that there were truffles on the land. She had seen a sign clearly planted in her vineyard, scrawled on a small wooden board, announcing *INTER-DIT DE TRUFFER* and had asked Yves about it. Yes, he had admitted. But there aren't many and they aren't the best quality. No matter, she said. She wanted her share.

The truffles grow in the edge of the vineyard at Chanteduc, at the end of the roots of the scrub oaks that form a natural hedge around the vineyards. Truffles also grow better if the earth has been cultivated, which the vineyard is.

Yves introduced us to the truffles at the beginning, perhaps as a way of staking his claim and perhaps because we had responded with admiration to his cleverness as a woodsman. He liked to perform, and that is surely the reason he showed us the truffler's skills. A friend of his had a dog, a mongrel named Penelope, that had been trained for that specialized hunt. Her technique was to range between the rows of vines, sniffing the earth and wagging her tail. When she found a spot where a truffle grew underneath, she paused and gave the earth three or four quick pats with her front paws. Her job was finished, and she got her reward—a big cookie crumb. Then it was up to Yves to dig up the delicious nugget. Yves had a small pick, and he drove it into the earth just beside the spot that Penelope had identified.

Yves was a man of few words, though he tended to say them a lot. Long before rap's baleful, angry singsong made its way to the French provinces, Yves was jivin' with his unusual patter, a mantra that both filled silence and gave away his excitement about the topic of the moment. For instance, talking to and about Penelope as she marked truffle spots, Yves encouraged both her and us with his chatter:

"Elle est pas folle, celle-la. Non, elle est pas folle du tout. Pas celle-la. Non, pas elle. Idiote c'est pas son type. Non, elle est pas folle."

His chant meant simply "that dog's no fool" and he said it over and over as he scooped handfuls of earth from the hole that his short-handled pick had opened. He sniffed and snorted over each handful, to see if he was getting closer to the truffle. Sometimes immediately and sometimes more slowly, he would extract a clot of earth and announce, "There it is, and it's a beauty." All the while, he never interrupted his praise of Penelope. "I told you, she's no fool."

For a neophyte, the thing was that the truffle looked exactly like every other clot of clay. Nothing about its appearance identified it as a truffle, though its earthy fragrance was unmistakable.

Once when Yves was working his friend came up alone with Penelope. We had been out with him and Yves several times, so surely we could do what Yves had done. But we couldn't. Penelope would pat, and we would dig, taking the earth into our cupped hands and snuffling as we had seen Yves do. We could tell that there was a truffle somewhere nearby, but we were unable to extract anything except the redolence. At one point, snorting around like coke heads, clay up our noses, I asked Patricia, "Do you want to change holes?" We had a laugh, but no truffles.

The other fruits of the vineyard are much easier to harvest.

Eventually the Reynauds moved to the other side of town. Their landlord wanted the house for himself, so Yves and Suzanne found another farm to rent. We lost touch except for occasionally seeing Yves in Vaison. We miss his jingling dog pack, especially in the late summer when the wild boars root out parts of the garden. If Yves were still around, I say to myself, we wouldn't have this problem. I can hear his emphatic description of the terrine he would turn the boar into: "*la meilleure des meilleures*" (the best ever).

We learned not long ago that Yves had died. Taken away by a cancer, he was buried in a grave that his former *mairie* colleagues dug for him. He was laid to rest next to his grandparents, who were identified in the newspaper as being "of Chanteduc." Their names were Léon and Victorine, and, like Yves's patter and his dogs, their sweet self-conscious smiles in the photograph we have make me glad that in our restoration we have been faithful to all that has gone before.

That we have the photo is a small measure of the pull that Chanteduc has for the people who have lived there or visited. One of Yves's elderly cousins brought it once when he came to call. He had seen a bottle of our wine, Clos Chanteduc, somewhere and arranged an introduction so that he could see what had happened to the place where he had spent many summers in his youth.

He led us through the house and told us how each room had been used and what animals were kept in each corner of the barnyard. He brought the portrait of Léon and Victorine, and told of Victorine's fresh cheeses and her cured olives. Vaison's mayor visited too, and talked of Léon's well-respected stud goat, which was housed in the room now appropriately called "the goat room" that we converted into a second kitchen.

Time passes. There are other poachers now, other hunters, most of them anonymous. And, frankly, they are not unwelcome. Aside from a tool or two (which I may well have lost myself) nothing has disappeared except the truffles and the mushrooms. Even that infestation of wild boars was cleared up once hunting season opened. My attitude of inclusion turned mean in one case. Competing truffle hunters tried to use us to take sides—and because of the tension between them, and absence of any truffles from either of them, I thought it would be interesting to tell them both that they had been chosen. My newsroom experience involved a lot of creative tension. The poachers fought it out for a while, then both stopped coming. I was as *méchant* but less inclusive the Sunday morning that I looked out the window and saw still another party of trufflers in the vineyard, two men and a child. I knew who it was, a neighbor who had never returned my wave when we passed on the road. So I pulled on my big rubber boots and trudged down to greet them. "Allow me to introduce myself. I am Walter Wells, the owner here. And who are you?" Grunts exchanged and then names, I asked: "Don't you think you might have said '*bonjour*' before coming to dig my truffles?"

"I just wanted to show my boy how to find them," the young man said.

"Don't you want to show him how to ask permission also?" There was no response, so I wound it up. "*Bon dimanche,*" I said, "*cavez bien.*" I was pleased to know the vernacular for digging for truffles: "*caver.*" They continued a while longer, then later stopped by the house with their meager haul. I opened the crumpled plastic bag, took out two of the chunks and gave the rest back. I had made my point.

So had they. Even after twenty years we were new at owning the land. They and their families had lived there for generations. A tight-assed no-trespassing policy would be pointless, nor would it honor Yves. We were both right.

SCRAMBLED EGGS with TRUFFLES

Walter makes the best scrambled eggs. He learned this method from French chef Roland Passot of La Folie in San Francisco, when Roland prepared this recipe for a crowd of twenty-five one weekend in January in Provence. We had all been invited to the home of Hervé Poron, our truffle producer, who of course had quite a larder of fresh black truffles. Roland taught us all this easy trick: Mix all the eggs and half of the truffles together, put everything in an unheated frying pan and add the butter, then stir and stir and stir with a wooden spoon. You end up with a luscious, creamy, golden mass. Of course these can be made without truffles, but they won't be the same.

EQUIPMENT: A wooden spoon; 2 very hot dinner plates.

> 1 fresh black truffle (about 1½ ounces)
> 6 ultra-fresh large farm eggs
> Fleur de sel
> 2 tablespoons unsalted butter, cut into small pieces
> Hot buttered toast for serving

Halve the truffle. Mince one half and cut the other half into a fine julienne. In a large bowl, combine the cracked eggs (do not break the yolks), half of the minced truffles, and a pinch of salt. Pour the mixture into a large frying pan and add the butter. Over low to medium heat, stir gently but constantly with a wooden spoon until the yolks break and the eggs form a creamy mass. Do not overcook—the entire process should take about 4 minutes. Stir in the julienne of truffles. Taste for seasoning. With a large spoon, transfer the mixture to two very hot dinner plates. Serve with little rectangles of toast spread with butter and dotted with the remaining minced truffle.

2 servings

23

{ Vineyard Tales }

WALTER:

We never thought of ourselves as Francis Ford Coppola. In the beginning we just wanted a well-tended vineyard. Someday, we thought, we could make our own wine, but the idea was very much in the future conditional. When that time came, we would want a wine that didn't fall into a Côtes-du-Rhône stereotype, the banal red you got in a French bar when you ordered a glass. We could even imagine a distinctive expression of Chanteduc's *terroir*, a wine that would be peppery, with traces of raspberries and ripe cherries and a hint of tobacco.

Might we also fantasize that the wine would be distinguished? Hope indeed springs eternal.

When we bought Chanteduc the vineyard merely rounded out the package. It was an attraction but not a factor in our decision. Certainly we liked having a house with a terrace that overlooked its own vineyard. We liked it too that the vineyard, six acres of rocky limestone and clay, was planted in Grenache, the workhorse variety in Côtes-du-Rhône. And we liked it that those gnarled black vines spoke of character and experience. They had been planted in the 1950s after a historic cold snap froze the olive trees, and thus qualified, in wine label terms, as *"vieilles vignes,"* or old vines. If French regulations do not address the issue of just how old *vieilles vignes* must be, the law is very specific about agricultural leases. And because of the law, we bought the vineyard three times.

The first time was when I gazed into *La Comtesse's* green eyes and asked her how she had such clear skin. We paid her a lot of money and took possession. Or thought that we did—it turned out that we had gotten not only the house and land, but a farmer who tended the vines. Having a built-in farmer seemed like an advantage, especially since the farmer was a *brave type*, a regular guy who asked little of us.

But it was that *brave type* whom we paid for the vineyard the second time. A French agricultural lease is essentially for life. The way out involves money, *bien sûr*. The amount he was asking was surprisingly close to what a Mercedes Benz would cost, but we plunged ahead and asked for a meeting with the farmer and his wife.

We wanted to make our own wine—that was going to be our story. The truth was that we were fed up with the way he tended the vineyard. I thought that if it had been cotton—a crop I knew something about—he would have had to pay it more attention. The crisis came one summer when he allowed an infestation of thistles to become so dense that they had to be dug out with an old-fashioned plow. Instead of a mule to pull it, he had his son drive a tractor with him behind the plow. I felt tugs of sympathy as I watched him going after the stubborn thistles one by one, their pretty purple blossoms winnowing away in the wind.

It didn't help either that at harvest time, the grapes were hauled like piles of Chinese cabbage to the local cooperative and dumped into a very banal brew. There was a point of defensive embarrassment when visiting friends asked if they could taste the wine from our vineyard. Yes, we would say, at one of the bars in town.

So with our story well rehearsed, off we went to our meeting. The discussion was polite, a slow and predictable volley with no spin. As I explained my desire to take over the vineyard, they talked of how much they wanted to continue tending the vines.

In conversations like that there is a "but" that allows you to relax. It isn't a "but" that challenges but that concedes. Giving up the vineyard wasn't their desire, *mais*—the important "but" and the expensive one—for the proper amount of money, they would not stand in the way of my dream.

I relaxed, the worst being over. But it wasn't. Monsieur left the room to look for the papers he just happened to have prepared that indicated how much my dream might cost, so Madame had the floor.

"Mr. Wells," she said, "if my husband had any courage you wouldn't have Chanteduc and I would." She pronounced "*courage*" carefully, so that I wouldn't confuse it with "*couilles*" (balls), but her tone left some room for semantic confusion.

She looked as though she expected a response, but words would indeed have failed. Instead, I looked away and pulled my thoughts back to our vineyard and how we were about to buy it again.

We recruited a new winemaker, and as he got to work the next spring the old farmer and his wife put in a swimming pool. Patricia calls it the best pool we ever paid for.

When the harvesters came that fall to gather "our" first vintage, Patricia rushed into the vineyard to join them. With her secateurs and big black plastic bucket, she spent a back-breaking day clipping off bunches and loading them into plastic boxes that when filled were dumped into a *benne* that had been newly scrubbed out and white-washed with alimentary paint. I joined in for a symbolic thirty minutes. Having grown up in the rural Deep South, where my first work-for-hire was picking cotton for a penny a pound, I didn't share Patricia's romantic notion of agricultural labor. For me the big thrill came a year later, when the first vintage was bottled as Clos Chanteduc, our very own brand.

Fifteen years and several winemakers later, I took possession of the

Patricia returns from her one and only day of harvesting grapes.

vineyard a third time, and the price was only a series of conversations. In the time between that first bottling and those discussions, there had been four winemakers. The first tended the vineyard for a decade and when he retired we were pained to see him go. Then came another winemaker, who bottled three vintages before selling his own property, ostensibly for health reasons. Being a wily peasant he arranged for the purchasers to claim rights on our property as well, without exactly involving us in the details.

Quickly those new owners set out to prove the axiom that the way to make a small fortune in wine is to start with a large one. But their fortune was already small. It soon disappeared and they were forced to sell, too. Within six years our little vineyard was on its third set of vintners, and we had lost our American importer in the process. The importer, the celebrated Kermit Lynch, was once lovingly described to me as "pure," and that was my experience indeed, because he never let our long friendship influence his decisions on our little wine. I save as a souvenir Kermit's fax after tasting the first vintage, the one I had paid the price of a Mercedes to be able to label as Clos Chanteduc.

"Not only will I not import the wine," his fax said, "but I advise you not to let anyone else import it. It will ruin your reputation."

I thought he might have a point—the fruitiness hinted at bubble gum more than at raspberries or cherries, and the spiciness was maybe a shade like Dr Pepper. But somehow the reputation survived that clumsy beginning and, happily, so did the friendship. Eventually, when we had moved on to winemaker number two, Kermit did import Clos Chanteduc for a couple of years, but when he canceled an order for the 2004 vintage, perhaps the *chef d'oeuvre* of winemaker number three, I decided to short-circuit winemaker number four and make the vineyard ours again. Which brings us to those weighty conversations.

We could have taken the classic way out, the one we had learned fifteen years before and coughed up a lot of money. But that didn't appeal. And Patricia and I held two trump cards—our registered brand and her signature on the label. Nothing kept us from stopping the use of both at will.

I made an appointment to meet with the new winemakers, and in the days leading up to the meeting I kept saying to myself: "If you had any courage, Mr. Wells, you'd have Chanteduc and they wouldn't." Again the conversation was civilized. I was talking to two men whom I liked personally and whose résumés suggested ample competence as winemakers. But we hadn't selected them and we had had it with being shuttled around. The deal was done quickly, and the cost this time was only palaver. In other words, cheap at twice the price.

In a separate piece of luck, Eric Solomon of European Cellars agreed to import the wine. We are wildly excited about that associa-

A snowstorm in the vineyard.

tion as well as the new winemaker, Yves Gras of Domaine Santa Duc in Gigondas. When he came up to talk about taking over the vineyard he plunged into it physically, pulling at the vines and explaining what was wrong with the pruning, the cultivation, the trellises.

When our deal was official and Yves went to work, it was with dazzling energy. He put all the vines on trellises for better canopy management. He cultivated deeply between the rows to encourage more roots to sprout, and he pumped iron into the soil because that's what the analysis showed it lacked. No previous winemaker had ever even had the soil analyzed.

He replaced 1,500 vines that had died out, planting Syrah to reinforce the wine's structure. Grenache still dominates, but the varieties have evolved over the years. When the original farmer pulled out a dozen rows of table grapes he replaced them with Cinsault, a pump-up-the-volume variety. It can add silkiness as well as bulk to a Rhône blend, but on our terrain we found Cinsault's fruitiness to be much too forward. Like bubble gum. So the first winemaker we hired ourselves grafted Syrah onto the same rootstock. He also added a few rows of Mourvèdre, but on a parcel that has about twelve inches of soil directly on top of bedrock. With the passage of time the Mourvèdre manages to produce a few bunches, but it will never be a huge influence on what goes into the bottle.

In front of the Clos Chanteduc aging tank,
with the winemaker of the moment.

With Yves' work we're confident of that distinctiveness we aspired to long ago, and think there's a chance even of distinction. "I worry about a lot of things," Yves said to us recently, "but I don't worry about being able to make a better wine here than anyone has made before." Energetic and thorough, Yves has earned altitudinous ratings for the Gigondas from his own Domaine Santa Duc from the wine pope himself, Robert Parker. Parker also included Yves in his book on the greatest wine estates in the world. The Santa Duc–Chanteduc association is a nice one.

Yves Gras is more than twenty years younger than I am. Finding another wine grower is not something I'll likely have to do again—God willing.

Vines are for more than grapes: Walter collects spent vines for firewood.

GRAPE HARVEST CAKE

When we moved to Provence I surely had an overly romanticized view of many things, including the grape harvest. I had visions of young girls in Souleiado print skirts singing as they gathered grapes into neat wicker baskets. The truth is, grape picking is hard on the back and the hands as the scissors continues its repetitive motion, bunch by bunch. The year we made our first wine I couldn't wait to get out there and pick with the rest. I lasted one day and could barely move the next. Now I'd rather cook dinner for the grape pickers! This is a favorite on our table through the seasons. I usually use either 100 percent Syrah grapes or Grenache, the workhorse grape of the Côtes-du-Rhône.

From May to September, I prepare this cake often: In spring, Chanteduc's crop of fresh cherries come into play, while come September I take advantage of whatever clusters of grapes I can find on our vines after harvesting. Note that the cake is prepared with olive oil, producing an unusually light and moist cake.

EQUIPMENT: A 9½-inch springform pan; an electric mixer fitted with a whisk.

> Olive oil and flour for preparing cake pan
> 2 large eggs, at room temperature
> ⅔ cup sugar
> ½ cup extra-virgin olive oil
> ⅓ cup nonfat milk
> ½ teaspoon pure vanilla extract
> 1½ cups unbleached all-purpose flour
> ¾ teaspoon baking powder
> Pinch of sea salt
> Grated zest of 1 lemon, preferably organic
> Grated zest of 1 orange, preferably organic
> 2 pounds small fresh purple grapes
>   (such as Champagne grapes)

1. Preheat the oven to 375°F.
2. Lightly oil and flour a 9½-inch springform pan, tapping out any excess flour.
3. In the bowl of an electric mixer fitted with a whisk, beat the eggs and sugar at high speed until thick and lemon-colored, about 3 minutes. Add the oil, milk, and vanilla, and mix just to blend.
4. Combine the flour, baking powder, and salt into a large bowl. Add the lemon and orange zest and toss to coat the zest with flour. Spoon the flour mixture into the egg mixture and stir to blend. Set aside for 10 minutes, to allow the flour to absorb the liquids. Stir three-fourths of the fruit into the batter. Spoon the batter into the prepared cake pan, smoothing out the top with a spatula.
5. Place the pan in the center of the oven. Bake for 15 minutes. Remove from the oven and scatter the remaining grapes on top of the cake. Bake until the top is a deep golden brown and the cake feels quite firm, about 40 minutes more, for a total baking time of 55 minutes. Remove to a rack to cool. After 10 minutes, run a knife along the side of the pan. Release and remove the side of the springform pan, leaving the cake on the pan base. Serve at room temperature, cutting into thin wedges.

12 servings

PART IV

World Enough

A party during the early days at Rue Daru.

24

{ Right Bank, Left Bank }

PATRICIA:

There was probably no exact moment when we fell out of love with the Right Bank. Like marriages that fall apart, love for a neighborhood also can unravel little by little, often in quiet, subtle ways.

For the first twenty or so years in Paris, we both worked long hours most days, so the thought of changing addresses may have entered our minds, but if it did, so did the realization that neither of us had time for that. But bit by bit, the love eroded. Our elegant 1905 apartment building was sturdy, imposing, and *bourgeois*, and we always felt good as we opened the heavy painted doors that led to the stone and marble-pillared courtyard. The entrance alone made you feel grand and important, even if you were neither.

But 1905 was not 1995. The sprawling apartments were designed for another era, another lifestyle, and not the way we live today. There was too much hallway, too much living room, too little kitchen, too much wasted space. For us also perhaps the worst part was that we didn't own the place. The Wellses—whose favorite pastime it has always been to make a house a home—woke up one morning and thought, "What are we doing here?"

The neighborhood now seemed downright boring. The treasures of the Rue Poncelet outdoor market and the proximity of the elegant Parc Monceau had helped to keep us there, for sure, and we had a fabulous dry cleaner. But we wanted more. The surroundings were stuffy and dull. We felt worn down by the lack of energy. We found ourselves spending weekends on the Left Bank, visiting cafés and envying the street life that we did not enjoy on the other side of the Seine.

About the same time I realized that as much as I loved my work and never lacked the discipline to sit down at the computer to meet the day's deadline, I HATED that spare bedroom, where I had written every word in Paris since January of 1980. In truth, my work had pretty much spilled out into the rest of the apartment, and Walter liked to razz me, saying he had only one question: "Where does the office end and the apartment begin?" I was always AT WORK! But I was plain sick of that room and knew that repainting, redecorating, even changing curtains or furniture would do nothing to encourage me.

Deadlines and my workload were such that I would get up, get dressed (and I really got dressed and made up, as if going to a public office), and sit down to write: restaurant reviews for the *IHT* and *L'Express*, freelance articles for American publications, cookbooks, and updates to the guidebooks. Beginning in 1983, various assistants also shared my space. At one point, as I was finishing up *The Food Lover's Guide to France*, a trio of assistants spilled out into what was mistakenly called the dining room.

About the only time I got out of the apartment was to go to dinner to review a restaurant. I was, in fact, beginning to feel like a fraud. Here I was, Patricia Wells, supposedly an expert on everything Parisian and yet I spent almost every waking moment sitting in one Right Bank room. As commitments and deadlines piled up, I got out less and less and loved being there less and less.

So, as I generally do, I took matters into my own hands and acted. Walter and I knew that we could not afford to buy a place the size of the Daru apartment, a spacious two-bedroom of about 120 square meters—1,300 square feet. The housing market simply did not allow us to purchase something that large.

We decided that we would continue to live at Daru, but find a place for an office of my own. I calculated how much money we had, how much room I would need, and what neighborhood I wanted to be in. As I saw it, I did not want to change husbands, jobs, or cities. Changing neighborhoods seemed liked the most efficient solution to a need for a dramatic transformation.

I clearly remember the day I found my office/cooking school studio on Rue Jacob in the Saint-Germain neighborhood of the 6th arrondissement. It was August of 1995 and I had allowed myself only a few days to look for something. August of course is the worst time to deal in real estate in Paris, but it was the time I had. It was a day of a torrential downpour, and before cell phones.

I stood inside a phone booth on an island on the Boulevard Saint-Germain as the rain pelted the glass. I was calling about an ad for an *atelier d'artiste* (artist's studio), and I had visions of a brilliantly lit, top-floor loft full of charm and good luck. The ad was in the weekly *Du Particulier au Particulier*, a newspaper for selling property directly from owner to buyer without passing through a costly real estate agent.

The owner answered, and to my surprise, arranged to meet me at the apartment within a few hours. What good fortune! It was a Friday afternoon and this would be my last chance to look for months. The second I saw the downtrodden, ill-kept studio, I knew that I was in love. I thrive on restorations and I could already picture this as a private and personal "room of my own." I made the cardinal mistake of blurting out "I am in love!" The owner responded, as one who knew he had a mark, "Then stay in love."

I brought Walter to see the apartment the next day, and talked him into it. I was on my way! We found an architect to draw up plans to clarify the bones of the space—there were flues for four fireplaces within a 48 square meter (520 square foot) area—so that we could begin demolition.

With the help of the architect we put together a fantastic band of artisans: Nino the carpenter, Cosimo the Sicilian mason and his deft crew, and Cosimo's son, Serge, a talented painter. We brought our good friend and plumber Jean-Claude Viviani and his wife, Colette, up from Provence, as well as their son, Marcel, who had just finished training as an electrician. They had helped us through more than a decade of restoration in Provence, so we were certain that this was going to be a piece of cake. Fun, even.

A celebration at Rue Jacob: Jeffrey Garten, Ina Garten, Eli Zabar, Patricia, Walter, Devon Fredericks.

Demolition began in December. As I recall, that winter was one of the coldest on record in Paris, and as I visited each morning to check progress, I found the band of artisans there, unfazed by the filth, the cold, the cramped quarters. At one point the mountain of debris almost filled the small space. Little by little, they peeled away layers of history. Beams were exposed, strata of paint and plaster were chipped off, to reveal rugged stone walls. A brand-new heavy-duty metal and glass ceiling and wall replaced the flimsy structure that had leaked and welcomed all drafts. I combed the Paris flea market and found drawer fronts that once belonged to a grain store, with their handsome painted white metal labels noting the contents of each drawer, from *moutarde fleur* (mustard flowers) to *girofles* (cloves).

Shutters found at the Isle-sur-la-Sorgue flea market in Provence were cleverly adapted as pocket doors for my office, so it could be transformed into a small living room in a matter of seconds. But the *pièce de résistance* was the set of four huge, nine-foot-high doors from an 1890s café in Paris, thick and sturdy *fin de siècle* oak frames set with thick beveled glass. Nino turned them into sliding glass doors to cover the oak drawers and shelves he built to house my ever-expanding collection of French ephemera and kitchen necessities.

And then the hazing began. We sure didn't see it coming. Soon angry and disgruntled neighbors were at the door, pesky letters arrived, phone calls made, visits arranged. Even though we had reinforced the second floor space with steel beams, my five-burner La Cornue stove with gas grill was deemed too heavy and neighbors feared that I would bring the apartment down, and theirs with it. (The building's handyman laughed when he saw that big stove, announcing "What do you need with anything that big?" I serenely inquired as to what make of car he drove. Of course it was a Mercedes-Benz, giving me just cause to announce "I don't have a car in Paris. This is my Mercedes.") The building's designated architect came for a meeting with Cosimo, and was convinced by the mason's explanation that the reconstruction had rendered the apartment solid enough to hold up the stove.

That worked out, but various rules and regulations kept us from some of the changes we needed to make. We couldn't move the electric meter; it was questionable if we could move the fireplace a few centimeters; the gas furnace couldn't be vented in the most practical and economical way; and we had to abandon our carefully worked out system for venting the stove's exhaust because the look *gênait* (bothered) a neighbor. It was our first Paris Welcome Wagon experience, and we were not amused.

In time, life calmed down and the Rue Jacob studio became a little corner of heaven. It is a haven of quiet, and I can stay there for hours writing, testing recipes, conducting cooking classes in the spring and the fall. It is a tranquil space that encourages thought and creativity. A true Room of My Own.

It was the spring of 2001, we were still living at the Rue Daru apartment, and Walter had just celebrated his first *IHT* retirement with a joyous, elegant party in the ornate ballrooms of the French Senate overlooking the Luxembourg Gardens. I was up early that day in April, for I had a class in session at Rue Jacob. It was, in fact, too early for the delivery of the daily *Figaro* or *International Herald Tribune*. So I sat with my coffee at breakfast, poring over the previous day's *Figaro*, heading straight for the real estate pages.

Walter and I love real estate. We both find it the sexiest thing in the world. And owning the place you live in is a necessity for us. How was it that we were still renters, letting the Rue Daru apartment fall apart all around us?

On those pages of *Le Figaro* I circled ads for a half-dozen Left Bank apartments that seemed appealing. It was a lark I knew, but a harmless one. I left Walter a note suggesting that if he had time on his hands that day, to take a look at some of these. When I finished my class around four that afternoon, I picked up phone messages and there was an enthusiastic one from Walter. "Get over here right away, this is it!" I raced to the Rue du Bac address, a fifteen-minute walk away, thinking there was no way we would find the perfect place on the first day!

The ad had read "*comme une petite maison*" (like a little house) but even Positive Patty knew that had to be too good to be true.

Then I opened the giant door that led into the long, narrow, flower-filled courtyard. As I walked through the courtyard, I prayed that OUR apartment would be the one on the ground floor, the one surrounded by a simple yet verdant garden. Then I saw Walter in the apartment, on the phone. Could this really be IT?

Walter and I both have the ability to close our eyes and envision the ugliest of apartment ducklings turned into a swan. Twice now in France we had managed to turn an abused dwelling into one that shouts of true love and immense care. Consider us the rescue crew of housing. If it has good bones, is well located, and the price is right, we know how to turn it around.

The apartment was a perfect dump. The owner had died and no one had lived there for months. It had been decades since anyone had even cleaned up the place. The room arrangement was all askew, and there were no fewer than eight doors in the small, 70 square meter (750 square foot) apartment. Nothing made sense and the charm was hard to see in the jumble of tiny rooms.

But we closed our eyes and dreamed. There was a lovely old oak parquet flooring, laid in the familiar zigzag style, that could be restored. There were two private entrances, a front door and a back door, and in my biggest fantasy of all, I could plant the tiny pocket-size garden as a perfect herb garden.

Beyond the sad walls and welter of doors that turned the place into a worn-out, almost freakishly depressing space, the pinkish-orange walls and garish bathroom fixtures, and the lack of heat (save a makeshift gas heater poking into the living room), we could see this is as a Wells haven, a Wells heaven. But, above all, the light poured in: The windows in the living room, kitchen, and bedroom looked out on ivy-covered walls. Yes, we were on the ground floor, but we quickly saw that if there was a ray of light it would find its way into our little Left Bank cottage.

Once again, we were buying directly from the owner, without the benefit or fee of a real estate broker. We later learned that the lawyer who met us at the door was working for the stepdaughter of the recently deceased owner, and the young woman already had a place of her own in Montmartre. We'll never understand why, but after we agreed on a price and hand-drafted a simple statement that we intended to acquire the apartment, the lawyer handed us the keys and suggested we begin to plan our future.

Even before we closed we got on the phone to line up the same artisans who had restored my Rue Jacob atelier. Our first call was to Nino, the carpenter. Patches of the parquet floor had buckled and curled, and we wanted him to replace them as well as cover the floor to protect it as all the walls were ripped out and new ones put up.

At the same time, we rid ourselves of the burden of rent at Rue Daru. We sold most of the furniture, gave most of our books to the American Library, and shipped what was left to Provence, where we'd be spending most of our time until the apartment was finished. In Paris, we moved, grad-school style, into the tiny Jacob studio with its snug pull-out couch and foot-wide closet. It was only going to be for six months or so, we told ourselves.

The first rude awakening came soon after all the fantasies were in place. One night while we were having dinner at the Jacob studio, Nino rang. "I think you had better get over here," he said. "We have some surprises. There is no foundation under the floor." We had hardly put down the phone when another call came, this from a new neighbor at Bac, a distinguished retired professor of medicine.

"What on earth are you doing! Debris just fell from your apartment into my wine cellar, breaking several bottles of precious Bordeaux!" he announced with some alarm.

We apologized, and raced over to the job site to see what had happened. As it turned out, when the floors were laid sometime in the nineteenth century, the oak boards were pressed directly into hot tar poured onto compacted earth. Underneath it all are the building's foundations (solid) and the vaulted cellar, but the floor is on the ground. The hot tar technique, current at the time, sealed out moisture and allowed the wood to have some give, to rest securely in place, and to, well, last forever!

It was hard to imagine, but as we entered the apartment, the tar, then more than a century old, smelled as though it had just been poured. It glistened with freshness in the spots where Nino had pulled up the herringbone parquet. The wood was more deteriorated than we could have seen, but now that we knew there was nothing but dirt underneath we had to start over on our plans.

We also had to find some good bottles for the professor.

Full of confidence because the Jacob renovation had turned out so well, we expanded the project to include new marble floors, with the heating installed underneath. To our naïve surprise, the renovation took much longer than we had anticipated. Jean-Claude and Colette Viviani returned for the plumbing and heating, and Marcel returned too for the wiring. They moved into the Jacob studio and we went to Provence. They were the only part of the renovation that offered no surprise, no tension, no angst.

Not that the project offered any greater complications than that first discovery of what was under the floor. But we quickly learned the greatest disadvantage of living on the ground floor. Every single neighbor—always curious, always suspicious, and often querulous— could pass many times a day and comment on the work in progress.

One of the great bonds Walter and I have is that we are both nesters. In New York, even before we lived together, we spent weekends painting his kitchen or wallpapering my bathroom. We love to fix, to enhance, to put our mark on the place we're living in.

So when Vivi—as faithful a friend as exists—reported back to us on what the neighbors were saying as they came by to judge, we were dismayed and confused. What we considered a serious demonstration of our appreciation for the *patrimoine de la France* our neighbors dismissed as American overkill. What we considered enhancements to a beautiful neighborhood they viewed as wretched excess. "*Pourquoi ils font tout ça?*" sniped one neighbor. "Why are they doing all that?" as if

Patricia in the Rue du Bac kitchen, still under construction.

we should have moved into a dump and left it that way. Another verbally assaulted Walter—who was overseeing the work daily when we returned to Paris—over one detail or another every time he walked into the courtyard.

To be sure, there were friendly and considerate acts, too—several neighbors encouraged us in our rebuilding as we *peaufiné* (fine-tuned) and embellished the apartment, and sent bottles of wine to welcome us when we moved in. And so we got through it all, if not quite understanding the spirit of *mesquinerie* (petty meanness) that we had encountered.

As we moved in, we could not imagine being happier anywhere else in the world. To this day, when I am within a block or two of the apartment, I pick up my pace to hurry to the front door, punch the code, and enter the courtyard to look into our little cottage in the capital. We had turned a sad and run-down spot into a little jewel.

WALTER:

The Jacob renovation was Patricia's project. My *Tribune* job filled as many hours of the day as I allowed, and at that point I was willing to let it fill a lot. I spent Saturdays going with her to suppliers to obsess over faucets, I encouraged her to buy the big stove when her determination wavered, and I wrote checks and arranged loans. But I kept myself away from the battles with builders and neighbors.

The Rue du Bac job was all mine. It filled most of the eighteen-month interlude of my first retirement from the paper. We used Nino from the old crew, and Cosimo built the tiny fireplace in the kitchen. But the rest of the workmen were new. I worked with them in designing the new layout and determining the interior details. When Nino wasn't able to deliver all the woodwork, I found new carpenters who could. As the crew gutted the place and started putting up the new walls, I visited every day to monitor the work—and to hear the complaints of the neighbors.

It was a long project and I sympathized with them because of the noise. As the construction went on and on—it took us a year from closing to finish the work and move in, and all of that for only 750 square feet—I sent earphones and a CD of Eric Satie's music to a neighbor who was housebound with a broken ankle. I sent flowers to others, and when it was over I sent a rosebush to the neighbor who had momentarily dropped his considerable charm because of damage to the plants outside the kitchen door.

It wasn't a very smooth start, but in time, we came to feel at home, not just in our little apartment but in the building. What followed, of course, was full exposure to the life of the "*co-propriété*," and the realization that everyone gets hammered. Newcomers get hammered the most because they want to make changes and they have to be taught who's in charge. It's like a schoolyard, or a chicken coop—new arrivals have to be brought into line, to be pecked into order.

Having endured the process ourselves, we now joined in the stern warnings to later newcomers and entered the fights over plantings in the courtyard and improvements to the building. I didn't pretend that our counsel was sought, but our vote was solicited. We had not just moved in, we had arrived.

Rue du Bac Grilled Mackerel

Sometimes my enthusiasms carry me away, and others with me. We had just moved into our almost completed apartment on Rue du Bac. I had just spent the summer in Provence, where fresh mackerel grilled over vine clippings in our outdoor fireplaces was regularly on the menu. What a great recipe to inaugurate the grill on our shiny new Ilve stove. I fired it up, grilled the mackerel, and the ground-floor apartment instantly filled with a thick and fragrant fog of smoke. As anyone knows the aroma of grilled mackerel is not delicate. The next day, our upstairs neighbor reported that his wife, choking from the smoke, cried out to him "Where are we, in Africa?" From then on, I've limited our mackerel grilling to Provence.

EQUIPMENT: Scissors.

> 6 very fresh mackerel (each about 10 ounces)
> Several tablespoons of flavored mustard (either coarse-grain or Dijon mustard flavored with peppers, spices, herbs, or lemon)
> Fine sea salt
> Freshly ground black pepper
> Oil for the grill rack

1. Clean the mackerel: Rinse gently under cold running water, gently rubbing off the scales. Gently twist off the head, pulling the guts with it. Discard the head and guts. With scissors, gently cut the fish open from the back side, head to tail, pressing the mackerel open like a book. With your fingertips, gently pull the central bone head to tail, being careful not to tear the flesh. With the scissors, gently detach the bone from the flesh, leaving the tail intact. Discard the bone. Open the fish flat but do not cut it into fillets. Repeat for the remaining fish.
2. Place the fish, skin side down, on a platter, keeping them open. Slather the flesh with mustard. Season with salt and pepper. Cover securely with plastic wrap and refrigerate for 2 to 4 hours.

3. Heat a grill and spread the coals out when they are red and dusted with ash.

4. Lightly oil the grill rack and place it about 3 inches above the coals, allowing it to preheat for a few minutes. Place the mackerel on the grill rack, skin side down. Grill just until the fish turn white around the edges and remain a delicate pink in the center, 5 to 7 minutes. Grill on one side only; do not turn. With a spatula, carefully transfer the mackerel, still skin side down, to a platter. Season generously with salt and pepper. Serve immediately.

6 servings

VARIATION: A nice variation on this mustard-grilled version of my invention is to season the fish with just a touch of olive oil, lemon juice, salt, pepper, and oregano. For some reason the earthy flavor of oregano marries just right with mackerel.

25

{ Fame but Not Fortune }

PATRICIA:

It was 1995, and I had been freelancing and writing books for fifteen years. I had more work than I could ever desire, but the bank account was still slim. Walter and I did not complain—we had a comfortable life. But I was reaching a point where I wanted a little bit more free time, a little bit more insurance, or maybe assurance, that all would be well in the future and not just right now.

Part of the problem was that the freelance life had changed. In the early days I would call an editor with an idea and the quick, simple response was "three hundred dollars and it's due October 1." They trusted my instincts and the fact that I would give them a fine, publishable story.

Then something changed. I would suggest a story, it would be accepted, and by the time I turned the story in, the editor had changed and the new one no longer wanted the story or wanted major reworking. Later, editors began managing the stories in such a way that I was not reporting the story but writing to someone else's script.

The cookbooks clicked along at a steady pace and sold well

enough, but as I always said, they still did not pay the rent. I needed another gig.

Then one evening, after a dinner party in which the questions included "Patricia, tell us about sea salt!" "Patricia, tell us about olive oil." "Patricia, tell us about Châteauneuf-du-Pape!" I began to think, hmm, maybe I could make some money dispensing all the information I had digested over the past many years.

So we began, in a very small way, our cooking school. We called it "At Home with Patricia Wells" and settled on two one-week dates in the fall of 1995. We sent out press releases to various publications and filled the first two classes rather quickly. We didn't know if we would like doing classes and we didn't know if there was a clientele out there for our fledgling business.

Slowly but surely students enrolled. A couple from Houston came up to me after a demonstration in Aspen, Colorado, and handed me a check. Another couple from Palo Alto faxed and said they wanted to come, but only if I took total amateurs (I did and still do). We tried to

Patricia with students in Provence.

limit the class to eight students, but sometimes the count went higher as students begged to bring along a sister, a parent, a good friend.

I always felt that our little hilltop paradise was too wonderful to keep for ourselves, and the school seemed to be a fine way to share our blessings and also pay the rent.

When chef Joël Robuchon heard we were doing classes, he said in his giggly childlike way, "Can I come and teach a class?" I nearly fainted! The world's top chef wanted to come teach in my kitchen!

We agreed that he would teach the final Friday lunch class. In his typical, ultra-organized manner, Joël sent his assistant and his pastry chef down in a refrigerated panel truck the night before, with all the ingredients, most of them already prepped. Joël came down on the high-speed TGV, hauling even more goodies.

I pinched myself as I watched him demonstrate searing foie gras, trussing a chicken for the wood-fired oven, wrapping the incomparable langoustines in phyllo-like dough for deep frying. Philippe his pastry chef made elegant strawberry tarts as well as butter-rich miniature madeleines—delicate scallop-shaped teacakes—which he forgot in my La Cornue oven and burned to charcoal. I still have one blackened, burnt-out madeleine, as a reminder that even top chefs can make mistakes.

During the entire summer of that year before the first class, I traveled throughout Provence, visiting village markets, shops, restaurants, and artisans we might want to include as part of our cooking school program. That year houseguests were put into action as drivers and companions on my travels. We visited beekeepers and a multitude of olive oil mills, goat cheese makers, and *tables d'hôte* in search of the perfect Provençal experience. Menus were written and rewritten. Not only did I want each recipe to teach a method or make a point, but everything needed to be done within a certain time framework, and I needed to make sure that there was enough oven space to accommodate the meal. The juggling was fun, if not a bit hair-raising, and it taught me a lot about organization as well as how to showcase local ingredients. What we ended up with that first fall became a template we have followed—with some variations—ever since.

In the end, I didn't want to teach only cooking techniques and recipes. I wanted students to share our life, meet the artisans and farmers who made us love Provence and who, in the end, kept us in France. I wanted them to share the excitement of creating meals together, the joys around the table, the rhythm of our days. I also wanted them to come away with a better understanding of menu creation, of cooking with the seasons, the pleasures of plucking fresh basil, picking multiple greens for an ultra-fresh salad, to know what a just-harvested eggplant tastes like, and what it takes to put grapes in a bottle.

Our local butcher, the charismatic/charming/delightful Roland Henny, happily took us into his shop and taught us how to cut up a chicken, tie a roast, make local sausages. Cheese merchants Josiane and Christian Déal arrived as dinner guests bringing with them a selection of local goat cheeses at various stages of development. We visited the local Vaison market, as well as the more upscale one in Saint Rémy. Local bistros, top winemakers in Châteauneuf-du-Pape, artisan potters all received regular visits.

The weeks were—and still are—delicate balancing acts. I am to this day still amazed at the sheer volume of food it takes to create regular meals—sometimes two a day—for a dozen or more people. Students spend most of the day with us, but stay at small nearby bed-and-breakfast establishments or small hotels.

During the first years of the classes Walter was still tied to the office in Paris, but made it a point to appear at the first meal, Sunday night's introductory dinner, or the final lunch on Friday. Once he retired, he became an invaluable collaborator, doing the bulk of the shopping, keeping us well-stocked in staples and mineral water. He is also there for the daily disasters that happen in any old country house: clogged drains, too much water or none at all, lack of electricity, a busted water heater, excessive winds that toss giant umbrellas into the vineyard, students who need a trip to the emergency room.

In time, we added specialty weeks—truffles, wine, fitness, and fish—as much to push myself to know more about these subjects as to share them with students. Over the years, we did have a few trying weeks. Only once did I lose total control. It was a cranky group with a couple of truly miserable souls who spread their unhappiness like a fast-moving plague. By Wednesday of that week I began to wonder if I could continue the school. Thank goodness, it happened only once. I also found out that if there was a troublemaker every now and then, the rest of the group—happy in their own right—would snuff out any notes of misery.

Patricia is admitted into the olive oil society in Nyons.

By 1998 it seemed a good idea to begin teaching classes in Paris. My Rue Jacob office was designed with a kitchen that could take up to seven students. I fashioned our first Paris week in 1999 a bit differently from those in Provence, offering just daytime classes with a day of touring. Market visits—to either Rue Poncelet or the Wednesday farmers' market on the Avenue President Wilson—play a role, as do wine tastings conducted by wine expert and friend Juan Sanchez. We taste specialty oils, delve into France's fabulous world of cheese, and spend a morning in the famed Poilâne bakery, watching expert bakers turn out incomparable sourdough loaves. And of course, we visit grand restaurants—like Pré Catelan and Pierre Gagnaire—where very French lunches go on into the late afternoon.

An award from the French: the French Spirit Award.
Patricia with friends Johanne Killeen, George Germon, and Randy Henson.

From the beginning the response to the school has been positive, most of all from me.

There is a saying that to teach is to learn twice. I might make that three times. My life has been enriched by our school in ways I could have never imagined. Many former students are counted among our dearest friends. And without it we would never have developed the close relationship we have with local restaurateurs, winemakers, merchants, and artisans. Best of all, I can take turns paying the rent!

WALTER:

Patricia's dinner party realization followed not by long her return from a book tour that she had extended by several weeks by teaching classes in New York, in Boston, in Seattle, in St. Louis. I began pointing out to her that if she organized the classes herself in Provence, there would be less travel and more revenue.

An honorary degree from Patricia's alma mater,
the University of Wisconsin-Milwaukee.

Again Patricia's response was: "I'll never do my own classes." But she had designed a kitchen at Chanteduc that could handle a group of students and is now as enthusiastic about doing the classes as she was once determined not to.

My role in the school is to be present and to be the host. It's also to keep the knives sharp and the water flowing, both into the sinks and out again. And occasionally I step in as only a spouse can to shore up leaky emotions. That doesn't happen often, because Patricia is amazingly even tempered. But once in a while she too can lose it.

She has tried doing the classes with an assistant and without, and for her without is better. "Two different cooks give two different sets of ideas," she says. There is adequate help with keeping the pots and pans shiny, but Patricia is the only person on stage when class is in session.

Our guiding principal in life and for the classes is simple generosity. Food and everything associated with it, especially the quality of ingredients, should be marked by generosity. We also pour good wines with our meals. All of which is to say that we still aren't rich but we're far from the poor kids we started out as, living paycheck to paycheck.

CEVICHE

When we dine alone, when we entertain, and in our cooking classes, we eat a lot of fish. This is a fairly recent family favorite, and demands ultra-fresh fish. Ceviche is one of those miracle dishes: You can actually watch as the citrus juice turns the codfish from a translucent pink to an opaque white. The acid from the citrus changes the structure of the fish proteins, essentially "cooking" the fish without any heat. Besides fresh codfish, one could use raw shrimp, red snapper, halibut, sea bass, flounder, grouper, salmon, or scallops.

EQUIPMENT: A pair of tweezers; a fine-mesh sieve; 8 chilled salad plates.

> 1 pound ultra-fresh white fish fillets, skinned and cut into
> ½-inch cubes
> ½ cup freshly squeezed lime or lemon juice
> Grated zest of the citrus
> 1 teaspoon fine sea salt
> 1 teaspoon dried oregano
> 20 cherry tomatoes, halved
> 2 tablespoons minced canned sliced jalapeño peppers
> 3 spring onions or 6 scallions, white and green parts, cut
> into thin rings
> 1 ripe avocado, halved, peeled, and cubed
> 1 tablespoon canola oil or extra-virgin olive oil
> ½ cup fresh cilantro leaves, coarsely chopped

1. In a glass or ceramic bowl, combine the fish, citrus juice, zest, salt, oregano, tomatoes, jalapeños, and onions. Toss to blend. Cover securely with plastic wrap. Refrigerate for 10 minutes.
2. Remove the fish from the refrigerator and pour into a fine-mesh sieve, discarding the marinade. Return the fish to the bowl, add the avocado, oil, and cilantro, and toss to blend. Taste for seasoning. Use a slotted spoon to transfer to individual chilled plates. Serve immediately.

8 appetizer servings

VARIATIONS: Serve with a soft tortilla pinwheel wrap filled with guacamole. As another variation, add chopped celery, black olives, celery salt, and capers.

Josiane Déal, our cheese merchant.

26

{ Clients Fidèles }

WALTER:

"Anything special today?" Patricia asked Josiane Déal, our cheesemonger, after the obligatory three kisses on alternate cheeks.

"*Oui*," said Josiane, giggling, her finger in the air and suspense dripping from it. "Something really exceptional." Reaching under the counter, she pulled out a small flat cheese about five inches in diameter and not quite an inch thick. "I only got four of these and I saved one for you." On top of the crust of ash was the design of the Cross of Toulouse, rich in pointy serifs. "*This* is exceptional," said Josiane. "It's called *Cathare*, and it's a goat cheese from the Languedoc. It's supposedly made in the same way it was during the crusade that crushed the Albigensians."

That explained the cross, but not the finesse of the cheese, which spoke of bourgeois comfort rather than of fanatic intolerance.

It also spoke of devotion to a cause, and not a thirteenth-century one. Josiane Déal is officially recognized as one of France's *meilleurs ouvriers*, or outstanding trades people in France's proud culinary tradition. She was awarded the honor personally by President Chirac in

2004 and remains the only woman in our region of Provence to have received the flashy blue-white-red sash. She earned the distinction in a series of tough competitions after prodigious study of cheeses, their history, how they are made, how to age and store them, and what wines to serve them with. In the final test she had to put together a display of cheese that was judged for its aesthetic appeal as well as for her knowledge. Her study concentrated on France's celebrated 350 or so cheeses, but didn't ignore a few of the great ones from elsewhere, like Cheddar, Stilton, and Parmigiano-Reggiano. As a joke, we once gave Josiane a can of Cheese Whiz, but as amused as she was by finding cheese in a spray can (a *bombe*, as such things are known here) she wasn't sold on the texture or the taste.

We got the rare *Cathare* because we are regulars at the shop that Josiane and her husband Christian operate in Vaison—*clients fidèles*. If we consume cheese in Provence, we buy it from the Déals. Because we're loyal, they're accommodating and look out for us, even special-ordering hard-to-find *burrata* from Italy. For a shopkeeper, to be friendly and accommodating is to be *"commerçant,"* a quality that helps keep patrons coming back. We keep coming back to the Déals and the other traditional shopkeepers in Vaison's *centre ville* primarily because they are loyal to us but also because the center of the village, like most villages in France, is under threat from big discount centers on the edge of town. We like the town as a town, and not just a collection of boutiques that change year by year, though I admit that as parking gets crowded out in the village, the supermarkets hold appeal, with their hectares of parking lots.

But no supermarket meat counter would provide the same service and personal attention that we enjoy at our butcher's shop in Vaison. Shopping there with Patricia, Maria Guarnaschelli, a friend from New York, noted that whatever the order—a leg of lamb one day, an entire filet for *boeuf à la ficelle* the next—the butcher dismissed the cuts lying in his display case, went into his locker and pulled out a side of lamb or beef and began carving away.

"You originated the Dean & DeLuca lifestyle," she said.

It turned out to be better than that, because the butcher had one of his young employees deliver the order to Patricia's car, parked far away.

The champion of the quick reach back to the locker is Eliane Béranger, at the Poissonnerie des Voconces, and her attention to us loyalists has yielded many delicious rewards. Rare skate cheeks, for instance, and tiny cuttlefish so tender that they cook in an instant. She has also called to check on an order that she thought we may have forgotten to place, or one we did forget to pick up, thereby saving a meal with Patricia's students.

Being a *client fidèle* is more than a bond of commerce—it has evolved into a bond of friendship. We're guests in each other's homes and make outings together. Friendship means that shopping can take a while because each purchase is a personal encounter. In the early days of our life in Vaison the context was not yet friendship, nor was personal encounter always what you had in mind when you dashed

Patricia with Monsieur Henny, our butcher in the early days in Vaison.

down to pick up a liter of milk. But living our way into the village, as we now have, has made those attachments important.

And very convenient at times, too. A greengrocer—since retired—once lent Patricia a hundred francs because she had left her wallet at home. Josiane Déal takes in the deliveries from DHL and Federal Express when we're absent or the drivers can't find us. A call to the druggist when we're on the road can get a missing prescription delivered in the mail a day or two later. And one of our butcher friends in Vaison actually closed his shop one day to hunt the wild boars that were pillaging our garden.

In Paris, the city pace means less time for the same degree of personal contacts. But they exist there, too. When our Right Bank neighborhood began losing our favor, we used to say that we couldn't move away from Monsieur and Madame Lascar, our friendly and attentive dry cleaners. When eventually we did, the Lascars stored most of our winter clothes for free through the year-long reconstruction of our new apartment. On the Left Bank a week isn't complete without a brief chat with Madame Servouze at her linen shop on the Rue du Bac with the wonderful name of *Le Sommeil d'Orphée* (the sleep of Orpheus). She supplies all the aprons for Patricia's cooking classes, and she has been a fixture in the neighborhood for decades—a neighborhood that now churns all the time with new shops.

Nearby is the Café Varenne, and for a long time I thought that the highest honor I could have in life was to have my name on the wall over my regular table. That plus the staff's good-natured banter make me a committed regular.

Patricia reserves a particular form of loyalty for the Poîlane bakery on the Rue du Cherche-Midi. Patricia loves great bread—one restaurateur referred to her first *Food Lover's Guide to Paris* as "the bad bread book," so often did she take shops and restaurants to task for serving baguettes with the density, texture, and taste of Styrofoam. Good bread is not hard to find. But bad bread is a lot more prevalent.

Her fidelity was adequately rewarded in one trip to Poîlane when she came home with some of the starter for Poîlane's famous sour-dough bread. The shop is so well known and the bread such a cult object that there is a Federal Express office upstairs to handle daily shipments all over the world. One American was so loyal, in fact, that in his will he left each of his children a loaf of Poîlane bread each week for the rest of their lives, to be shipped by FedEx wherever they were in the world.

The starter was a significant score ("Don't tell Marie," said the baker who gave it to her) though she routinely buys flour at the bak-ery to make her own bread. Even cooked in our wood-fired oven in Provence, of course, the bread she made with the starter was not identical to the yeasty loaves from Poîlane. But it was delicious, and it was Patricia's own.

The bakery is run now by Lionel Poîlane's daughter Apollonia, a recent Harvard graduate. Her parents were killed in 2002 when their helicopter crashed en route to their private island on the Brittany coast. Apollonia was only eighteen at the time, and had begun work-ing in the bakery to learn the business, and when they were killed she took on the responsibility for the multimillion-euro business as well as going on to Harvard, as her father had wanted.

In the city not just shops change but staffs also, and it's destabilizing when a favorite shop turns into a French version of Crazy Eddie. As on one recent day at Augé, the famously good Right Bank wine shop near Place St.-Augustin. Passed on from one dismissive clerk to the next—on the basis of our accent, I was sure—we left the shop with no wine but an experience that changed a habit of two decades.

Visits to another famous wine merchant were another experience entirely. When we arrived in Paris perhaps its most famous *caviste* was Jean-Baptiste Besse, whose shop on the Rue de la Montagne Ste.-Geneviève in the 5th arrondissement was the destination of many wine lovers' pilgrimages.

The fame of the shop and the mystique that we attached to wine then suggested for us some sort of inner sanctum, but that's not what it was. The shop was laden with the treasures of the best wine producers, but it was an unprepossessing tumbledown jumble.

Monsieur Besse was already in his eighties when we moved to Paris, so we never had time (or good enough French, for that matter) to develop a friendship with him. But we went to the shop often, usually looking for a single bottle for dinner that night. "So it's a Côtes-du-Rhône that you want—well, do you want a good one?" he would ask.

Then like an alpinist but without ropes and pitons he would climb up a wall of bottles, inadvertently pulling some out of the racks and letting them break on the floor. He would reach his objective and climb back down clutching a dusty bottle.

"For this to be good, you should wait four years or even five," he would say. With embarrassment, we would explain that we planned to drink it with that night's roast or daube. "*C'est dommage*," he would say, "but it will be good anyway."

Both Augé and Monsieur Besse have been replaced in our affections by Juan Sanchez, an American who has operated a wine shop called La Dernière Goutte on a little street behind the St. Germain church for a decade or more. Juan not only looks out for our wine needs, he delivers and racks the bottles in our tiny cellar. And he lets us keep spare house keys in his shop and leave messages for friends passing through.

Living away from family and, for a time, apart from familiarity as well, the lesson for us has been that community is where you make it, and loyalty is the vital ingredient.

∽⌀∾

Corsican Ricotta Cheesecake

Our cheese merchant Josiane Déal always remembers to put aside the real fresh Corsican cheese, *brocciu frais*, made from raw sheep's milk. The Corsicans use it to make their traditional cheesecake, known as *fiadone*. Flecked with just a touch of lemon, and full of that lovely lactic tang from the cheese, this is many times lighter than a traditional American cheesecake. It can be served any time of year, accompanied by a favorite sorbet and fresh fruit.

EQUIPMENT: A 9½-inch springform pan; a heavy-duty electric mixer with 2 bowls, fitted with a whisk; a large rubber spatula.

> 1 teaspoon almond oil or vegetable oil for preparing the pan
> 1 pound whole-milk ricotta cheese, drained of any excess liquid
> 5 large eggs, separated
> 1 tablespoon whole-wheat flour
> ¾ cup raw sugar
> Grated zest of 2 lemons, preferably organic
> Fresh fruit and sorbet for serving

1. Preheat the oven to 350°F.
2. Brush the springform pan with the oil. Set aside.
3. In the bowl of a heavy-duty mixer fitted with a whisk, combine the ricotta cheese and egg yolks and whisk to blend. Add the flour, ½ cup of the sugar, and the lemon zest, and whisk to blend. Set aside.
4. Rinse and dry the whisk. Place the egg whites in the second mixer bowl. Whisk at low speed until the whites are frothy. Gradually increase the speed to high. Slowly add 2 tablespoons of the sugar, whisking at high speed until stiff but not dry.
5. Whisk a third of the egg white mixture into the cheese mixture and stir until thoroughly blended. (This will lighten the cheese mixture and make it easier to fold in the remaining egg white mixture.) With a large rubber spatula, gently fold in the remaining

egg white mixture. Do this slowly and patiently. Do not overmix, but be sure that the mixture is well blended and that no streaks of white remain.

6. Spoon the mixture into the prepared pan. Place in the center of the oven and bake until firm and golden, about 45 minutes.

7. Remove from the oven and transfer to a rack to cool. After 10 minutes, run a knife along the side of the pan. Release and remove the side of the springform pan, leaving the cake on the pan base. Sprinkle with the remaining 2 tablespoons of sugar. Serve at room temperature, cut into thin wedges. The cake should be served the day it is baked. Serve with fresh fruit and a favorite seasonal sorbet.

12 servings

At the Vaison Tuesday market, with our favorite vegetable vendor.

27

{ Life Lessons from Julia and Joël }

PATRICIA:

Besides family, there are two people who have most influenced my life: Julia Child and Joël Robuchon. Although the connections with each were ostensibly initiated by a common passion for food, the greatest ties were really about sharing lessons on how to live a life.

By the time I met Julia and Joël in the 1980s, both were well on their way to becoming icons. They had many traits in common, and both remained simple, humane, approachable, and full of what is really most important in life: character.

One of the most amazing of Julia's traits was her total straightforwardness. Once, as I bemoaned a friend's passing, she replied, in her distinctive voice, "But he had a good, long life!" No time for mourning. Move on!

It was totally characteristic that my first encounter with this *grande dame* was a fan letter she wrote me in 1984 upon publication of *The Food Lover's Guide to Paris*.

We met face to face that same year, in Paris, and even before then she had become a major influence. She was a no-frills gal who thought and said exactly what was on her mind. When we cooked together, she would peel apples deftly with a knife (faster than a trio of us could peel with a vegetable peeler) and expertly open oysters, not with a fancy oyster knife but a "church key" or old-fashioned beer can opener.

I make sourdough bread regularly and for years held on to a stubborn insistence that it had to be kneaded laboriously by hand, never by machine. That was until the day that Julia—who was then a guest at our home in Provence—came down for breakfast and found me hand-kneading a golden, wholesome dough.

"Get modern, Patricia!" she scolded, tossing her head side to side in bewilderment. I was forty-six at the time. She had recently turned eighty.

But the greatest lesson she taught me by her own example was of married love. Of patience, admiration, unflinching fidelity, and total companionship. Tammy Wynette had nothing over Julia when it came to standing by her man.

In 1985 she and her husband Paul were sitting next to me at the inaugural meeting of The American Institute of Wine and Food in Santa Barbara. The speaker was giving a lecture on the subject of peppers.

Paul, as a result of a stroke some years earlier, often spent much of his time in a quiet daze. He was not always alert and had difficulty fitting into the conversation. But Julia NEVER treated him as though he was not 100 percent there.

As the lecturer spoke, he turned to Julia and whispered: "Julie, what's a pepper?"

Without missing a beat she replied with a detailed explanation of what the vegetable looked like, how one found them in all colors of the rainbow, and how she used peppers in their own everyday cooking. There was no reproach for such a simple question. No impatience or embarrassment. As much as any other human being, Paul deserved a straight response to a straight question.

But Julia didn't baby Paul either. It was 1986 and the two were

Julia and Paul Child at Patricia's 40th birthday party in 1986.

leaving my fortieth-birthday celebration in Provence. They wanted a snapshot of Walter and me standing on the terrace overlooking the vineyard. Paul was the professional photographer of the pair, and as Julia began clicking away, he began to suggest how she should pose us, where the light should fall, where she should stand, and so on.

As only someone who had been happily married for decades could announce to a spouse: "Now Paul, we will do it two ways. My way. And then your way." And so they did.

Julia also taught me to never stop learning, never stop asking questions, never lose that naïve curiosity or youthful enthusiasm for life. When a reader would write that he or she was having trouble with a recipe in one of her books, she wouldn't just ignore it or demand the reader return to the kitchen and try again. No, she would go into her own kitchen, retest the recipe—and she sometimes found that, yes, it needed a bit of alteration.

Julia was human, and loved a good gossip fest. She loved to pull up a chair in front of the fire, a glass of red wine in her hand, and dish out bits of ire about those she didn't like.

But what she loved most was to cook! Whenever she visited us we seemed to have a house full of guests and she picked up an apron and a knife and went to work.

Once when we were lunching at Le Bernardin in New York, a table of half a dozen professional women, we began playing the game of What Would You Do If You Had All the Money in the World? Julia, along with the rest of us, agreed that she would have a hairdresser come to her house each and every morning, so that she could always go out perfectly coiffed.

And yet she liked to say: "As long as I have a good pair of shoes and a car that works, it's enough for me."

Julia was never one to give false praise. Chefs always came around and wanted to know how she liked the food, hoping for praise and encouragement. Unless she felt genuine enthusiasm she would withhold praise, choosing a simple, perfectly noncommittal response: "We had a lovely time," she would reply with a smile.

Once Julia and our friend Susy Davidson left a live *Good Morning America* show, had a quick lunch with the editors at *Food & Wine*, hopped the overnight New York–Paris flight, then immediately boarded the TGV for a three-hour train ride to Provence, a lengthy trip that would exhaust even a young and intrepid traveler. As Julia looked out the window of the train, watching the porter-less travelers struggling with their bags, she mused to Susy, "I wonder what old people do?" She was well close to eighty at the time!

In June of 1992 we were panelists at a Young Presidents' Organization convention in Cannes, on the French Riviera. The morning after the first evening's banquet Julia phoned my hotel room and bemoaned, "This is too much like a Shriner's convention. Boring! Tonight let's get out of here and go to a good restaurant."

That evening we had a magical fish dinner at Restaurant du Bacon in Cap d'Antibes, a place I loved and where I was well known. Julia loved all the attention that was showered on us, and begged to go again the next night "to a place where they know you."

The girls cook: Susy Davidson, Paula Lambert, Patricia, and Julia in 1992.

The following night we dined at Tétou, the glittery fish restaurant on the beach in Golfe-Juan near Antibes, a family place that has been there since 1920. Bouillabaisse is the specialty of this pristine blue and white restaurant, where female servers adorned with multiple bangles of gold on their arms have become the trademark. As a lean blonde waitress brought a platter of fish to the table and deftly began filleting the Mediterranean rockfish—more carefully and expertly than even a surgeon—Julia's interest was intense, as though she was seeing something for the first time.

Julia's eyes were set on the operation. When we praised the woman's expertise, the waitress replied matter-of-factly, in French, "I do it every night, and the bones are always in the same place."

It was on that trip, as we were coming up in the elevator of the Carlton Hotel, that Julia stared dubiously at my hair, which, once blond, had now turned a mousy brown, with curly streaks of annoying gray.

Julia looked me straight in the eye and said simply, "People say that women look younger when they don't dye their hair." Then she pronounced, in her booming voice, "Well, they are simply wrong!"

I got the message loud and clear. On my first morning back in Paris I called to make an appointment at Carita, then one of the most famous salons in town. I have never looked back.

When Julia lived near Grasse in the south of France during the 1960s, she outfitted her kitchen with a La Cornue stove, a shiny white Art Deco–style model. In 1992 she stayed with us at Thanksgiving, on her way to close down the Provence house for good. I asked if I could buy her stove. (For me, it would be like an analyst having Freud's couch.) She said no. But the next morning she came down to breakfast and said she'd changed her mind. I could have the stove if I replaced it with a new one.

Shortly afterward, we created a cool summer kitchen in Provence, adding a stone floor, a marble sink, and Julia's stove, a cantankerous butane gas model with an oven that seemed to have only one temperature, 450°F, no matter how you set it.

Now, in the summer months, I have a special ritual: I strike a match to light the oven in Julia's stove first thing each morning, then head for the vegetable garden to gather whatever is ripe that day. I prepare rustic tomato sauce and eggplant towers, stuffed squash blossoms, and roasted pumpkin, and arrange the dishes on the sturdy oven racks. I head for the gym on the property, and by the time my workout is over, lunch has been made!

Just weeks before her death, I e-mailed Julia to thank her once more and deliver news of her trusty La Cornue. As usual, she e-mailed back within seconds, saying she only wished that she could be with us and cook once more on that stove.

For years, I had saved mementos of her trips: pictures, letters, faxes, e-mails she sent over the years, family menus that we all signed, songs that students have written after cooking in Julia's space. For no special reason at all, on the morning of August 13, 2004, I decided to frame those pictures and mementos and hang them in Julia's kitchen. I was nostalgic and felt her presence more than ever. Then I got the call of her death. Sweet Julia did indeed live a good long life.

In the beginning, Joël Robuchon and I came together over a shared passion for the daily ritual of food—a source of satisfaction, joy, discovery, and renewal that offers each of us the promise of short-term happiness several times a day. I first dined in his restaurant, Jamin, in 1981. After several visits, I introduced myself and asked to spend time in the kitchen. He gave me carte blanche and I was invited to spend as much time there as I wanted.

Many mornings, as I stood drying my hair in our bathroom on Rue Daru, Walter would pass in the hallway and ask what I would be doing that day. Often, my reply was "I am going to church," which meant that I was going to walk the mile or so to the 16th arrondissement restaurant to spend the morning in Robuchon's culinary temple.

I don't have professional training as a chef, and I figured if there was a way to get a little on-the-job training, spending time with Robuchon would be it. We shared a passion for hand-crafted sourdough bread and many a morning I would arrive at the restaurant's door with a warm, freshly baked loaf from my Rue Daru oven.

Before long, those daily visits to the kitchen—where I tried to stay out of the way, observe, and ask questions—turned into the idea for a joint work we would call *Simply French*, a cookbook that would attempt to translate Robuchon's complex cuisine and distinctive philosophy for the home cook.

Robuchon was at the top of his game then. Even those who would have preferred not to, agreed that he was the best chef working in the world. I remember asking him one day what it felt like to always be touted as "The Best."

"It's easy," he replied. "If you do your best every day and look all around you and see that the others are not, you automatically become the best." A simplistic answer maybe, but one to ponder, for sure.

Patricia, Joël and Janine Robuchon, and Walter
at a Chanteduc breakfast on the terrace.

Joël always had to win. His single-minded mission was to excel and give the best of himself every day. How could not that not rub off?

He was also obsessed with perfection. He often said to me, "Perfection does not exist. But it should not stop us from attempting to achieve it each and every day."

As I watched him in the kitchen, I saw that he was always in search of greater purity of taste, finer technique, superiority of freshness, absolute harmony of ingredients, and resulting flavors.

In life as well as in his work, he never aimed for a big bang that would not endure. For Joël, life was about the importance and value of human work, and especially the resulting satisfaction of a job well done.

None of this was passed on like solemn liturgy or a series of rules for life. Ideas, thoughts, words, or values would just fall into place as they should as we went about our mutual work.

During those years, as we worked on the recipes for *Simply French*, Joël and his wife, Janine, often boarded the TGV for Provence, to spend

Joël prepares the potato gratin for the cover of Simply French, *working out of our temporary kitchen!*

weekends cooking. In our wood-fired oven we baked breads and tarts, gratins and whole saddles of lamb, brushing the meat with rosemary just picked from the garden.

One of my best memories is of that day in May when we photographed the cover for the American edition of the book. The photo session was long and arduous, with half a dozen people working meticulously to make sure that every herb, every vegetable, every leaf of salad, and every prop in the photo was picture-perfect. We finished our job around five in the afternoon and all headed for the cherry orchard, where for what seemed like hours we climbed high into the trees picking cherry after cherry, consuming our fair share along the way! The day had been extremely tense, but as a group, one by one, we became more and more relaxed and the tension was released. We giggled and laughed and knew our friendship was deeper than ever.

Joël and Janine always stayed in what was then known as *la chambre de tilleul,* so named because in days past the room was a loft used for drying *tilleul,* linden blossoms, and figs harvested on the property. Indoor shutters made the room very dark, but the Roman tiles on the roof let little slits of light through at dawn: The first night they slept there Joël thought he had awakened to stars. The room has since been renamed *la chambre des étoiles,* or bedroom of the stars.

But some of the best times we had together at Chanteduc were on weekends when we did no work at all. We would enjoy a long and leisurely brunch on the terrace overlooking the vineyards that provide grapes for Clos Chanteduc, our fruity red wine that has hints of pepper, raspberry, and ripe cherries. Then, I might bake my Provençal *brioche,* made with olive oil instead of butter, and very lightly perfumed with the sweet flavor of orange-flower water.

One day I served a variety of young, fresh cheeses, and Joël finally gave in to the sin of *gourmandise.* He fell so in love with the rich, creamy, lactic flavor of our cheesemonger's *brique de Brebis* that he ate the entire, brick-sized cheese by himself. When Janine and Joël boarded the TGV to head back to Paris, I handed them a week's supply of that marvelous sheep's milk cheese!

On one visit, I was in the development stage of my *bouillabaisse de lotte,* a colorful monkfish stew laced with a heady, garlic-rich mayonnaise. As Joël stood by my side as I prepared the dish, I was suddenly overcome by stage fright for the first time in my life. Up until then, I had only been trying to re-create, as a student might, the master's dishes. Now, here I was, offering the greatest chef in the world one of my original creations. What was I thinking?

I shouldn't have worried, for the soup, with all the dominant flavors of Provence—garlic and fennel, tomato and anise, orange zest and saffron, all enlivened by a rich *aïoli*—later inspired Joël to create a similar dish, one made, of course, with lobster.

WALTER:

Part of Julia's reputation was for unflappability when something went wrong in the kitchen. That and gutsiness, because her early PBS broadcasts were live. Once at dinner when Julia was visiting I told her how much I admired that imperturbability, using something I remembered from the show as an example. A salmon had crumbled as she took it out of the poacher, and she said: "I'm so glad that happened, because now I can show you how easy it is to reassemble a fish."

Julia looked at me with an even regard for longer than an instant, then said: "It's amazing how many things people *thought* they saw on that show that simply never happened."

Patricia and I often watch Julia's *The French Chef* on DVDs and I still haven't seen the salmon trick. So maybe it didn't happen after all. But whether it did or not, I appreciated Julia's calm certitude as the demeanor of a great professional.

In the 1990s, an era when it seemed that anything that cost money was possible, at least for big wealthy companies, Patricia had a consultant's role in organizing an international conference on tourism that American Express sponsored in Paris. Patricia and her colleague Susy Davidson were responsible for all the meals that the participants and their spouses ate throughout an entire week. The participants included only CEOs and their wives, from Disney, American and United Airlines, Qantas, Trusthouse Forte, etc. Patricia even persuaded Joël Robuchon to close his exclusive Restaurant Jamin for a CEO lunch, where Henry Kissinger was the main speaker.

The *grand finale* dinner was prepared by Robuchon and served in the rococo opulence of private reception rooms at the Opéra Garnier. Patricia was a presence, but there was no invitation for me. So Joël issued one—he invited me to work the line sending the plates out. On one of the warm-up dishes in the long, delicious menu, there was to be a *brin* of fresh chervil as the finishing decoration, a tiny branch of three tiny leaves. He assigned me to put it on.

No problem, I told myself, confident of my elemental kitchen skills. Anyone can do that. Except that I couldn't do it, not very well. The plates came through rapidly—there were scores of elegant people waiting for the master's long and delicious tasting menu. You had to keep up with the pace in order not to slow the service.

It was quickly apparent that pinching or clipping a miniature bunch of precisely three leaves from a damp pile of chervil required more skill than I had in my jittery fingers. Sometimes I managed three leaves, but more likely four, or even five or six—big bushy branches, not tiny shoots. And then Joël would say reproachfully: "I said three leaves of chervil, I mean three leaves."

"*Oui, chef,*" is the only permissible response, and I used it a lot that night. We got through that part of the service, and then I got "to relax," and to touch nothing else.

I felt spared. In his kitchen I had witnessed scenes when suddenly everything got very quiet. Anyone who could scurried out of sight, and Joël would explode. "Who did that to my lamb!?" "Eric!?" he said to his second, with outraged disbelief. "You did that!? I don't believe it. You'll never touch my lamb again!"

The tense moment blew over of course, and Eric remains one of Robuchon's leading chefs. But the effectiveness of wrath as a management tool had been memorable. It was not a lesson my placid personality ever let me use, but it was a performance I had admired.

~✺~

MUSSELS with TOMATO SAUCE

Whenever Julia or Joël visited us, cooking and eating took up most of the time. We'd shop together, peel, chop, braise, roast, deep fry, and open a few bottles of wine while we were at it. We've always been big fans of mussels, and this utterly simple dish often found its way to the table when such gastronomic kings and queens graced our home.

EQUIPMENT: A large frying pan with a cover.

> 2 pounds fresh mussels
> 3 tablespoons extra-virgin olive oil
> ¼ teaspoon hot red pepper flakes (or to taste)
> 3 plump garlic cloves, finely chopped
> 1 cup dry white wine
> 1 cup tomato sauce
> Freshly ground black pepper to taste
> Crusty bread for serving

1. Thoroughly scrub the mussels, and rinse with several changes of water. If an open mussel closes when you press on it, then it is good; if it stays open, the mussel should be discarded. Beard the mussels. (Do not beard the mussels more than a few minutes in advance or they will die and spoil. Note that in some markets mussels are pre-prepared, in that the beard that hangs from the mussel has been clipped off, but not entirely removed. These mussels do not need further attention.) Set aside.

2. In a frying pan large enough to hold the mussels, combine the oil, hot pepper flakes, and garlic. Cook, covered, over low heat until soft and translucent, about 3 minutes. Add the wine and cook, uncovered, over high heat for 2 minutes to cook off the alcohol. Add the tomato sauce and the mussels and cook, covered, over moderately high heat until the mussels open, about 5 minutes. Do not overcook. Discard any mussels that do not open. Season generously with freshly ground black pepper. Serve immediately, with plenty of crusty bread to soak up the sauce.

4 servings

28

{ Another Kind of Interlude }

WALTER:

Two decades after I landed at the *Trib* there was another period of momentous change at the paper and premonitions of a colossal one in journalism, but I was most aware of the upheaval in my head. Through a series of five executive editors I had remained number two. With each new editor in chief my title had changed too—I had been called associate editor, deputy editor, editor, news editor, and managing editor. But whatever my title, I was always the operations guy. Many years before, Katharine Graham had passed word that I would never be executive editor, inasmuch as the *Post* and the *Times* would always need that spot as a reward or perhaps an exile. I had long since made my peace with being the person who knew where the light switches were and what had been hidden in the broom closets, and life had been good to me and to Patricia.

By 2000 the *Trib*'s ownership had been pared to a *Times–Post* equal partnership and would be pared again to just the *Times*. Before the last paring I quit, surprising myself as much as everyone else. Patricia wasn't surprised, but she was a little anxious about paying the mortgage.

I was not surprised either to have been passed over one more time for the chief editor's job, although it was the only time in twenty years that I thought I had a serious shot at it. But that wasn't the reason I quit. I simply felt burned out. I was unable to gin up the enthusiasm I was obligated to give the new editor, a very talented man whom I personally liked. And more than that, I had lost faith in a reinvention process that a new publisher had launched. I wasn't alone in thinking that the consequence of his tinkering would not be the wheel but the buggy whip.

By 2001, when I left, a lot had happened that impacted on the *Trib*. There was a new editor and a new publisher in Paris, and within the previous year both Katharine Graham and Punch Sulzberger had moved to emeritus roles, putting their sons in charge: Arthur Sulzberger in New York and Donald Graham in Washington. At this point the *Times* and *Post* were not just newspapers but major media enterprises in competitive markets with clamoring shareholders. Sulzberger and Graham would be measured by how they built shareholder value, and what was perceived as a stagnating little property in Paris didn't contribute very much to that.

This was still before—by months, not years—the Internet took over information delivery, providing everybody anywhere in the world all the news they could tolerate. But there was already another big shift in reader demands that the *Trib* struggled to keep up with. After the end of the Cold War, the surge of capitalism had created demand for instant share prices and financial tips. The *Trib* didn't have the resources of its two rivals, the *Wall Street Journal* and the *Financial Times*, in appealing to those readers.

There was all that, and there was also the crucial fact that Patricia's cooking classes could support us. I thought I'd enjoy acting as her assistant and host, and so after twenty-two years out I went.

I had been gone for half a year when the Al Qaeda attacks brought down the market for international advertising as well as America's sense of invulnerability. The *Trib* now moved from its familiar fragility to a position of serious jeopardy. Previously a self-sustaining journalistic protectorate, it now needed monthly cash subsidies from the *Times* and *Post* and was pressed to cut costs sharply, which meant shrinking space and staff.

Late in 2002 there were rumors that something bad was about to happen to the paper. A successful national strategy at the *Times* had given the paper a growing circulation and advertising base outside the Washington–New York–Boston corridor. In looking for ways to continue its growth levels, the *Times* had focused on foreign potential. "We've found considerable demand for *Times* journalism outside the United States," Howell Raines, the *Times* executive editor, said to me in one of the early conversations that led to my returning to the *Trib* as editor.

The *Times* had scores of well-paying international clients for its news service, and it had recently started selling its content overseas in another way, on complete four-page sections that were produced in New York and transmitted to newspapers abroad for their weekend editions. The first of those in Europe was *Le Monde*, and the project was launched without the *Times* telling the *Trib*'s executives in Paris. That deepened suspicions that the *Times* planned to shutter the *Trib*.

Instead, the *Times* bought it. That was a really good thing for the *Trib* and not just because the *Times* brought me back as executive editor. The *Trib*'s global franchise now had "ownership" and not just absentee owners. And while it took a while to reassure readers that the paper still merited their loyalty, in time circulation climbed as the value of the *Times* investments became clear.

I had agreed to return for six months, but the interlude lasted nearly three years, until August 2005. In those years, with *Times* investment and guidance, I was in charge of the greatest journalistic expansion in the *Trib*'s history. We restored space that had been cut and hired reporters, editors, and art designers. We rationalized deadlines and editions. And we added content that would delineate the paper and enhance its identity. The efforts worked, but in the end my *Trib* credentials gave me only an accessory's standing in New York. When the time came for the next stage of the *Trib*'s development, a fuller integration into *New York Times* identity, the *Times* wanted one of its own insiders in charge.

Leaving the *Trib* twice, I had two extravagant goodbye parties. The Champagne flowed at both and so did the tributes. Though truly moved both times I kept thinking of the lines from Robert Frost's biting poem, "Provide, Provide":

> No memory of having starred
> atones for later disregard.

But no atonement would be needed. As I always had, I live in other ways and for other things. When I returned to the *Trib,* Patricia and I had put a lot of personal plans on hold for an interlude that lasted much longer than we had expected. My second career at the *Trib* had been intense, satisfying, and redeeming. But once again I was glad when it ended. I was more than ready to get back to our life together.

Modern Salade Niçoise

Walter's job and mine would sometimes clash at dinnertime. When I reviewed restaurants, he tried to get there on time, but often a last-minute crisis would mean that I would order for him and hope he'd come before the first course was on the table. When I was testing recipes at home, I learned to keep it simple, for I never knew if he would walk in the door at eight, nine, ten, or sometimes eleven. Late-breaking news meant that there was not always time to call the wife at home to say you'd be late. I learned to be patient, and not depend on testing dishes that needed to be eaten the second they came off the stove. This is the kind of salad that offers sustenance but also can be eaten at any hour. It's a modern *salade niçoise*, made with the best ingredients: Spanish *Bonito del Norte* or prized white tuna cured in olive oil as well as the mildly spicy wood-roasted red peppers, the *Pimientos de Piquillo de Lodosa*. I sometime embellish this a bit, adding freshly steamed green beans tossed in olive oil and salt, and maybe a few spring onions, to the green salad. No matter how you prepare it, make sure you serve this on large, generous plates.

> About 6 cups mixed greens, such as butterhead lettuce,
>   curly endive, radicchio, romaine, and oak-leaf lettuce
>   (5 ounces)
> About 2 tablespoons Classic Vinaigrette (page 33),
>   or to taste
> Two 6½-ounce cans or jars Spanish tuna packed
>   in olive oil, drained
> 4 hard-cooked large eggs, peeled and halved lengthwise
> 8 whole roasted red peppers, preferably Pimientos de
>   Piquillo de Lodosa in a jar
> Fleur de sel
> Toasted country bread for serving

Trim the greens, discarding the outer leaves. Wash and dry the leaves and tear into bite-size pieces. Place the greens in a large bowl and toss with just enough vinaigrette to coat them evenly and lightly. Divide the dressed greens among four large dinner plates. Arrange a portion of drained tuna at one edge, two halves of a hard-cooked egg at another, and two roasted red peppers at a third. Season with fleur de sel. Serve with plenty of toasted country bread.

4 servings

WINE SUGGESTION: We are most likely to sample this with our own red Côtes-du-Rhône, Clos Chanteduc, but any good daily drinking red will do!

29

{ Mrs. Walter Wells }

Walter and his paper.

PATRICIA:

I have very vivid, detailed dreams and tend to remember them in depth the next morning. My favorite Walter dream took place while we were learning to dive and planning our trip to the Red Sea. I dreamed that we were to leave from shore, diving and swimming to an island, across very deep and treacherous waters. I was not a timid diver, but in this dream I just didn't have the courage to make the crossing. Walter saw my fear, so he dove down, pulled a plug and emptied all the water so that I could walk across to the island in complete safety. Is there greater married love than that? Since then, I've called him my plug puller.

Many years later our friend Jeffrey Garten came to Walter for advice. His wife, Ina, was about to publish her first book and they both saw that fame might be in her future. Jeffrey asked Walter how to act as the husband of a famous woman. "Stand by the sidelines and applaud" was Walter's counsel.

I tease Walter that I only married him for my byline. I love the neat, orderly look of the name Patricia Wells on paper. When we married in 1977 it was not stylish for a woman to take the name of her spouse. If you had been married it was okay to return to your maiden name, or to jointly go by a hyphenated name. At the time I went by my married name—Raymer—a name that never suited me at all. My maiden name is Kleiber, and I had no desire to go back to that. So I became Mrs. Walter Wells. There is something more than just visual about sharing a name. I also find it a deep psychological bond.

The saying is that opposites attract, and that is definitely true in our case. I feel fortunate that I have an eternally sunny outlook on life, sometime too sunny for many. I remember when we had just begun to live together in New York. I bounced out of bed with my usual energy and spirit, shouting about what a great day it was. Then I asked Walter how he was. "Too early to tell," he replied, eyes half open. After that, I tried to tone it down, but with little success. A friend calls us Miss Sunshine and Mister Grumpy.

When we moved to France and I began writing for the *IHT*, I intentionally distanced myself from the office and paper. I didn't want anyone to think that there was any favoritism. (I know for a fact that Walter rarely read my columns, and never before they were printed.) I worked at home and almost never ventured into the office. So for almost thirty years I observed Walter the editor from afar. I admired his ability to manage people and his general calmness. His staff included a large team of copy editors, a special breed of human being that is paid to find fault—and not just in copy. But maybe once a year I would show up at a *Trib* party and it was with great surprise, as well as wifely pride, that I saw how all these highly critical individuals looked up to Walter and admired his quiet leadership. They called him their mild-mannered managing editor, though I knew better.

When Walter quit the *IHT* in 2001, I wasn't really consulted. Even I didn't think that he would follow through on his threat. I felt as though I was being pulled off the high dive again, just as in 1979, not sure if I would belly flop or not.

But before I had time to dwell on the new life, the paper held an amazing retirement party in the elegant gilded rooms of the French

Walter receives the French Legion of Honor.

Senate. It was one of the most memorable evenings of my life. It was spring, the weather was fine, windows were open looking out onto the flowering Luxembourg Gardens. For once I was the one who could stand on the sidelines and applaud. Friends flew in from all over to celebrate his twenty-one years at the paper, and it was a true lovefest, a toast to Walter Wells.

When a staff member leaves, the tradition is to print up a mock newspaper, with stories and photos from the person's life. Years before the Internet and the World Wide Web, we nicknamed him Wonderful Walter Wells. In that mock paper one colleague wrote "For one thing, he is independently, and extremely wealthy. WWW actually stands for Walter Web Wells and he receives four francs each time that's punched onto your screen."

Other nicknames that came up in that edition included Walter Well-ordered Wells and Walter Wellbred Wells, Walter Wellappointed Wells, a nod to his appetite for fine clothes, especially shoes. They applauded him for handholding needy reporters, soothing enraged editors, and contending with crafty compositors on both sides of the ocean. And I applauded him for just being Walter.

Hand-Cut Saturday
Surprise Beef Tartare

One day I was standing in line at my local butcher's in Provence, ready to purchase his delicious butterflied leg of lamb. Gilles marinates the lamb in extra-virgin olive and local herbs, then vacuum seals it to allow the flavors to mellow. It's delicious grilled or roasted and we can never get enough of it. But that day the woman in front of me began asking him about a "very rare and special cut of beef." "It's the *surprise*," he replied. "There is only one, and most butchers don't bother with it because it has a lot of gristle and sinew that take a lot of time and talent to remove." I told Walter about it, we ordered a *surprise* the following week, and fell in love with beef again. This former vegetarian was clueless as to what the cut might be in American lingo, and a Google search in both French and English were hopeless. Finally, at a dinner with meat expert Bruce Aidells in San Francisco, he confirmed that Americans called it a flatiron steak and that the cut comes from the tender top blade roast cut from the shoulder. This is one recipe that is great for just two people because it does require a bit of dexterity. Walter is the man who sharpens knives in our house, and hand-cuts the beef for our favorite lunch on Saturdays.

EQUIPMENT: A very sharp knife; 2 chilled bowls; 2 chilled salad plates.

> 8 ounces lean flatiron, top-round beef, or trimmed filet mignon, or very lean trimmed sirloin, chilled

ACCOMPANIMENTS, SET IN SMALL INDIVIDUAL BOWLS:
French mustard
Finely minced shallots
Finely minced celery leaves
Finely minced parsley leaves
Drained capers
Extra-virgin olive oil
Quarters of fresh lemon

Fleur de sel
Freshly ground black pepper
Hot pepper sauce
Worcestershire sauce

Toasted thick-crusted bread for serving

Using a very sharp knife, chop the beef by hand into small cubes. Mound the beef into two chilled bowls. Allow each person to select from the number of garnishes, as well as their quantity. Transfer the mixture to chilled salad plates. Serve with toasted thick-crusted bread.

2 servings

WINE SUGGESTION: A favorite Saturday lunch wine comes from our winemaker Yves Gras. His sublime, complex daily red, Quatre Terre, a Côtes-du-Rhône from his Santa Duc winery is a blend made from grapes from four different villages in Provence. This spicy, unfiltered wine is a blend of Grenache and Syrah grapes.

30

{ It's Not About the Marathon }

PATRICIA:

My sixtieth birthday—November 5, 2006—was one of the most exhilarating days of my life. I completed my first marathon, in New York City. It was, one might say, a thirty-eight-year journey.

The journey started in 1968 when I was married to a different man. He was an army lieutenant stationed in El Paso, Texas, and I was teaching first grade at the local Catholic school. A friend had returned from a life-changing experience in a program called Outward Bound. He came to visit and turned me on to a new sport that they called jogging. (Before that it was called roadwork, when athletes such as boxers customarily ran several miles each day as part of their conditioning. Not until a decade later did Jim Fixx's book *The Complete Book of Running* turn jogging into a household word.)

I began running then and pretty much never stopped. It was never an obsession, just something I did on a regular basis. That is, until the year 2000, when my life took a change. During a January visit to the Golden Door Spa north of San Diego, I learned that I had all the motivation in the world but not the information. I was then fifty-three and wanted to lose some of the weight I had gained in the past decade.

By April I had lost fifteen of the thirty-five pounds I was to lose in the next four months, and a marathon seemed like a natural thing to do. My new friend Marcella had just run the London marathon (where she lost a toenail, as many runners do, and swore never to run another) and we decided that Paris should come next for the two of us.

So we signed up for the Paris half-marathon in October, a glorious course that begins and ends at the Eiffel Tower. We finished the race in personal glory. As the two of us, both blonds, arrived at the first water stop an elderly, robust Frenchman cheered us on, shouting "*Allez les Barbies!*" ("Go Barbies!") Under other circumstances we might have slapped him in the face. But on that glorious fall afternoon, we took it as a compliment. To this day, we refer proudly refer to ourselves as *Les Barbies*. We celebrated that night in a Paris bistro with oysters and Sauvignon Blanc, proudly wearing our hard-won medals.

And so I began to train in

Patricia and Marcella Butler, ready for their Paris 20K—just short of a half-marathon—in October 2000.

earnest. And that is when I realized that marathon training is really a metaphor for life, and it's not really about the marathon at all.

There are classic eighteen-week training programs for aspiring marathon runners that, if followed to the letter, pretty much guarantee you a place at the finish line. The goals are specific, as to the distance to run each day, imposed rest days, and advice for cross-training.

O that all of life would be this organized and would come with such a guarantee! Two tough days each week, two easy days, two days off, one for cross-training. It's a great mix, no two days or distances are ever the same. You push your body to places you never thought it could go (and back to places it might never want to go again). You learn to push it to the max and then better your best over and over again. Imagine the sense of accomplishment in cutting the time of a hilly run in Provence from an hour and twenty minutes to a mere fifty-six minutes!

But, no, it wasn't about the marathon at all. It was about jumping off the high dive, daring to make myself go farther, be better both on the road and off. The training is about goals, small and large, met and then reset and made bigger and harder. It is about the self-satisfaction of setting a goal and meeting it head-on, with success as well as soreness.

The discipline of training moved quickly into the rest of my life. Who wants to sit all day tied to a computer, writing? But if you are a writer that is what you have to do. Write. Walter calls them Iron Pants Days. You put on your weighty iron pants and sit there until the job is done. After that, a few hours' run in the park seems as though you've been given a Get Out of Jail Free card!

Motivation is a big part of keeping up a running life. I long had a note pasted to my bathroom mirror that said, simply, "Either you worked out today, or you didn't." Even my running shoes give me a good shove; the slogan on the soles of my red and white Saucony shoes reads, "Running is a way of life . . . a commitment to yourself . . . judged only by yourself." In other words, you quickly learn that you can't cheat yourself. And if you do, why bother?

Running the 20K in October 2000.

But the euphoria of 2000 did not last. Only a few months into se-rious training (for which I stupidly had no formal advice, just my own iron will to run farther and faster) I suffered my first major injuries. After a ten-mile run I could barely walk, and the skin around my hip turned black and blue. I ached with every step. (Stupidly, I thought if I just increased my stride, I would automatically run faster. My body did not agree.) Then one late winter day before I even passed the elegant gilded nineteenth-century gates into Parc Monceau for a daily run, I heard a crack and limped back home, dejected and depressed. It was a torn meniscus that sidelined me for several weeks. It was clear I would not be in shape for the April marathon. Marcella's body let her down, as well. But she had her ticket to Paris, and so we spent the weekend not running at all, but engaging in a little Retail Therapy, mostly at the corner Armani store.

So the metaphor continued. As did the learning curve. I learned to be more patient. Not to be so smug. To listen to all those who came before me. To listen to my body. To learn to wait it out. I learned that sometimes NOT running ten miles or fifteen is harder than running them! I wondered if I needed another cardio sport, if treadmill and running were not enough—should I take swimming lessons?

So in 2001 I gave up the marathon dream. I kept running, usually five miles five days a week, each run taking me about an hour. I kept running half-marathons in Paris, loving the Eiffel Tower to Eiffel Tower run in October, vowing never again to run the March half-marathon: The only one I ran began and ended in a horrendously icy late winter snowstorm.

But my resolve changed in 2005, when I discovered that in 2006 the New York Marathon would take place on my sixtieth birthday! Clearly it was meant to be. This time, I trained smart, followed the classic eighteen-week program, and learned even more about life and my body. Following the training program, I was actually running fewer than the twenty-five miles a week I ran on my own before serious training. Only once did I have to train on the treadmill, a mind-numbing, boring twelve-mile run one rainy, windy day in September in Provence.

Training became my new metaphor. If a detailed eighteen-week program could help me run the twenty-six-plus-mile course, why couldn't the same program help me reach other goals? In fact, I applied a training program—with detailed dates and deadlines—to finish this book!

I found, also, that a five-mile run requires little preparation. But as you get up in miles, you need to consider liquids, food, and bodily functions. In Provence I ran my normal, hilly four-mile course, hiding water bottles at the bottom of the hill. (Only once were they stolen, brand-new Golden Door bottles soon to be replaced with recycled plastic Perrier bottles.) As advised I experimented with liquids (gels, pure honey, just water, sports drinks), food (energy bars of all flavors and brands) and learned to pee in the woods in Provence or carry forty centimes in my pack for *Madame Pipi*, guardian of the public restrooms scattered in the chalets in the Luxembourg Gardens.

I trained well and I trained smart. I ran the required three shorter three- to ten-mile runs during the week, adding a six- to twenty-mile run on the weekends. After one horrific experience in the heat of Provence's August weather—dry heaves and pain as a result of de-hydration—I learned my lesson. The day before a long run I drank plenty of water, relinquishing my daily ration of red wine. I never got in trouble again!

As I trained, running longer and longer on each of my weekend runs, I realized what a gift the marathon dream was. How often, at any age, can one witness such enormous progress from week to week? There is a great reward in realizing, "A week ago, I could not have physically or mentally done this."

Or as my trainer Mike likes to say, "It's not too often that a person can realize what they are truly made of and not be in their twenties."

One of the best parts is the way I feel the day after a long run, one of ten miles or more. For the entire day I have an almost spiritual calm, an afterglow, a personal sense of achievement and inner peace. Just another runner's bonus!

The funny thing about a marathon is how little most people know about the challenge. Nonrunners assume that cities have marathons of different distances. They call it a marathon because it is 26.2 miles, just like the original one in ancient Greece! Likewise, the uninformed think that you run the 26.2 miles in training. No! You TRAIN in hopes that on the big day you will make it to the finish line.

Nonrunners also think it is the most boring thing in the world. Wrong again! I have always used running as a time to solve problems. To create. To plan. To dream. If I have a problem with someone or

The New York Marathon, November 2006:
with Kathy Griest and Marianne Tesler.

something, I either work it out on the run, or the problem sort of dissolves, goes away. Most of my book ideas come on a run. I have even thought of book topics for friends who are also authors.

When the big day came, November 5, 2006, I was ready. Two girlfriends ran at my side, and though it took me six hours, six minutes, and six seconds to cross the finish line in Central Park, it seemed to be no more than a challenging day's run. The crowds, the energy, the euphoria of the day carried me through. At least, until the next challenge comes along. (Coincidentally, this was also cycling champion Lance Armstrong's first marathon, and he finished in exactly half the time it took me!)

How great to be sixty and still find that you can improve, physically and mentally, day after day!

The marathon turned me into someone else, one set apart from the pack no matter how long it had taken me. I felt that at sixty I had new credentials, mine for life, never to be taken away. That first marathon changed the way I looked at running, at myself, at the structure of life. Before I engaged in structured training, I just ran for the heck of it, to keep my weight in check, to keep those endorphins racing about, to get outdoors and absorb a bit of sunshine, to feel younger than I really am.

But serious training gave me tangible goals, greater daily structure, greater daily discipline. Now quite overnight, I thought of myself not as a recreational jogger, but a runner. (While there is no clear definition or difference between the two, generally a jogger is considered a recreational jogger who runs for fitness, while runners race, if only with themselves, and keep track of their time. Or as someone else once said, "The difference between a jogger and a runner is a bib number.")

Walter always says that I run because I was raised Catholic. The daily run is like going to confession, then saying my penance. He is probably not far from the truth. Running does have a cathartic affect, and finishing a successful run gives a feeling of forgiveness.

The week after the New York marathon I signed up for the Paris marathon scheduled for the following April, and completed it in record 86-degree heat. Yet the run was magical, with the route taking us past every monument in Paris. The best part was the free massage given by two gorgeous young French students training to become professional massage therapists. Leave it to the French to add this final touch. Who said running wasn't fun?

WALTER:

1. I saw this coming, and was powerless to stop it. Once Patricia embraces something, her enthusiasm for it is boundless.

2. There's nothing done in public that's quite like the instant when the endorphins kick in during hard exercise. That's addictive, they say, but I've never been a substance abuser.

3. If running is religious, I was predestined not to. Though I did have a religion-related breakthrough a couple of years ago when I stopped lying to myself that I too would soon be back in the park pounding along with Patricia and the others.

ED BROWN'S
WHITE TRUFFLE RISOTTO

The night before the New York Marathon in 2006, my running mates Kathy and Marianne joined Walter and me and our friends Marcella, Rita, and Yale for a veritable feast at the hands of talented chef Ed Brown. I chose his Sea Grill in Rockefeller Center for my "carb-loading" dinner the night before the big event. Actually it was protein I had in mind and knew that we would sample his marvelous crab cakes as well as other delicacies from the sea. I hadn't counted on this incredible white truffle risotto, the most memorable dish of the evening. When we crossed the finish line the next day, we agreed that we were probably the only three of some 30,000 runners who had feasted on a truffle risotto the night before.

EQUIPMENT: 6 warmed shallow bowls; a truffle shaver.

> About 4 cups homemade chicken stock
> Extra-virgin olive oil
> 1 small onion, peeled and finely diced
> Sea salt
> 1½ cups Arborio or Carnaroli rice
> ¼ cup dry white wine
> 1 tablespoon white truffle peelings
> 1½ tablespoons softened white truffle butter
> ½ cup freshly grated Parmigiano-Reggiano cheese
> About 1 ounce fresh white truffles per person
> Fleur de sel

1. In a large saucepan, heat the stock and keep it simmering, at barely a whisper, while you prepare the risotto.
2. In another large saucepan, combine 2 teaspoons oil, the onion, and a pinch of salt and cook, covered, over low heat until soft and translucent, about 3 minutes. Add the rice, and stir until the rice is well coated with the fat, glistening and semitranslucent, 1 to 2 minutes. (This step is important for good risotto: The heat

and fat will help separate the grains of rice, ensuring a creamy consistency in the end.)

3. When the rice becomes shiny and partly translucent, add the wine and stir to coat the rice. Add a ladleful (about ½ cup) of the stock. Cook, stirring constantly, until the rice has absorbed most of the stock, 1 to 2 minutes. Add another ladleful of the simmering stock, and stir regularly until all the stock is absorbed. Adjust the heat as necessary to maintain a gentle simmer. The rice should cook slowly and should always be covered with a veil of stock. Continue adding ladlefuls of stock, stirring frequently and tasting regularly, until the rice is almost tender but firm to the bite, about 17 minutes total. The risotto should have a creamy, porridge-like consistency.

4. Stir in the truffle peelings. Remove from the heat and add the truffle butter and cheese and stir vigorously. Taste for seasoning. Divide the risotto among six warmed shallow bowls. Generously shave the fresh white truffle over the risotto. Drizzle with extra-virgin olive oil and fleur de sel. Serve immediately.

6 servings

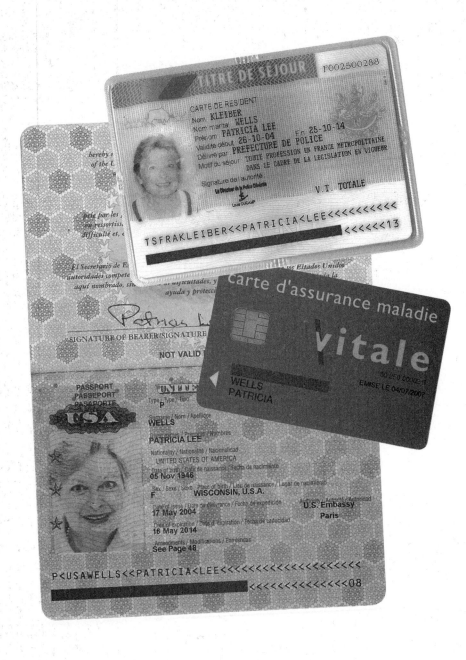

31

{ You and Me, Babe }

WALTER:

A list of phone numbers, a couple of postal codes, and a hefty taxpayer ID number—those are the basics of our French identity and they're all we'll ever have. Just as we accepted that the language would never roll flawlessly off our tongues, we accepted that we would never be French. Did we want to be? No, our pretensions were made of far lesser stuff, though in staying on in Paris it's clear that more was involved than just a job. It's logical that we hoped maybe that some Frenchness would rub off—the sophistication, the elegance, the culture's general delight in pleasure. But it didn't take long to figure out that whatever rubbed off wouldn't penetrate deeper than the pores.

We still laugh about something that happened in our earliest days as Parisians. Patricia and a friend had waited first in line at a taxi stand for more than a few minutes during rush hour, and were happy to see an empty cab pull up. As she and her friend got into the backseat from the curbside door, an elderly couple scrambled across the street and jumped in from the other side. "But we were here first," said Patricia, in her still rudimentary French. The gentleman offered no arguments about need or priority for old folks. He said simply and dismissively: "*Vous n'êtes pas du pays.*" You're not French.

I wish she had sat there calling the old turd names until he relented—the taxi driver refused to take sides—but she didn't. She backed out of the car, stunned into silence by the unvarnished bigotry.

We not only laugh about the incident still, but we use the line whenever there's something going on that we don't quite understand. And there's still a lot that we don't quite catch on to.

There's a big harrumph of a sign on a gate hidden away inside the Luxembourg Gardens that I think about in moments of ironic reflection about the country where we chose to be interlopers. *ENTRÉE STRICTEMENT RÉSERVÉE AUX PERSONNES AUTORISÉES* says the sign. Perhaps the gate leads to a service area, with potting sheds and piles of compost, or perhaps it leads to some exclusive and private area. Whichever it is, the warning leads me to an understanding of France and the French: Only members are eligible for membership.

France is a destination in every conceivable way—it is by far the country most visited by tourists; it is generous in taking in political refugees (if not the economic ones), and its graceful seductions have beguiled many foreigners and turned a lot of us into residents. Despite all that, true membership comes only as a birthright.

We turned that into an advantage—being kept out of the club helped us to remain not just happily together but symbolically joined at the hip. We're a stalwart club of two, certainly not beleaguered, but enduringly exclusive.

Well, sometimes beleaguered. Even a fantasy life has its share of uphill struggle, and buying and remodeling an apartment turned into a steep grade in our climb. We thought we knew what to expect—we had owned our house in Provence for twenty years and had bought Patricia's studio a decade before. But there were new lessons when we bought our second apartment. Even before the legal folderol was finished, we encountered both the grand gestures—a bottle of chilled

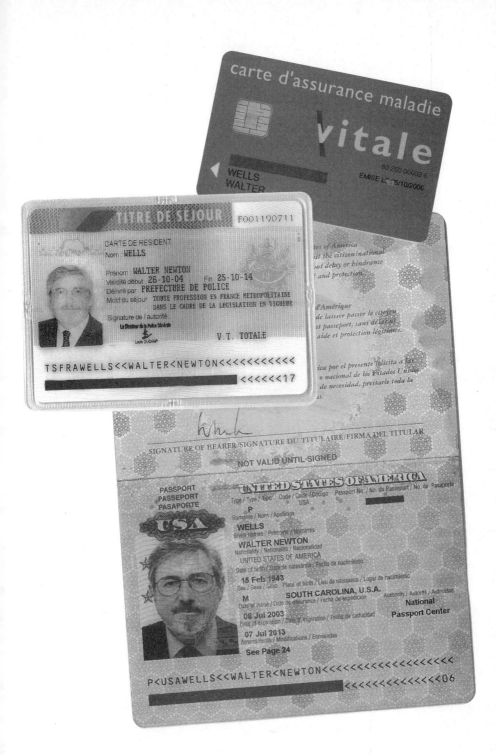

Champagne delivered personally—and the petty reminders that we were interlopers.

For instance, soon after moving in we came to experience the joys of the sunlight in the tiny garden and charms of birdsong outside our door. We also learned that only two authorized residents could prune the ivy, though the vines had run rampant in the neglectful final years of the previous owner's life. Because of the jungle, our shutters had to remain propped half open. "*C'était toujours comme ça,*" was the only part of the explanation I could understand, and my French is fluent.

Exterior woodwork had to be repainted twice to meet the exacting eye of the neighbor who claimed inspector's rights. Costly paving stones we had tracked down and brought in to match the ones that were there had to be ripped up and repositioned.

I felt seriously excluded. Not enough to go out and torch cars—of course not. But even with a deed in my hands I was on the wrong side of that "*défense d'entrer*" sign.

Then the rejection process slowed and the foreign body—us—was accepted. There was a momentary glitch when overly enthusiastic grilling on the kitchen stove sent smoke billowing into the courtyard. Our upstairs neighbor thundered down immediately to remind us with emphatic, well-practiced politesse (which bears no relationship to courtesy) that under the house rules objectionable odors were not tolerated. After his stern finger wagging he said, "We're not odious, you know." At that point I was thinking of not an adjective but a very specific noun.

Not long afterward on a flight back to the United States I happened to see a French film that gave me a new perspective. *Mille Millièmes* (*The Landlords* in English) recounts the resentful coexistence of the occupants of a small Paris apartment building. The pettiness and absence of warmth among them is remarkable. An expression I first heard in the context of the Japanese—"the nail that sticks up gets hammered down"—is probably true in any society, but I know it's true of the French. We got hammered, and it had less to do with our accents or passports than with a sort of apprenticeship, similar to being college freshmen and going through hell week.

Despite the negative incidents, we have consistently encountered graciousness and hospitableness over the years. The warmth is not necessarily touchy-feely, but it is unpretentious and genuine. On 9/11 it was emotional and truly heartwarming as neighbors called or stopped by.

In the decades since 1980, our own private clubhouse has been a redoubt against neighborly scolding and a hospitable cocoon to welcome them in acknowledgment of their friendship. We have seen economic parallels to that, too, with the dollar at parity with the euro, and at two-thirds that. We have been here when Americans loved France more, and when they loved it a lot less.

Constancy has marked my own feelings since an early age. When I was growing up in the Carolina hill country, my mother loved to quote phrases from her high school French *dictées,* and a mother's endorsement might explain any early affinity. There was also a Huguenot branch of our family, "the Martins of Martinsville," as we said. The distinction set me apart, or so I thought, from all the Scotch-Irish kids I played with.

One of those playmates was the son of an artist. They were "from off," in local parlance, rare new arrivals in our village. They lived in a big house and had real paintings on their walls, not copies. They served wine and beer at their parties, unlike us Presbyterians. In a word, they were sophisticated, and as much as I liked my new buddy, my cultural inferiority was a source of discomfort.

A couple of years ago my boyhood mate called. We hadn't spoken in maybe fifty years—different high schools, different colleges, very different lives. He was coming to Paris for the first time and wanted advice on where to stay. I told him how pleased I would be to see him after the intervening lifetime. I ran through my spiel about hotels on the Right Bank and the Left. He listened, and then said, "Walter, what's the Left Bank?"

"World enough," I could have replied, and Patricia would have agreed.

~⚬~

WALTER'S BIRTHDAY CHICKEN
with TOMATOES and FETA

Like most food professionals who are surrounded by an embarrassment of gustatory riches, Walter and I still tend to turn to simple
fare as comfort food. On a recent birthday I asked Walter what he
wanted for his celebratory meal. We could have taken a day trip to
Champagne, dined at a Michelin three-star restaurant, or made a
dinner of truffles and foie gras. He wanted a version of the chicken
we used to make in New York City when we studied with cooking
teacher Lydie Marshall.

EQUIPMENT: A large frying pan with a cover.

> 1 fresh farm chicken (3 to 4 pounds), cut into 8 serving
>   pieces, at room temperature
> Sea salt
> Freshly ground black pepper
> 3 tablespoons extra-virgin olive oil
> 1 tablespoon unsalted butter
> 1 small onion, minced
> 2 ribs celery, thinly sliced
> ¼ teaspoon hot red pepper flakes, or to taste
> One 28-ounce can crushed tomatoes in juice
> 2 bay leaves, several sprigs of fresh parsley, 2 stalks of
>   rosemary, and several celery leaves, tied in a bundle
>   with cotton twine
> About 6 ounces Greek feta cheese

1. Season the chicken liberally with salt and pepper. In a large frying
   pan, combine the oil and butter over high heat. When hot, add
   several pieces of chicken and cook on the skin side until it turns
   an even, golden brown, about 5 minutes. Turn the pieces and
   brown them on the other side, 5 minutes more. Do not crowd
   the pan; brown the chicken in several batches. Carefully regulate
   the heat to avoid scorching the skin. As the pieces are browned,
   transfer them to a platter.

2. Add the onion, celery, hot pepper flakes, and salt to the fat in the pan and cook over moderate heat until the onion and celery are soft and translucent, 4 to 5 minutes. Add the crushed tomatoes. Add the herb bundle, then stir to blend, and simmer for about 5 minutes. Bury the chicken in the sauce. Add any juices that have pooled on the platter while the chicken rested. Cover and simmer until the chicken is cooked through, 25 to 30 minutes more. Remove and discard the herb bundle. Top with crumbled pieces of feta cheese. Cover and let simmer until the cheese melts, about 3 minutes more.

3. Transfer the chicken to warmed dinner plates, along with the sauce. Serve immediately.

4 to 6 servings

WINE SUGGESTION: If we are having this dish as part of a major celebratory meal, we'll most likely pull out a special bottle of red Châteauneuf-du-Pape, perhaps one from the cellars of Château de Beaucastel.

Captions for Endpapers

Beginning at top left, reading left to right:
At home on Rue du Bac, 2002.
Walter's first retirement party, at the French Senate, 2001.
At the Pyramide of the Louvre with Richard Reeves.
French ceremony: Patricia and Walter are inducted into a Côtes du
    Rhône wine society.
Signing books with Nancy Barr and Susy Davidson, 1994.
Second row:
Twins: *Food and Wine Magazine* editor Dana Cowin and I show up in
    matching outfits at the Aspen Food and Wine Festival, 2000.
A press portrait, 2001.
With Susan and Michael Loomis in August, 2000.
Patricia portrait, 1987.
Walter on assignment in the Soviet Union.
With George Germon and Johanne Killeen at their restaurant in
    Providence, Rhode Island, in 1994.
Third row:
August, 1989: Walter, Mel Brooks, Harry Lorayne, Howard Blank, Wendy
    Blank, Anne Bancroft, Patricia, Renee Lorayne.
Walter resting at Chanteduc, 2005.
Fourth row:
Walter's mother made this apron for Patricia.
With George Germon celebrating a July 4 Junk Food Party in
    Provence.

The ancient bread oven door in Provence: No More Bread!

Eli Zabar, Devon Fredericks, and Walter on his fiftieth birthday in 1993.

Ina Garten and Patricia on a boat ride, 1999.

Walter receives an honorary doctorate from his alma mater, Presbyterian
College.

Bottom row:

A cold night in Provence with Susy Davidson and Judith Symonds.

Patricia and Susan Loomis celebrating at Rue Jacob.

Christmas, 1984: Michael Loomis, Susan Herrmann Loomis, Patricia,
Walter, and Larry Altman with our freshly baked sourdough bread.

Patricia's fortieth birthday party, 1986.

Flying to lunch in 1994 with Richard Peterson, Patricia, Eli Zabar,
Oliver Zabar, Sasha Zabar, Walter, Devon Fredericks, and Ellen
Flamm.

Walter and Anne Bancroft: Lots of drama!

BACK ENDPAPER

Beginning at top left, reading left to right:

A Chanteduc portrait.

Walter in Provence with his parents, Mary and Newton Wells, in 1985.

A weekend in Provence with George Germon and Johanne Killeen
(*center row*) and Lisa and Lou Ekus (*back row*) in 1994.

Andrew Axilrod and Walter, in Provence, 2007.

In costume, in Venice, 2007.

Second row:

Fitness class in action, Provence, 2003.

Andrew Axilrod, Walter, and Juan Sanchez during Wine Week in
Provence, 2001.

Patricia and Johanne Killeen.

A midnight hike up Mont Ventoux in Provence in 2000 with Johanne
Killeen.

Rolando Beramendi and Patricia in 2001.

The boys in white: Walter, Yale Kramer, and Eli Zabar in Provence.

Third row:

An autumn hike in Provence, the rain, Patricia and Johanne Killeen.

Lieutenant Captain Wells celebrating his honorary degree from
Presbyterian College.

A Chanteduc weekend with Steven Singer, Fanny Singer, Gail Scoff, Walter, Kermit Lynch, and Patricia.

With Ina Garten at book signing in 2001.

A plane ride to Providence, Rhode Island: Eli Zabar, Devon Fredericks, Patricia, Yale and Rita Kramer.

Walter, Sandi Getler, and Art Buchwald in Paris in 1999.

Susy Davidson, Julee Rosso, and Patricia, just friends.

Fourth row:

In Paris at the restaurant Fish in September 2004: Andrew Axilrod, Colette and Jean-Claude Viviani, Patricia, Walter, and Allyson de Groat.

On a trip to Sicily with Rolando Beramendi and Ina Garten, 2000.

Patricia with Marcella Butler on a joy ride.

Patricia with her parents, Vera and Joseph Kleiber.

Very bottom:

With Stewart McBride and Martha Rose Shulman in Provence, 1985.

Steven Rothfeld and Patricia in Provence, 2006.

Andrew Axilrod, Steven Rothfeld, and Walter in Provence in 2000.